940.54   Roebling, Karl
R   Great myths of World War II : a shattering
          revelation that will change the way you view
          the world / by Karl Roebling. -- Fern Park,
          Fla. : Paragon Press/Dynapress, c1985.
             261 p. : ill.

          ISBN 0-942910-11-7 : 14.95

          1. World War, 1939-1945.

                                   37258

                                              S85

                                                  19

IF WE ARE EVER TO FACE THE RUSSIANS IN
COMBAT WE MUST FIRST ACCEPT THE TRUTH
ABOUT THE SECOND WORLD WAR

GREAT MYTHS
OF
WORLD WAR II

**A SHATTERING REVELATION THAT WILL
CHANGE THE WAY YOU VIEW THE WORLD**

by
KARL ROEBLING

PARAGON PRESS/DYNAPRESS
P.O. BOX 866 FERN PARK, FL 32730-0866

FIRST EDITION

LIBRARY OF CONGRESS #85-60763

Printed in the United States of America
ISBN 0-942910-11-7

iv

To The Allied Merchant Seamen Of World War II
— Especially September 1939-May 1943

CONTENTS

ACKNOWLEDGMENTS

The rewriting of the War in the 1970s was the "second time around." Vast accumulations of data were available — and were sifted to produce super-compilations: the books and film documentaries upon which I have drawn most heavily. Examples of this extraordinary research are:

World War II Almanac 1931-1945 (not published until 1981, and having the advantage of drawing on all data, released secrets, and settled arguments to that time), lists more than 575 books in its bibliography. Another source, *Bodyguard of Lies* (published in 1975), perhaps tops all for references. In addition to listing some 350 books in its bibliography, it presents fifty-two *pages* of "Sources and Notes." Next, it introduces the reader to what archival research means, by listing sixty-two "Archivists, Historians, and Librarians" whose keeps were thoroughly examined. Incredible lists enumerate more than 600 archive-type source items with titles such as, "Historical Sub-Section, Office of the Secretary, General Staff, SHAEF, *A Short History of COSSAC 1943-1944,* May 1944, Center For Military Studies, U.S. Army, Washington, D.C." (that's all one title!), and "Abwehrstelle Paris to Military Governor France and C-in-C West, 'Report Concerning Foreknowledge of Dieppe Raid,' EDS, NA," and "Speidel, Ms. No. B721, *Background for July 20, 1944, Ideas and Preparations of GFM Rommel for an Independent Termination of the War in the West and for Putting an End to Nazi Despotism, OCMH,*" and on and on, for interrogations, lectures, unpublished manuscripts, captured documents, etc. To these enormous lists of sources, that author has added seven pages merely to list code names and alphabet names such as "XX-Committee" and "SOE."

Thus, for my book, I follow an unusual procedure — and list no standard footnotes.

My book is — in part — a compilation of the less than two dozen super-compilations shown below. For this reason, I list these works in the front of this book, not, as would be customary for a standard bibliography, in the rear.

I also acknowledge encyclopedias and other standard references, biographies, clipped news items and articles containing hundreds of interviews or quotations from interviews in my files, and telephoned answers from patient library reference desks.

The sources listed below are more than the recipients of an acknowledgment, and are more than a bibliography and filmography. Once my comments are added, they are, in effect, giant footnotes.

I have also relied upon my own deep, instinctual feeling — dating back to the War years — that there was a disparity as large as opposite poles between the truth and the stories the "home fronts" were being fed.

Through the decades, beginning 1941-45 with my extensive scrapbook of *Herald Tribune* and *New York Times* war reports, and 1950-53 with my own military service, and travels, and to the present, I have pursued relentlessly both the fragments and the full composite true picture of the conflict. I have conducted hundreds of conversations with U.S. veterans from all fronts. (I have even interviewed some German vets — all of whom seem to say, "We lost the War," not "We shouldn't have started it").

I knew, or sensed, the emerging truth of many of the important segments of the War long before the numerous rewritings began to hammer away at sculpting new images. New views of the North Atlantic, North Africa, Rommel in France, Allied massacres of prisoners, and on and on, were finally summarized, I feel, in the books and films I have selected for this bibliography.

The public was willing to modify its concept of individual segments — one by one. But its *overall* concept of the War didn't change. That remained the tightly-knit wartime presentation.

My conclusions in this book are of two types. First, by my presentation, I corroborate the conclusions of the rewriters of the 1970s, and bring these into sharper focus by relating each author's work to the others.

Second, I present my own conclusions — the leading one of which is that we must see the combined rewriting of the War as one whole entity. And from there, we must accept the new picture, and displace the entire old, knitted, mythological lump — not just a myth here and a myth there.

On the way to that conclusion, I arrived at some revolutionary lesser conclusions when assembling various of the segments. The reader will find these in the text. They are entirely my own.

Here and there in the text, I have placed the name of one or another of the below listed sources in parentheses. Whereas all of the bibliographic sources on a topic are used to support that subject in the book, occasionally one reference work has brought the facts into such special clarity (or added a few extra tidbits of fascinating documentation), that it deserves a distinct mention.

Also, particularly in the matter of numbering troops, I sometimes select the claims of one source over others, and will note this source in parentheses. This does not necessarily indicate disagreement between major sources. Some sources include combat divisions only, and some include combat and close support, or combat and theatre support troops. In these and other matters where it might be useful to the reader to know the exact source, I denote it in parentheses.

Also, where there is open disagreement between sources, I may mark the differing sources in parentheses. Material disagreement is seldom, however. About eighty percent of the post-1970 data is in general agreement. About fifteen percent has variations that could be interesting. Regarding only about five percent is there occasional open disagreement germane to this book.

Regarding disagreements still remaining forty years after the War these leave a few intriguing avenues to be settled someday — or relegated to that ever-diminishing stack of "this will probably never be solved." One thing appears certain, however: the unsolved items are all on side roads, and any final resolutions which we might have surmised, or which might come later by surprise, will not change any main element of history.

I shall list below eight books and two documentary film series which comprise, in my estimation, the cream of the "rewriting of WWII" in the 1970s and early 1980s.

I have supplied each with my comments as to its special focus, plus my opinion of the work. I also show, in parentheses, the short "handle" which I use when identifying it in the main text of my book.

World War II Almanac 1931-1945   1981   *(Almanac)*
Robert Goralski
Perigree Books, New York

Focus: Broad, but thorough, compass of entire War
Opinion: Superb day-by-day "just-the-facts-ma'am" digest-form record, plus some nifty special compilations, features, and graphs.

Atlas Of The Second World War   1973   *(Atlas)*
Peter Young, maps by Richard Natkiel
Paragon Books, New York (1979 ed.)

Focus: Broad, war-map and short-text compass of the War from 1939 to the end; arranged by major fronts, major actions.
Opinion: Utterly engrossing WWII history in maps with color, showing attacks and defenses by arrows, and significant units; backed by solid, brief, text and some photos. Indispensible. Only editorializing is that he (a Britisher) believes Ike should have followed Montgomery's plan and raced for Berlin. (Watch out for an erratum or two on dates — hard to avoid in a book so jammed with

exact data: Dresden is shown as February 1944, a typo, it was 1945; and a couple of "1941s" mixed in with the invasion of France in 1940; and others. As with any research, it's wise to make that double check — but this book is one of the ten great, late super-compilations.

War On The Eastern Front 1941-1945　　1979　　　*(Eastern Front)*
James Lucas
Bonanza (1982 ed.)

Focus: The German soldier in Russia, firsthand accounts from infantrymen and gun crews.
Opinion: Stupendous. Since that Front was almost totally obscured on both sides by lack of press reporting (due to absence of any press on both sides), censorship, destruction of record-keeping systems and procedures and the actual records in the near-total combat chaos, and later "official histories," this compilation fairly trumpets to the reader across the decades with fragments of the never-told greatest war story of all time — in peril of vanishing forever.

Stalingrad The Turning Point　　　　1968　　　　*(Stalingrad)*
Geoffrey Jukes
Ballentine (1978 ed.)

Focus: Stalingrad.
Opinion: We already knew it was the turning point, but this book is great because it sees through the eyes of both German and Russian combatants — including generals. It reveals in very close focus the mistakes Hitler made. Particularly, it reveals the psychological key that defeated the Germans — the key which the Russians discovered, and used to turn the tide, and which has never been broadly reported elsewhere.

Decision At Sea: The Convoy Escorts　　1978　　　　*(Kemp)*
Peter Kemp
Dutton, New York

Focus: The North Atlantic War
Opinion: Best yet at showing for the first time anywhere the very wide array of weapons, detection systems, and attack methods, and their slow, incremental development, which — instead of a few zip-ah-dee-do-dah dashing advents — alone won the toughest, meanest, war of all time. In my opinion, this is the first book, and the only book, to lay open the whole system — and to stay away from trying to credit one or two aspects just to make a good story. And, of all books, the author touches a chord closest to my heart, commending in three different places, in remarkable paragraphs, the volunteer merchant seamen, who took the brunt for four terrible years before the turnaround, and who set records in unsung heroics and the fact that, in all the War, no ship was ever delayed in an English port for want of a crew.

Bodyguard of Lies   1975   *(Bodyguard)*
Anthony Cave Brown
Bantam

Focus: Twin foci: First, the Ultra story of cracking the German Enigma code told in *full* for the *first* time (Brown caused the release of a lot of the secrets which had been withheld even from Winterbotham's book *(The Ultra Secret),* and obtained interviews from the last living secret operations executives, who were finally willing to let go their oath of secrecy not for personal gain, but that the world might know the incredible story before it passed irretrievably into history's grave). Second, the full story of the British planned war of deceptions, the details of which were largely unknown until this very comprehensive book, conducted by various organizations so numerous and secret some didn't even know the others existed, and directed by Churchill himself; and which had a profound effect on winning the War. Also, he spans the entire period from before the War to after, in depth, and in tapestry detail — to give us an entire picture from that viewpoint, touching all sides, all fronts, all overt and covert activities, all major personalities.

Opinion: I stand in awe of the revelations in this book — and declare that the War cannot be understood in the slightest without this information, and that all WWII histories previous are obsolete. This book confirms, more deeply than I ever could have imagined, my thesis that everything accepted by the general public about the War up until the mid-1970s was *not the real story* — and adds the fillip that *an enormous chunk of the story had not even been told, anywhere.* I had drafted my manuscript, and was on the third rewrite when I read *Bodyguard* for the *first* time. It reinforced every point I was making, and contradicted none, but added much. The type is small, the pages 800-plus, and the writing such that the subject can't be "scanned" without missing threads of the picture. But the other side of the coin is the reward for the investment of three or so full days of time. Where I disagree with Brown, I mention this in my text. Where I feel he overemphasizes the role of Ultra or of the deceptions, I say so. But this is seldom. Only in the North Atlantic do I find a major part of his story incomplete. (Only Kemp's book fills in that desperate campaign in all its major parts). Brown was a wartime reporter, and is a damn good storyteller. Thus, although he's got a compilation of facts, facts, and more facts, that would reach halfway to the moon, if you put the book down (which you will have to do, because it can't be read in one sitting), you'll pick it up again.

Brown editorializes seriously in only one category: that "Unconditional Surrender" was (in his opinion, not mine), stupid. This comes from his natural bias in favor of the deception programs and extraordinary Ultra intelligence schemes, which he felt could have ended the War early had we not held out for Unconditional Surrender. (The position of Roosevelt, not entirely agreed in by

Churchill, was that he didn't want any temporary end to German aggression such as between WWI and WWII — a temporary end foreseen by Marshal Foch in commenting on the Treaty of Versailles, "This is not Peace. It is an Armistice for twenty years").

A Dictionary of Battles	1977	*(Dictionary)*
Peter Young		
Mayflower Books (1978 ed.)		

Focus: Sharp focus on great battles 1816-1976.

Opinion: Good basic reference and cross checking reference. Under World War II, the battles are alphabetically listed. This presents some real difficulty in using the book easily, because, whereas some battles can be easily located (such as "St. Lo Breakout"), others are more difficult (such as "Germany, West, March-May 1945). The more I familiarize myself with the book, though, the more I use it. However, an index would be a great help.

Iron Coffins	1969	*(Werner)*
Herbert Werner		
Bantam (1979 ed.)		

Focus: The North Atlantic submarine war from early until the end, told with real names and dates by a U-boat commander, who, unlike a cat with nine lives, had at least 99 — or 999.

Opinion: Can be read for adventure-only (super — none more gripping), or for facts-only (a dandy — especially marking dates, types of equipment, states of morale, and so on), or both. This book is an absolutely necessary ancillary to Kemp or other authors noted herein, because it corroborates them from the enemy side, and also gives the German viewpoint of the effectiveness of stratagems, equipment, weapons, etc. Particularly, it absolutely corroborates the tremendous point (which even Brown missed totally, but which Kemp brings out (though naturally reluctant to shift any focus from his great love for the immense saga of the North Atlantic), that, after all the twenty or so Allied factors had finally, incrementally, and agonizingly, tilted to the position of advantage, the U-boat war was won not in the North Atlantic at all, not at the convoys, but in the Bay of Biscay — and there, not incrementally, but in wholesale slaughter. Werner's chapter, "Above Us, Hell," is an unforgettable firsthand account of how only the very wily (as he was) could get in and out of the Bay. (On just one occasion, slipping out of the French ports, he took 300 depth charges in just one of several attacks on his boat. (I thought this might be overstating things a bit, but in one of the strictly factual books put out by our side, a figure of more than 100 depth bombs as an average to attack one sub (not sink it in most cases, just attack it) was normal, especially from the Spring of 1943 forward, when the Allies were able to take the offensive in the U-boat war). Our public perceptions are naturally (and understandably) riveted still on the North Atlantic and the convoys.

There are many books on these. But my book is the first to put foremost the fact that the U-boat war was won in the Bay of Biscay. This was not just the final tad of the victory. It was the slaughter of virtually the entire German U-boat fleet beginning in March of 1943 — a fleet which was *not* worn down by the North Atlantic and the convoys (a very important point usually ignored or put to one side), but was *at an absolute peak of numbers and strength.*

TV DOCUMENTARIES

World At War (Series)   *(World At War)*
PBS

Focus: Each segement focused on a different part of the War.
Opinion: Excellent. With the obvious opportunity for use of the photograph (movie and still), and the brevity of time, it is logical that these would not be long on detailed information. But the cream of the facts is presented. Also interviews with some of the old participants are fascinating. Add extensive use of archives, lots of different opinions, insights, and viewpoints, and little if any editorializing, and these total up to "state of the art" for this mode.

The Commanders   *(Commanders)*
PBS

Focus: On the different top commanders of WWII.
Opinion: Excellent.

Immediately below, I have listed another film documentary series which does not qualify in the arena of the important rewriting of the War, although is often taken by observers as factual — or as finally explaining that greatest of world mysteries in modern times, the Russo-German conflict 1941-45.

However, the film corroborates several of the important points of my book — including that such a significant segment of the War could remain (to use their term) "unknown" for such a long period of time (unfortunately, from their report, it is still unknown); and that there was no factual (only political) reporting from the Front (a fact they don't state, but which is obvious from viewing the series in light of what is known about the conflict). There are important corroborations of things we can assume are accurate because gained from the actual wartime film footage — including the feeling of the peasant nature of the big, dumbfounded land; the method of attack in battle; and other things which are important to confirming the veracity of, for example, *The War On The Eastern Front* by Lucas (see above). And lastly, there were a lot of things already known (but always interesting) — including Leningrad's heroic holdout, and Stalingrad's titanic struggle.

The Unknown War (Series)   *(Unknown War)*
PBS

Focus: The Russian-German conflict.

Opinion: A poor job of facts, but some excellent wartime photography, and, overall, some useful aspects. Little factual data came out of either the German or the Russian side of this greatest war in the history of the world. The Russians had no press. They placed political commissars at levels as low as battalion. These "reported" to Moscow — taking care to present "facts" so as not to endanger their heads (a distinct possibility if battles were lost!) *Nothing* of value in the way of reporting came out of the Russian side of the War *except* their remarkable film footage shot by camerapeople accompanying the troops. The *words* accompanying the footage would be added much later, so we often mix up fact and fiction!

The documentary traveled to Russia with Burt Lancaster to get the "Russian Story." The main item used was some of the amazing Russian film footage — a real treasure. But the words the Russians wanted said by the documentary — words the producers were pretty much obliged to use, in that they were, after all, getting the prize footage and being received hospitably in Russia — were of the same genre as the political pap and "official history" stuff and nonsense. One episode said Russians, in "Barbarossa" (the original German offensive), fought to the last man. In fact, Germany took some 3,300,000 uniformed prisoners (a number larger than the entire lean, mean, German invasion army of about 2,500,000 — and a number so huge that Hitler thought he had wiped out the entire Russian army), in that brief June-November 1941 opening drive! (The misstatement in the documentary was so colossal that the makers put a sort of "aside" in a later episode, in which, in rapid voice, many real facts were stated! That was an attempt at redemption). As to interviews with Russian generals, these were, of course, very interesting — but again, mainly from a visual, not an audio, standpoint. It's always interesting just to *see* a Russian general who participated in WWII in any capacity. But the words had to be "party line." The idea that these were open interviews (as with personnel of some other nations), was absurd. The Russians were not going to give their opinions — they were going to give the "official" statement. I don't think highly of this series as a *documentary,* but *visually* it is interesting, and even fascinating at times (a bit too many big males kissing other males mouth-to-mouth, though — and young soldiers being kissed by old grannies that way — despite the fact 'tis the custom). I will commend one high point of inspiration in photos taken on the trip: the scenes from a plane circling the incredible monument at Stalingrad (now Volgograd) — the woman with the great arm with the sword raised in glory, not aggression. One wouldn't even have to be told where that is — but would know instinctively that here Mother Russia was saved from the beast.

xvi

In addition to the above, I would like to add to this bibliography several more books from which I drew concepts, special insights, and facts. These I list below in typical bibliographical style, and without further comment:

Churchill, Winston S. *Memoirs of the Second World War.* An abridgement of the six volumes of the Second World War. New York: Bonanza Books, 1978.

Coffey, Thomas M. *Decision Over Schweinfurt.* New York: McKay, 1977.

Doenitz, Karl. *Memoirs: Ten Years and Twenty Days.* New York: World, 1959.

Goerlitz, Walter. *History of the German General Staff.* New York: Praeger, 1953.

Goodenough, Simon. *Tactical Genius in Battle.* New York: Dutton, 1979.

Goodenough, Simon. *War Maps.* New York: St. Martin's Press, 1982.

Hughes, Terry and John Costello. *The Battle of the Atlantic.* New York: Dial Press, 1977.

Price, Alfred. *Battle of Britain: The Hardest Day.* First American Edition. New York: Scribner, 1980.

Vonnegut, Kurt. *Slaughterhouse-five.* New York: Delacorte Press, 1969.

Winterbotham, F.W. *The Ultra Secret.* New York: Harper and Row, 1974.

PREFACE

Reporting by anyone allowed to go near the Western side of the War or its councils, was collected through censors on its way to military and government propaganda officials who performed surgery, and then grafted on new material to make "presentation" packages for the public. These were designed with several specific purposes in mind, including: keeping the "home front" happy; maintaining outrage at the enemies; providing motivation to produce more; and nurturing the willingness to make sacrifices without complaining. As this reached the *publishing* end of the press (which, in the U.S., was obviously free), the publishers were "leaned" on — in a spirit of patriotism — to feature the material which had been released, and to not ask too many questions. This applied generally among the Western Allies.

The rewriting of World War II came decades later — and it came in pie slices, so to speak, each dealing with one portion of the War, such as, for example, the North Atlantic. My book assembles all the new portions, with the result that a *new overall picture* emerges, revealing many of our most popular War concepts to be myths, and demanding that the entire structure of old information give place to the new.

What caused the revolutionary new information to come out after decades? Many factors. Actually, the true information began entering the U.S. when floods of servicepeople returned after the War. But the public didn't listen. The most interesting war stories are still swapped only among servicepeople who were there. For example, the general public (by contrast to a selected public) would not accept stories about the Jewish extermination camps until the 1970s and the TV series, "Holocaust."

There were several stages of progressive awareness by the general public.

Immediately after the War, the "home fronts" were no longer fed sanitized, specially prepared, "picture-painting," information. The "intermediate" role of government and military propagandists receded, and vanished for everything except secret projects or intelligence-gathering efforts that were current. In general, reporters could flow their material directly to publishing and broadcasting firms. Immediately, or soon, after the War, a lot of the material that would later appear in the "rewriting" of the 1970s, was published — but ignored by the general (not select) public.

By the 1960s, huge archives were functioning on both sides, in many nations. The amounts of material were so vast as to appear unmanageable. However, with the progress of computers, microfiche, and other modern library techniques — plus the application of enormous amounts of time by skilled librarians, and the financial support of governments — the entire mass of material gradually came into a form that could be readily accessed by researchers. But the process was an ongoing one! Previously classified material was being released almost every year. This had to be added to the various archives.

The Vietnam and Watergate eras produced and encouraged a new breed of skeptical, deep-questioning, and even mistrustful reporting. Topmost leaders, the Pentagon, and other departments — once nearly "sacred" in WWII — were now fair game, and, in fact, suspect. Vietnam had other effects — producing the world's first reporting by TV direct from the battlefront into living rooms, via the evening news. The "glory of war" fell, "hors de television." Thus, the basic, age-old myth of the glory of war vanished. The censor and "packager" were bypassed. The press could legitimately *de*glorify war. Following this, the U.S. public became more able to accept bad things about Allied actions in WWII — such as Hamburg and Dresden.

After 1970, the U.S. became more able to accept former enemies in a social framework. This resulted in some extraordinary interviews and books. Albert Speer's book appeared in 1970. Japanese war pilots who bombed Pearl Harbor (invited to be advisors for the film, "Tora! Tora!"), German generals, Nazi pilots who participated in the Battle of Britain, all became, somehow, part of our lives. Today, some reunions invite their former enemies. The recent D-day celebration included a number of defenders.

Returning to the early 1970s, there was a tremendous new appetite for World War II data. Television in the U.S. and Great Britain was hungry for film. Plenty of funding was available. There was a deep sense that we should get all the information we could acquire before all eyewitnesses died or vanished. Not just leaders, but all kinds of average people — former military and civilian participants on all sides — were interviewed. Prisoners released from Russia in the mid-1950s were sought out for information about that front.

In the mid-1970s, Anthony Cave Brown pursued the full Ultra and British deception story — finding the door ajar, but gaining little from British Intelligence. It was said that any special agencies which had functioned during the War had simply closed up shop at the end, and left no records! So Brown went to find people he knew had been involved. Many were dead. Some wouldn't talk. All had sworn an oath to secrecy.

The great difference between the Briton and the American in matters of oaths of secrecy is that the Briton will continue to know nothing, even if a book contract is offered! The British people who finally talked with Brown, and led to his unravelling of the entire, amazing, story (which had been declassified — but just try to find it or get past the oaths!) were few. Their motivation was not personal gain or even personal mention. The greatest and most sacred thing in their lives was that they had been able to help preserve the country in its direst hour. But they divulged some information in order that the story — to which they felt the world was entitled — not pass into the grave with them.

Brown's book, *Bodyguard of Lies,* made obsolete the entire history of the War to 1975. Not only had the histories — including official histories (which had been deliberately distorted) — been inaccurate, but they had lacked enormous chunks of utterly vital information which had remained as silent as some tweedy British professor somewhere, smoking his pipe, and sworn to his oath.

(Lest the Sphinx-like Briton appear unreasonable, there was a concrete reason for years after the War to keep the secret of the Enigma decoder: other nations were using the Enigma encoder, or had plans to use it, unaware of the extent of British decoding capability. *Also,* there is a written law in intelligence work: never let anyone know either what you know or what you don't know. Once the entire Ultra story was out, the U.S. had to vastly revalue upwards Great Britain's role in the War — a role the U.S. public had simply not thought the British *capable* of. And that was part of the British cover. "You see, old chap," to have let the story out would have mean Britain could no longer play a certain type of role).

Full declassification of Ultra in 1975 made obsolete the entire history of the War to date (even the official histories — which had been deliberately distorted).

Did all this revolutionize public opinion about the War? No.

Why? For one reason, separate pieces of the rewriting have been accepted, but have not been assembled — until now — to challenge the entire, old, wall-to-wall mythology network which is still in place.

For another reason, the media files are jammed with the old fables, and thus when an editor sends for "background" on an anniversary of some WWII event, the stories produced during wartime make up most of the information. This is then repeated for today.

For another reason, the old wartime story was engaging. It was designed that way. It made one feel good. And, if the news was just a disaster, it was presented in a way that made one feel good about going down to the factory and producing more planes.

For another — and the most sensitive — reason, the loss to families, or disablement to individuals, or loss of friends, in the War, was often closely tied to one or another event which human nature had exaggerated in order to make the sacrifice seem more bearable, or even glorious.

It's time now for the unified mass of true information to take its rightful position — replacing the entire old picture.

Not just nostalgia, hard-dying dreams, and the definite factor of sympathy for those whose deep sacrifices or losses may have been attached to a myth, are involved here.

Peril is involved, for it we don't understand the last war — our true role and the true role of others in it — we could lose the next one (or be put unnecessarily into a very deep hole for a very long time before winning).

GREAT MYTHS
OF
WORLD WAR II

Myth One

That The War News Gave A True Picture

The Western Allied War news censored no-no's, but more significantly, padded the remainder with pleasant items, and generally wrote a stage story for the "home fronts" — one designed to keep morale, production, outrage, and willingness to sacrifice, at high levels.

Western Allied reporters — under the free press in the West — could *report* anything.

However, first they had to get access to battle areas, or to other important places such as, for example, Ike's headquarters. Next, their reports had to go through a sort of hamburger grinder — on their way to becoming palatable meatloaf. Material was taken out, and, worse, from a pure news standpoint, material was added. This was then cooked up by "official news bureau" employees into a dish designed to accomplish specific ends: the consumer of the news — the populace — must feel reasonably good about the War; must feel like producing at high levels; must stay angry with the enemy; and must be willing to sacrifice.

Although basic news — such as an air attack on a city, or a new offensive — could not be hidden, everything else (including timing, emphasis, and amount of padding), could be manipulated for effect.

The reporter had no control over the report once it left his or her hand.

Publishers in the U.S. and U.K. were — under our Western free press concept — free to print anything they wanted to print.

1

However, war news was "owned" by the military or the government, which alone had or controlled the access and release! Hence, news came to the publishers in a controlled form, from a controlled outlet.

(In England, there was a Government limitation on publishers — not to print results of the Nazi bombings. However, the populace could gather most of this with their own eyes, hence the limitation was not as harsh on free press as might appear on the surface. But one source said the British "censored press could only hint at chaos" — *World At War*).

Hence, the press was free (or, in England, relatively so), but the *data* was controlled.

Certainly, many top publishers knew far more than they printed. They had the right to aggressively question the truth of controlled data — but seldom did so.

The reasons for the passivity of publishers were numerous. They were under many overt and subtle pressures within themselves and from outside. The first of these was patriotism. The second was the simple fact that breaking a story, failing to keep a secret (or even a portion of one, or even a suspicion of one), or contributing to a loss of confidence in government or leadership, could cost lives, delay the effort, contribute to poor quality control on bomber assembly lines, etc. The third was the simple fact that reporters from newspapers and wire services, and any other press media, had to be credentialled in order to get into the front areas or main headquarters. Publishers naturally wanted their reporters to have the highest standing possible with the governments, so they went along with the rules.

Why couldn't reporters just quit and go home and "tell all"? They could. However, they were allowed at all times to "tell all." The telling, however, didn't survive the hamburger grinder.

Reporters felt flattered to be in the important positions they were in; understood the reasons for much of the censoring; didn't understand how their material was being padded out into important mythologies; felt they were as much a part of the War Effort as the warriors (for example, Ernie Pyle, a special hero to me, and to many readers, was indeed a battlefront reporter in every way); were *uniformed* (yes); felt the entire thing to be a duty; and were sworn to a special honor code. Under all these combined circumstances, had any reporter attempted to go against the tide, the response would have been quite drastic. Also, no publisher of any standing would have printed the complaints.

The press honor code extended from the reporters through the publishing functions. It was a very high code — carefully maintained and practiced. In simplest terms, it was "off the record" secrecy. (We hear this term today, but it is often used in a trite way. In the War, the stakes were much higher. For example, Ike revealed the Sicilian invasion date and plans to the uniformed (but civilian) press corps in Africa — off the record. It was a rash move, and later often criticized. And it also displayed Ike's idealism. But, Ike was not crazy. He knew that the group he addressed consisted of only a handful who had been carefully screened, and who had demonstrated their trustworthiness in the past and over a period of time. Particularly, he knew these were actually *inside* the military establishment, and, further, a long way from civilian land. He knew too that they were not able to just trot off to the nearest palm tree intercontinental telephone booth and get the news to the U.S. to the editor or the wire services. He knew also that there was no nearby bar, where the beans might be spilled over a few too many drinks. And, on top of all that, he knew he had the press "off the record" honor code. There probably wasn't a reporter in that room who wouldn't have died before releasing that information).

The press honor code permeated the entire reporting and publishing functions in the U.S. and U.K. during the War. Many editors with contacts at the highest levels of the governments knew *what* was going to happen, and many knew approximately *when*. For example, the invasion of France was a known factor to half the U.S. public and all the British public, and to all the German High Command, certainly from the fall of 1943 forward. But when, how much, who, etc. — all the other standard press questions — weren't answered. Did the publishers respond by printing stories *attempting to guess* the time and place and strength? No — this normal function of the press was absent,

No palm tree intercontinental phone booths in North Africa.

and rightly so. Sometimes, top editors were given information by Congress, the military, or some bureaus, under the "off the record" limitation, in order to forestall speculation.

The press was free, but the data was controlled.

An aspect of distortion in which the U.S. publishers avidly cooperated was the natural one of "proportionality." Who won the War? Daddy did. National egotism is similar — but whereas we can laugh at ourselves as individuals, we retain a fierce pride in our estimation of our national role *in proportion* to all others.

The press also didn't have to be asked to magnify our local perspective. "Local news" is news. That's an axiom. One local boy wounded gets more ink than the Battle of Kursk. And it never ends, on a local or — as an extention of local — a national level. Sometimes it was truly excusable — for example, when Stalin's great Winter Offensive (which drove Hitler from Moscow's gates, denied him his main goal, and popped the balloon of German invincibility) coincided with the Japanese attack on Pearl Harbor, naturally, we learned very little about the Russian front at that time — being forgiveably absorbed in our huge Pacific problems and our entry at last into the War.

But, in less excusable circumstances, has the press ever learned the lesson of local perspective in reporting the War? Nope. In 1984, on D-Day's *fortieth* anniversary, report after report in the U.S. featured the U.S. and how it invaded France. The reporting was accurate, and there was no government bureau standing in between. But somewhere, we forgot the British Commonwealth — which just incidentally landed more men that day than the U.S. did: 75,000 to 57,000. Does that take anything away from the U.S.? No. But does it change the proportionality? Oh, yes. And does it embarrass our provincial perspective? Yes, again.

The U.S. press also eagerly cooperated in making the public feel happy about itself — good about the War, justified about hating the enemy. From the standpoint of the general public, there was no hard questioning of Allied acts (until *long* after the War — for example, when the general public learned, in the late 1960s, about Dresden). In the war years, there could still be "glory" in war. (I am not criticizing the good heroics of saving the world from evil. I am pointing to the mistake most publics make of actually feeling that *war* is glorious — a mistake promoted by governments. That mistake was corrected by front-line television reporting of the Vietnam War — for the first time in history).

WWII had a spirit which the Russians caught when they termed it, "The Great Patriotic War." So — in waves of real patriotism, and a sense of clear-cut good versus clear-cut evil — it was easy and natural to promote the war as clean. Betty Grable, war bonds, U.S. Navy officers in white, Clark Gable in his U.S. 8th Army Air Force uniform climbing out of a B-17 — these things symbolized the War. We overlooked the oil-grimed merchant seaman sunk for the fourth time, the paraplegic (the U.S. didn't even know these people existed — despite "Best Years Of Our Lives" — until a couple of Vietnam era movies and Max Cleland), and the civilians massacred necessarily in many cases, unavoidably in others, but horribly, by bombers.

Did the press hide the bad, and show only the good? No, the propagandists fed the press some bad items, while hiding many, many others. Some bad items couldn't be hidden. The Bataan Death March was a horror — but it was turned very thoroughly into a strong stimulant (which indeed it was) for public fury against the Japs. Such things as the sinking of capital ships could not be hidden, so were turned as best as possible into memorable events. The "Life" magazine picture of the stricken *Lexington* in the South Pacific was one of the great photos of the War. With the ship's towering column of smoke, her list, her ropes over the cliff-like sides, with hundreds of men getting off, the picture had dignity, power, and dedication written all over it. Any patriot seeing that would want to go at once to work to build a new one! I find no fault with that — but a study of the bad things that were revealed, shows that we hid many bad things, and released ones that could be used to produce a studied effect!

That was, of course, not the case in every instance. The sinking of the *Juneau,* for example, with all hands, the loss of the five Sullivan brothers, the two days in the shark infested waters as survivors were picked off — this was just a horrible disaster, and we all knew it.

As mentioned, the press was not fed many bad items which could not be "managed" to produce one or more of the desired effects on the "home front." We were not told about the Slapton Sands training disaster, for one example. We were not told of the big losses to Jap Kamikazes (only our big, "one-sided victories" in shooting down large numbers). We weren't told the bad things our people were doing — such as obliteration bombings of cities such as Hamburg and Dresden (only that "military targets" were hit with "precision bombing"). The above are just a few examples of vast amounts of things kept from the general public during the conflict — and which that public didn't want to hear about once the War had ended.

Where Allied operations were progressing well, the press was always fed a "shiny" story — covering the grime. Bill Mauldin knew this. After D-Day, he lived and drew his cartoons for the Army press from the front areas. One famous "Willie and Joe" cartoon showed dog-tired, dirty, slumping, unkempt U.S. troops moving in bad weather and mud through a French village. In the hand of one was a newspaper whose headline declared something like this: "Fresh, victorious U.S. troops chase defeated enemy!"

The public really didn't want War truths. (Even after the War, most returning servicepeople could not really tell Mom, Pop, and the home folks about the War). At barrooms, people would set up the returning serviceman's drinks all night — but wouldn't listen to his stories. I saw this routine a hundred times. Only among groups of others from the same theatres, or same campaigns, would the real stories flow. However, if a wife or other family member came in, the storytelling would switch at once to the funny — to jokes and amusing incidents, so that the

War seemed a colossal good time. But just among groups of servicemen, or one on one, I heard some amazing stories — almost all of which have proven to be true, though after twenty, thirty, and, for some, forty years!

A major area of press neglect in the U.S. was discussion of the "buffer." England, for example, didn't have a buffer, once France fell. The British were hammered from midsummer of 1940 forward to virtually the end of the War nearly five years later. But the U.S. was so insulated that, in midsummer 1940, it was still eighteen months away from active participation — a participation which took Pearl Harbor to bring it to pass. Thus, the U.S. was "buffered" by England, by the wide ocean, by time, and by the feelng that the German planes could not get here. In the First World War, the U.S. came in only at the very end — and tipped the scales. This is seldom mentioned in our *First* World War reporting, which sounds very much as if "we won the war." As to any *large* scale troop involvement in the *Second* World War, the U.S. didn't confront Germany until D-Day — less than a year from the end, when Russia was already back into Poland, at the Bug River. These related matters — our buffer, and our ability to be fresh and reaching our peak when the enemy had been fought out against others — were seldom, if ever, mentioned by our general press (although some of the more intellectual press with a select public printed discussions); and certainly these factors were not only well known to our high command, but played for all they were worth in diminishing our cost in blood. Stalin fumed much of the War, because he said we were letting him fight it out with the Germans before we got involved with large scale troop actions. We covered up some of our lack of large scale troop involvements by featuring our truly colossal contribution of war materiel. My point here is only that the U.S. press did not go into this matter in any full sense during the War — or since.

I would add the point that, in the next war, the U.S. may not have any buffers of distance, other nations, or time. The nation may learn for the first time what it is like to catch the initial brunt of an equipped, militaristic, ambitious enemy — and to have to fight the entire period of the war, from start to finish.

The public *liked* the War fed to it in a way that made people feel good — and (not incidentally) that was good for the commercial and economic side of the press. I don't say the press put money first. But a "feel good" war was natural, in demand, and available. So the press didn't have to be *asked* to feature the "glory" side — even the "glory" magnification — of anything from production to the battle fronts themselves.

Out of all this came a mythology that was deeply ingrained in the psyche of the nation. Too, it was all deeply ingrained in the files on the War — so that any story (even many current ones), just repeat some of the old factual myths, and the overall mythological magic of the period.

Most sensitively, the mythologies are intertwined with the sense of sacrifice and loss by families, friends, and individuals related to the War. The more vital to the War Effort was the action in which someone died or was crippled, the easier the sacrifice was to bear. Every commander who ever wrote a grieving mother knows that. Many a man killed by his side's own fire, or by his own stupidity, died "a gallant hero, of whom you and the nation can always be proud." And, in many ways, that is true — but it doesn't tell the whole truth. In previous wars, many a warrior dead of disease was presented to bereaved families as a combat death. In a very real sense, anyone who signs up and puts his or her life on the line is a national hero. I won't diminish that. But to say that the serviceperson died in an important action makes the loss easier for the families at home to bear. And many a Mom who knew better has told others her son died in battle.

In my demythologizing of the War — and in my putting an entire new structure in place — I do not wish to diminish the value of the sacrifice of anyone. The overall facts are still there — we won the war against evil forces.

But the battle in which the loved one died or was injured may not have been as important to the U.S. — and the U.S. action may not have been as important in proportion to the overall effort by others — as we thought.

> **A mythology was produced that became deeply ingrained in the psyche of the nation.**

What about Russia — which was an *Allied* nation (though hard to believe today)?

Russian press was nonexistent. There were no private publishers and no private reporters. There was no reporting arm at all (with the exception of uncaptioned, remarkable, combat film footage), and the reports of the political commissars who were assigned to battle units as low as battalion level. For any war releases to the world or the nation, State propagandists manufactured most of the substance and color, dressing out some inescapable event such as the Battle of Kursk.

What about our enemies — Germany and Japan?

Germany had some private press, but it wasn't free, and no reporters went to the front. War releases were wholly controlled — censored and padded out into elaborate stories by the propaganda bureau. Goebbels had the worst concept on record — the attempt to control not just the news and information, but the *minds* of the population!

Japan had press, but no free press, and no reporters who went to the front. News was censored, reshaped, and padded, into electrifyingly good war news. One source quotes a high Japanese government official as saying, "It was customary for GHQ [in Tokyo] to make false announcements of victory in utter disregard of facts, and for the elated and complacent public to believe in them." *(Almanac).*

☆   ☆   ☆

Neither public nor propagandists knew about "Ultra" during the War! Ultra was the secret decoding system by which the British *regularly* read the German High Command coded messages from about 1938 forward. Although here and there, during the War and afterwards, it was known that "we had broken the enemy code" for this or that battle or occasion, no hint of the titanic scope of Ultra came out until Commander Winterbotham's "approved" book in 1974. By this time, Anthony Cave Brown was hot on the trail of the whole story — and got it from individuals, and from the declassification of U.S. documents in 1975. He set forth the whole story in *Bodyguard of Lies*.

No record of the War was true or complete until *Bodyguard* was published.

THE "ULTRA" SECRET — BEHIND THE SECRET . . . BEHIND THE SECRET!

When the British hide a secret, they *hide* it!

The Ultra secret was hidden so well that if one discovered all about it — or what one might have thought was all — there was another secret behind that. And lo — another behind that!

After nearly forty years, it would appear that the entirety of Ultra (all except many of the individual stories which have gone to the grave), is out in the open. Is there still another secret apparatus — and series of amazing revelations about the War — hidden? I don't think so. The reason is an old one in intelligence work — most of the gaps are filled in; and those that aren't are not very important in the overall scene of the greatest conflict in history.

From about 1938 forward, the British regularly read the German High Command coded messages. For the details, read all 800-plus pages of *Bodyguard of Lies*.

The Germans used a rotor encoder called "Enigma." There were several models. It could not be cracked because there were nearly an infinite number of settings possible — and the Germans changed settings each day.

Therefore, how did the English achieve their great triumph — a triumph which saved hundreds of thousands of U.S. lives alone?

The Enigma machine was in existence from the early 1920s, having been built from the plans of Hugo Koch of Holland. The machine was on the open market. Not a commercial success, the patents were sold, and the device came to the attention of Fellgiebel, who would later become Hitler's chief signals officer. In

1937, a German sold data on the military model to French Intelligence for money. The French were able to build a replica at a cash register factory. With this replica, the French could read German High Command ciphers — but *only* as long as their source provided the ever-changing "keying" the Germans were using.

In 1938, the British were approached by a Pole who had worked in an Enigma factory, and who offered to sell them the machine plus the technical expertise regarding the *wiring* of the machines. "Lewinski" is the Pole's fictitious name. At this pont, such other legendary names in this field as Alfred Knox, Wilfred Dunderdale, and, particularly, Alan Turing, began to come into the picture.

(As a side note, for those people who think Poles are stupid, the Poles were the most brilliant cryptanalysts in the world. Rejewski and Zygalski first cracked the Enigma machine. And, the Pole "Lewinski" understood the wiring of the rotors — which turned out to be the most important basic ingredient in the decoder).

Britisher Alan Turing, a pioneer in computer theory, then built, with the assistance of others and the British Tabulating Company, a machine called the "Turing Engine," or, simply, "The Bomb." Eight feet tall, eight feet wide, it could — by matching the wiring of the encoders — determine the "keys" in which the messages had been sent. From there, to use Brown's words, "cryptanalysts at Bletchley could then 'unbutton' the messages."

As the War came on, Churchill set a firm rule that no other nation was to learn of the Enigma decoder. The secret was kept from Stalin (though Churchill, without mentioning the source, warned him of the June 1941 invasion — warnings Stalin ignored, at great cost to Russia. The U.S. learned — but only at the highest intelligence levels).

Churchill also had a firm rule that any information gained from the decoder must be attributable to *another* intelligence source, if it was to be used! For example, when the British learned from decoded Enigma messages that a warship was sailing, they would next send out reconnaissance planes which would be spotted by the Germans. Only then would the British attack! And the Germans would attribute the loss of secrecy to the recon planes. This absolute rule applied in some agonizing situations where the use of the information would have saved lives. The most famous case (which had been rumored, and which Brown confirms as fact), was that of Coventry. Churchill knew from Ultra that the attack was coming, but he provided no more than the normal defense — lest the decoder be compromised.

Late in the War, he occasionally set the rule aside — establishing his "cover" by, in one instance, radioing to a nonexistent Italian band of partisans, thanks for the intelligence! The Germans picked up on this, and attributed their loss of secrecy to "Italian traitors."

Despite all efforts to hide Ultra, the Germans often suspected their Enigma had been compromised. Investigations would be held — and the machine upheld time and again! The main culprit was believed to be "traitors" — particularly people from occupied countries who manned telephone switching points around the Reich.

(As a side note, the Germans never fully realized that Admiral Canaris was talking with the Allies from before the War until he was killed late in the conflict. His "Schwarze Kapelle" (Black Orchestra) secret group had tried to assassinate Hitler from before the War, and regularly fed critical information to the Allies. Canaris could never understand why the Allies largely ingored him! The reason was that they already had the information from Ultra).

After the War, rumors flew about code-cracking. However, only the specific cases such as the breaking of the Japanese code at Midway, were these nailed in as fact. Gradually, it was accepted that here and there, now and again, we cracked the enemy codes, and vice versa.

The British "never heard of" Ultra or Enigma. Anybody who knew of these by name, and printed something, would find the various intelligence offices admitting only, "Oh, you are probably talking about codes — that sort of thing."

In fact, no one agency of which the public ever heard, knew all about Ultra. That was part of the reason for its success.

MI-5 was British counterintelligence and security, while MI-6 is their Secret Intelligence Service. Right away, one can see the possibilities for endless passing of any "hot potato."

But, during the War, Churchill operated his supersecret deception war — involving such things as the "LCS" (London Controlling Section), and "SOE" (Secret Operations Executive — which maintained patriot armies in enemy-occupied lands). LCS just vanished at the end of the War! Convenient, one might say.

All these were heavily involved with Ultra information. Their top people all knew the decoder existed — but maybe knew very little else about it.

One man might have known more than anyone other than Churchill. That was Menzies. He was titled as head of MI-6, but in fact, he was much more. He was almost a secret organization unto himself, in addition to his command role.

It might be added that only in Great Britain, with her traditions, and only in a country under the bomb day and night, could such organizations and such secrecy have existed in a democratic society (although the U.S. didn't do badly with its colossal "Manhattan Project").

So what happened immediately after the War? Did those in the "know" rush for their publishers? No — Ultra was still hidden. Why? For one reason, it was thought that many nations might use the Enigma for *their* secret messages — and thus Britain could listen in covertly! The biggie in all this was Russia itself! Suppose the Big Red Bear had decided to use the Enigma for its intelligence work! Russia didn't (and later revelations that Kim Philby, the Russian spy, worked for British intelligence, might have had something to do with that).

Immediately after the War, the LCS personnel were *sworn* to secrecy. They took an oath. They were periodically reminded of it. This held up for a long time.

The years passed.

By 1962, Brown had "completed" *Bodyguard of Lies.* Or so he thought.

Filing his manuscript with the Office of the Chief of Military History (OCMH) in Washington, he discovered there had been (officially) *no* "cover and deception" operations regarding the Normandy invasion! Astonished, he inquired, and found that in fact there had been thirty-eight such operations, but that the *British* had the data — and that, furthermore, the *official history* of the Normandy invasion had *not been permitted to mention these!*

Going to SHAEF, he found some records — but these were still classified after nearly twenty years!

At this point, he knew he was onto something big.

He had some luck with the British Foreign Office, which answered some limited questions. But he was warned "not to go too far."

So the reader can see that "some" secrets were let out after the War, and "some" secrets were discussed — but in a limited way. This was supposed to satisfy public curiosity. But behind the divulgence of the "secret" was — the secret being protected.

And Brown would find — when he got to second base — that there was another secret being protected at third base!

He had an interview with Sir Stewart Menzies — and learned enough to whet his appetite. But Menzies had drawn a line too.

By 1965, the trail was cold.

By 1968, though, Brown had possession of one document which had (he says, "unaccountably") been declassified. He pursued further information. A military man told him in 1968, "Your people and ours were reading the German and Japanese command ciphers for the better part of the War." He also heard the word, "Ultra."

This was revolutionary — and known to so few twenty-three years after V-E Day!

He went on an interview campaign. Included were General Gehlen of Nazi Intelligence! And General Omar Bradley, and many other names mystical and famous.

The case was cracking fast.

In 1971-72, the U.S. relaxed its protection of many old secrets of WWII. But *getting* the information — even though it was declassified — was another hurdle! (This, apparently, is one way governments protect their secrets in an open society. The open society — after, say, twenty-five years — clamors for the truth! The government says, "OK — you're right, we're no longer classifying that." The public rejoices. But the next step is trying to find where the documents are — and prying them out!) Brown credits many librarians and archivists in getting this information.

In 1974, F.W. Winterbotham's book, *The Ultra Secret,* was released. He was certainly one of the very few people privy to the topmost secrets. His was an "approved" memoir. Material which could no longer be held back was released. However, even in the introduction, the author states that much was *not* released. It is an outstanding book, on its own. It is more important as a stepping stone and integral brick in the new structure of truth coming into place. It is vital as a facilitator and dam-buster.

The word "Ultra," was declassified only in 1974.

In 1975, the barriers in the U.S. toppled. None of the information sources claimed by Brown in the areas of cover-and-deception, and cryptanalysis, including Ultra, came from the British, who were still closemouthed. Included in the declassified and available documents was an *agreement* by the U.S. to G.B. to *prevent* access to the specialized areas mentioned above. In documents, Brown read of the censorship of someone's manuscript in 1944. He read an agreement by the U.S. Joint Chiefs in 1945 to *not* provide material, and to *not* let material be published. This agreement also acceded to the LCS request that acceptable *British* people write the accounts of certain battles — for inclusion in *official histories in the U.S.!*

The Joint Chiefs had issued a directive, Brown says, which "muzzled" news of Ultra and the cover-and-deception activities for thirty years. Furthermore, the data was committed to a permanent TOP SECRET classification.

The cult of "secrecy for secrecy's sake" has some foundation in need. Further, it was staffed, during and immediately after the War, by people who, many times, put their lives on the line for the secrets — and who knew friends would die if the secrets got out. That type of secret has a way of remaining hidden for long periods. But after thirty years, the old warriors were going, at least from their desks, and the new need was for revelation — before graves hid the facts forever.

In praise of the British, they knew how to keep their mouths shut. Had the U.S. developed Ultra, the leak would have been out early, newspapers would have run features on it, reporters would have gained their "spurs" by breaking secrecy, and employees and secret service people would have quit and written books and appeared on talk shows. Not so with the British. And through the decades after the War, they endured also with silence America's bragging about how it won the War! — and how the Brits were just kind of nice, defeated, broke people who were dependent on the U.S. for everything.

After reading *Bodyguard of Lies*, one will watch less television and fewer football games. One will contemplate more the real world. For if such was the state of trickery's art in 1940-45 — far greater than any spy movie has ever portrayed — then what might it be today?

Every line of 1975's *Bodyguard of Lies* tells us the pap we were fed for news — and *even official histories* — was fabricated only partly of whole cloth, and mainly of fiction; and that *the truth came out* in the *1970's rewriting* of the War.

☆   ☆   ☆

The war news did not give an accurate picture of the conflict. Long after the War — and particularly in the 1970s — the War was "rewritten," presenting an entirely new picture, including the proportional input by various Allies, vast amounts of information previously known but unaccepted, plus much irrefutable data unknown until the Ultra declassifications. The true picture of the War is now present. Assembled, it topples the mythological and tailored war news of the first half of the 1940s.

Myth Two

That The People Taking Bows At The End Of The War Are The Real Victors

> In the wars between good and evil, there are usually two phases. In the first, good — pressed to the wall — reaches desperately for divine strength, and produces the turnaround, "miracle," victory. In the second, mere human strength, weapons, and planning progressively take over, produce the final victory, and assume the "braggin' rights."

Ancient battles between, for example, barbarians and Babylonians, were *not* between "good" and "evil" — although each side may have clothed its nationalism, aggression, and greed in vestments of good, justice, and local material religions; as some do today!

Some of the old Bible battles were between a degree of divine good and some obviously evil force. When Gideon led the Israelites against an immense horde of invaders, God guided him. God also made certain the victory would be phase one *all* the way. He required Gideon to cut his forces to a mere handful, "lest Israel vaunt themselves against me, saying, mine own hand hath saved me," afterwards (Judges 7 KJV).

Gideon's undermanned attack caused a great change to occur in the minds of the enormous enemy. They imagined large forces had entered the camp. Fearful, they fled — and, terrified, fought destructively amongst themselves!

All that is important to our story.

World War II was essentially a struggle between a degree of divine good and some deep extremes of evil. As to first and second phases, it was about halfway on the scale — the first phase produced the turnaround victories, and the second the final victory.

The initial victories were through prayer having the top priority; but then prayer's primacy was replaced by physicality, and the final victory claimed in the name of arms and men.

Prophets say the final victory at "Armageddon" will be by prayer — as Gideon's final victory was by prayer — without a second phase. If readers stick around for a couple of decades, they might find out!

But to return to the Second World War, good was frequently pressed to the wall.

In the middle portion of this chapter, we'll mainly discuss the central prayer-turnaround victory of the entire War. This frustrated the enemy drive, confused it mentally, and sent it in the opposite direction into a self-destructive conflict with another Godless force.

On theatre levels in World War II, there were also "miracle" first-phase, turnaround victories — such as the *Miracle at Midway* (the title of Gordon Prange's book), which outlined the astonishing series of "breaks" which produced the turning point in the Pacific War. The main reason for the victory is not credited by the world, or permitted, even by the U.S. to take its proper bows. The movie, *Midway* — accurate in most details — attributed the victory to "planning, error, courage and pure chance." It left out prayer, the winner.

At campaign levels, there were also "miracle" first-phase, turnaround victories. In this, we can't overlook the *Miracle at Dunkirk* (another book title, and the common "handle" by which millions still refer to that campaign-ending battle).

There were countless "miracle" first-phase, turnaround victories at the battle level, including convoys and small actions.

There were untold individual experiences. There's hardly a warrior who, when facing horrible danger, has not said, "God, get me out of this one, and I'll serve You forever!" — and has been delivered. (And then, later, has attributed this to luck, John Wayne and the cavalry arriving, coincidence, or some other physical or mystical thing! Probably every one of us can blush a bit in that department).

Why are great prayer victories ignored, forgotten, covered, or set into secondary positions with faint (or "quaint early days") credit? Why aren't the principles investigated — and the type of battle utilized therein placed thereafter at the top of the list? After all, prayer worked when all else had failed, or would have failed — and produced the victory!

The answers include several reasons — all related to the human ego: We don't like to be reminded of the days when the cold sweat was running down our backs and into our shoes — of our weakness and helplessness and desperation — even though those things produced our upward search and prayer victories; we feel foolish and embarrassed — when later celebrating phase two victories in our barrooms with the new victors who are sleek, supplied, and who never knew the desperate days — in crediting prayer; and we unfortunately like to — as quickly as possible — recover our human egos and footings and bragging stance.

The balance of this chapter will direct attention to the central prayer victory of the entire War — August 15-18, 1940.

This prayer victory saved the West intact, addled the mind of the German leadership, and oriented the Nazis in the opposite direction into a suicidal conflict of philistine vs. philistine with atheistic Russia.

We all know the "Battle of Britain" was a general tide-turner, and that the entire period from the invasion of France, through Dunkirk, through the terrible bombings of London, Coventry, and other civilian areas, continuing into the spring of 1941 — was prayer-filled.

Some define the "Battle of Britain" as the struggle against the bombing of civilian areas. This focus is quite understandable, due to the horror of these massive, demolition and incendiary raids.

However, there was something else — something precedent, distinct (though usually overlooked), and more important — which produced the central tide-turning victory of the entire War. This battle was very physical, but the victory was by prayer — resulting in a colossal German mental error at a time when British physical resistance was about to yield.

In early July, Hitler was set to invade England — but needed to destroy the RAF (particularly the day Fighter Command), as a prerequisite, to assure aerial superiority over the Channel. Neither the Army General Staff nor the Navy under Admiral Raeder (which had to transport the troops, weapons, and supplies), would proceed without this. Goering assured them the Luftwaffe could knock out the RAF by August 15 — and Hitler issued directives tying the invasion to that accomplishment within that timetable.

But after this one-month maximum effort to *destroy the RAF* (a program precedent to and totally separate from the later attacks on cities), was extended three days to August 18, Germany fell back in the belief it had been unsuccessful, gasped, and *dropped* the *primary* mission of destroying the RAF to clear the way for the invasion.

So, for all intents and purposes, the invasion was finished August 18. No air superiority, no invasion.

This was not announced — for a variety of reasons.

Britain was still pounded, though.

The Germans had been hitting the seaside — ports, coastal defenses, and airfields on a broad but shallow front relative to the invasion. Now, in a renewed air offensive August 23, the Nazis went after deeper targets of industrial and rail areas in the interior port of London. These new attacks were on a narrow front. Destruction of the RAF was still a goal, but at best only a shared top priority with the bombing goals — and only in a narrow band, incident to clearing the way for the bombers, not for an invasion. (Churchill wrote that the air offensive between August 24 and September 6 against RAF airfields had the object of breaking down the day fighter defense of the capital, London).

By September 1, or the days immediately thereafter, the German mission changed again. Now it was the bombing of civilian areas to break British morale. This program included night and day raids (with the last big daylight raid September 15), on into the spring of 1941.

September 15 is frequently credited as the day that terminated the German invasion.

However, this chapter will conclusively show that the invasion was given up after August 18, when the Germans fully realized they could not *eliminate* the RAF — which was the prerequisite for any invasion. And this chapter will show that this was clearly evidenced by the change of primary air mission from elimination of Fighter Command.

After August 18, the Germans kept their forces positioned for an invasion, but they were merely saving face, quartering troops (which had to be quartered somewhere anyhow), and hoping for some unplanned break.

The events precedent to the almost unseen August 18 turn-around were filled with desperation and prayer victories — such as Dunkirk.

From the last week of May, Hitler was encountering something he had never met before, and had no defense for — prayer power.

He made the first of his very bad military decisions at the end of May, just prior to Dunkirk. Twelve weeks later, after August 18, his military decisions never again made *any* sense. It was as if his entire mind-set could no longer reason through to any goal. His invasion of Russia was goalless — as this book will point out.

Up until late May of 1940, Hitler had experienced only stunning victories. But suddenly, with his armored forces under the famed Guderian only miles from Dunkirk, he ordered the spearhead to stand down! The general was stunned. No explanation was offered to him.

One widespread analysis holds that Goering — fearing the glorification of the armor after the French-British rout — had demanded the right to use airpower to eliminate the British on the evacuation beaches! There are interesting quotations in various histories and biographies which could back this theory up — but still, does it make sense militarily? No.

The Luftwaffe indeed went in. But — strangely — despite their astonishing advantage, it was almost as if most of the attacking pilots wouldn't pull the trigger. Newsreel after newsreel shows thick, winding, lines of Tommies (and almost as many French), standing helplessly, waiting for transport large and small to take them across the Channel. Overhead flew the German fighters and Stukas (short for dive-bomber) firing — it seemed to me — directly into the packed lines. But no one fell. I remember it well — though I was only ten. I would ask my mother, "Why don't they fall?" She would reply, "They are protected."

Did the British defend in the air? Yes, mightily. Every available plane flew continuous sorties to try to keep the Luftwaffe out of the beach airspace. The British lost 180 aircraft in the entire Dunkirk operation *(Almanac);* while the Nazis lost 179 May 27-30 alone *(Atlas).*

Meanwhile, German artillery moved onto the perimeter. By itself, it could have destroyed the troops on the beach, and the vessels! But it didn't seem to be organized, or have orders to destroy the evacuation.

Any one of three offensive arms (armor, air, artillery) — even without the others — could have finished off the evacuating forces. But none did.

Some analysts after the War — unable to credit this to the power of prayer — said a possible explanation was that Hitler didn't want to antagonize the British because he hoped for a peaceful capitulation by them. (If that theory held water, Hitler should have captured the forces on the beaches, and then negotiated!)

The troops got off with what — under the circumstances — could only be called light casualties.

They lost all their materiel — 75,000 vehicles, 1,200 artillery pieces, 1,250 antitank and antiaircraft guns, and more *(Almanac).*

After a crucial two-day delay (plus a day to get cranked up again), Guderian was unleashed — but too late.

The British people simply call it, "the miracle of Dunkirk." Walter Lord's book is entitled, *The Miracle Of Dunkirk.* An imposing British figure on a recent TV show told about the evacuation, and called it, "the miracle at Dunkirk."

I remember the events well. The umbrella of prayer power could be felt in the U.S. In fact, much of it emanated from the U.S.

Something caused Hitler to halt his troops, miss timing, ignore the advice of one (Guderian) or more of his top generals, accept the bad advice of another of his top generals (Goering), use less than one third of his available forces, and so on.

(For a slightly contrarian view, some believe Dunkirk was a colossal defeat — dressed by the Allied government press departments to look like a *victory.* The recent book, *Dunkirk: The Patriotic Myth,* calls it "victory by propaganda."

(Personally, I don't believe I've ever heard Dunkirk called a British *victory.* It was a defeat — but the point was, it was saved from being an utter disaster by events not explainable in physical terms. The men got home when, instead, the beaches could have been red. Of course, a "propaganda" aspect was openly functioning — but, in my perception, it admitted both the scope of the problem and the miracle aspect. Therefore, I think whatever propaganda existed in this case, mostly had to reflect the perception of the public — instead of issuing what it wished the public to believe. There were just too many servicepeople returning from the beaches, and too many pilots, and too many boat crews — plus a great closeness to the actual war scene itself — for the British people to have received or believed distortions of the event).

Churchill knew, from Ultra, that Germany would attempt an invasion. In his June 4 speech, he said that "civilization" would be defended by a few thousand airmen. (The U.S. at that time was still eighteen months away from entering the War — and had not yet even sent the fabled fifty destroyers! So England was indeed alone).

✝ During the balance of June after Dunkirk, Hitler was pre-occupied with taking the remainder of France. Paris fell on the 14th, and the nation officially surrendered on the 22nd.

Admiral Raeder, whose German Navy had taken a poudning in the invasion of Norway, told Hitler there could be no invasion of England without both air and naval superiority in the Channel area. That was a tall order. England was a natural air base; the British Navy was still the world's greatest; the German Navy had been severely limited by the settlements after WWI, and had only managed to build a few ships since breaking free of the sanctions; and the submarine fleet was, at that hour, very small.

Goering, who never understood the concept of cooperation between air and sea forces during the short life of the German invasion plan, had about 2,800 bombers, dive bombers, and fighters ready to go against RAF Fighter Command's 500 to 700 planes. The idea of nailing British warships, mine laying vessels, radar stations, gun emplacements, and other items which had to be cleared for a successful invasion, didn't appeal to him. He performed those tasks only with reluctance. He perceived his task in the universe at the time to destroy the RAF, and generally prove the Luftwaffe to be the principal arm of German might.

Still in June, Hitler — impressed by his quick defeat of very large French and British forces, felt that England would make peace. The Swiss in London were feeling out the British Government, but finding no inclination to make peace, even on an unoccupied basis. (Hitler is reported to have commented several times that the British would not keep a peace agreement anyhow, and would have to be conquered later).

On June 30, the Swiss told Halder (Chief of the German General Staff), that there was no basis for peace negotiations. *(History of the German General Staff)*.

On July 2, Hitler issued his first orders for "Operation Sealion" — the invasion *(Bodyguard)*. (Also known as "Sea Lion").

It was important that Hitler act fast. Bad weather in the Channel lasts late and starts early.

July 11, in official session relating to planning the invasion,

Goering told Halder that the Luftwaffe would knock the RAF out of the skies in "a month or less." As a direct result, the Staff announced plans July 15 to invade England a month later — sometime after "August 15" *(Almanac)*. Hitler informed the Staff July 16 that he had definitely decided on the invasion.

The aerial offensive began July 10. Churchill credits this as the opening day, and mentions attacks on shipping and towns where troops might land, with the purpose also of drawing the RAF into combat, to "deplete" it. The RAF Official History shows the first phase beginning July 10.

Continuing with a discussion of July, Hitler had thirteen divisions prepared to invade England, with twenty-six in reserve. There would be two main landings. However, the German Navy said there was no hope of landing such large forces with the warships, transport vessels, and landing craft, available. (Germany, being a land-army nation, had not bothered to consult the Navy up until then, and the Nazis simply didn't have the training or equipment for two big landings). (In my personal analysis, they should have invaded immediately after Dunkirk, irrespective of losses, while England was stunned and disarmed. Every day after that, and every prerequisite established, diminished their chances. As a side note, the leading *generals* were totally opposed to an invasion at all!)

The Navy told Hitler that, once landings were made, troops and supplies would have to be brought in at a rate much lower than planned.

Halder said that, in this case, the invasion wouldn't work, because it would be like putting the troops through a "sausage machine."

The Navy was also understandably nervous because Goering — who would provide the air cover — didn't believe in roles other than pure air force work. Fighting, bombing, and strafing were all right as long as the Luftwaffe was in the featured (or at least headline-grabbing), role — not merely supporting the army or the navy!

As late as July 19, Hitler, in a public speech he knew would be reported in England, made another offer of peace. He didn't receive a reply. Basically, his "track record" with peace accords, his deceiving of Chamberlain and others, his vacillation between murderous threats and pleasant olive branches depending on his moods or temporary needs, and the obvious fact that he would just use "peace" with Britain to invade some other nation, left him without credibility!

A compromise was reached July 31 to make *one* landing instead of two. (Data on divisions, Navy, and landings from *History of the German General Staff*).

Also July 31, Hitler said to Raeder, "If after *eight days* of intensive air war the Luftwaffe has not achieved considerable destruction of the enemy's air force, harbours and naval forces, the operation [the invasion] will have to be put off till . . . 1941" *(Churchill)*.

August was climactic. This fact was duly recorded by historians, as I will show in this chapter. However, due to bloodier phases of the cross-Channel war that erupted afterwards, this was overlooked; or, if observed, not given proper context or deserved stature.

On August 1, many immense factors (including the issue of "civilization," as Churchill put it), were coming into one tiny time frame — one small "window." If Hitler eliminated England, then the big natural base at his back was gone forever. If not . . . ? Then all his generals said sooner or later the British would be back.

One of Hitler's biggest problems lay in his own inability to make the required decisions within the limited time-frame.

The Fuehrer was not an intrepid leader! When his troops had met unexpectedly stiff resistance in Norway, he had spent two days wanting to pull them out! His hand on the throttle of the great German war machine was unsteady. His vision was either too grandoise or too puny. Could he take England? He didn't want to be defeated at arms. He didn't want his soldiers thrown back into the Channel in an English "Dunkirk" — and without help from above! All reports tell of his vacillation, hesitation, and irritating changes of plans, orders, and timetables.

Surely he had many advantages. The British Lion was

wounded, the U.S. was asleep, the Channel weather was good, the Luftwaffe was at its peak, and the RAF was beaten down in numbers of units and experienced pilots.

One thing complicating his offensive was the sheer number of different types of targets assigned to the Luftwaffe. These included shipping (listed by almost all sources), the RAF (listed by all sources, and usually meaning the day Fighter Command), ports where troops and supplies might land, and the Royal Navy (shown by only a couple of sources). There seemed to be no priorities. For example, why waste valuable time and sorties on Channel shipping? That could be left for another day. And meanwhile, there was no concentration on the Royal Navy — which *was* important! A couple of tough cruisers could have torn up a lot of invasion ships! Even the orders to "bomb ports" didn't take into account the hundreds of miles of estuarial and harbor coastlines in the world's number one maritime nation.

Too, in all this, there was little mention of such things as gun emplacements, radar stations, and the like — or of the difficulty of spotting these from the air, and further difficulty of hitting them.

The Germans had the notion that by attacking ports, for example, the RAF would come out and fight — and thus be blasted from the skies. The first part was correct — the RAF came out fighting. But the German losses exceeded their estimates — and exceeded the losses of the RAF! (The net for August and September was about two German planes to one RAF plane destroyed, after adjustments made long after the conflict).

Goering had given his "one month" timetable for destruction of the RAF, and, by August 1, he had only two weeks remaining!

The Luftwaffe was scattering its fire.

Therefore, it is logical that, around August 1, orders became more specific.

As quoted earlier, Hitler told Raeder (July 31), "If after eight days of intensive air war the Luftwaffe has not achieved considerable destruction of the enemy's air force, harbours and naval forces [the invasion] will have to be put off till . . . 1941."

That didn't address specificity, but it did address the immediate timetable.

August 5, Hitler issued "Directive No. 17" authorizing a stepped-up air war against England.

August 8, the Fuehrer told the Luftwaffe of "Eagle Day" (Adlertag), August 15, saying, "within a short period you will wipe the British Air Force from the sky" *(Almanac).*

Now the focus was intense — get Fighter Command and get it fast.

In addition to bringing the RAF into the skies, the Germans attacked airfields, the vital air net control centers, and factories as well.

The arena was very small — all things considered. Spitfires had a range of only about 180 miles (before coming 180 miles back), in level fight. Once a little dogfighting was tossed in, the planes didn't go far before they had to refuel and rearm. German bombers (twin-engined Heinkels) had a longer range, but ME-109s had a shorter range than the Spitfires. Thus the arena — from all standpoints of offense and defense — was Southeast England, no more, no less. And the target was — Fighter Command, particularly the bases.

The British had their usual secret — Ultra. By routinely reading the German coded military traffic, they knew just what to expect, where, and when. This enabled them to increase the "arena" a bit, by pulling defensive aircraft from the North and Midlands which would normally have to remain on alert there!

The British also had their radar. The Germans knew about it, but their Air Minister Goering was reported more than once as giving its destruction a low or even no priority.

Building up steadily in the preceding days, the Germans struck on "Eagle Day," August 15, with 1,786 sorties, mainly directed at RAF bases. The Germans lost seventy-five planes to thirty-two of the RAF *(Almanac),* or seventy-six to thirty-four *(Churchill).* (During the War, both sides tended to exaggerate — often unwittingly, due to reports by several witnesses — losses inflicted on the enemy. However, by the time of the appearing of histories decades later, the figures had been adjusted within a very small margin for error. Even then, however, there can be differences because "losses" could include planes "put out of action," which, some weeks later, flew again).

Despite some sources which indicate "August 15" as the main day of that period, it was only one important day in a string of a few days precedent, and three days subsequent.

On August 16, the Nazis were back, hitting with 1,720 sorties. *(Almanac)*.

The 17th was clear and bright — perfect for more German attacks.

But nothing came over the Channel on the 17th.

This day has been heralded in stories and movies as evidence that the German attack had been broken. A British official broadcast a rather triumphant speech — one that later drew criticism as perhaps stirring the Germans to new efforts!

On the 18th, the Luftwaffe was back again in force! In fact, the well-documented book, *The Hardest Day,* shows it was the roughest of the entire year — later months included. The enemy put up 1,000 sorties — again directed mainly (as were the raids of 12, 13, 14, 15, and 16) — at RAF Fighter Command airfields that could impact a German invasion.

This group of several days of furious raids — particularly the "Eagle Day" 15th, followed by the 16th, and capped finally by the 18th — produced the "prayer turnaround" victory of the entire War.

After the 18th, the invasion was no longer *possible,* because the destruction of the RAF (mainly the Fighter Command), had been proven not possible!

After August 18th, the invasion was no longer possible, because the destruction of Fighter Command was proven impossible.

A very significant break in the action occurred for four or five days from August 19-23. There were only isolated actions.

How significant a break? Churchill saluted the RAF with his famous "never have so many owed so much to so few" speech.

The RAF Official History gives the four-day break special notice by classifying it as a full "phase" of the summer and fall air battle — the "Interim Phase" — with very little action.

The significance of the break was far more than just relief from attack. It was felt in hearts and minds. It was a great psychological moment. In my opinion, this break was the prayer victory. Germany had been denied the destruction of the RAF, and hence denied the invasion — and hence would shortly reorient on its self-destruction in the east.

How badly was the RAF Fighter Command hurting when the action broke off? It was on the ropes. A British ex-official interviewed in a TV documentary said that if the mid-August attacks had continued "one more day," Britain could not have put an adequate defense into the air.

Trained pilots were in short supply, but serviceable aircraft was the critical category. Two RAF planes were put out of action for each RAF pilot put out of action *(Churchill)*.

A RAF survivor interviewed in a TV documentary said the Germans destroyed most of Fighter Command's airfields in Southeastern England, along with their repair facilities, spare parts supplies, etc.

In quoting sources on these points, one must watch for the phenomenon of defiance mixed with admissions of helplessness. The same sources which say England was not in trouble, are the sources for information about how close to the edge the great nation lay! This is a natural thing.

Planes had to be repaired, refueled, and rearmed for, sometimes, three or more sorties in a day. This could not be done from bombed-out buildings — or by dead or wounded ground personnel. A source citing the wreckage of fields said the fighters could continue to fly "from any pasture." That was defiant and grand, and true — but they could not be repaired, refueled, and rearmed from "any pasture." The fields were essential.

The control of Fighter Command was by a sensitive network taking inputs from intelligence, radar, and patrols, and dispatching — with the maximum economy of force — the best effort to the right place at the right time. This was one great key to the British defensive successes. The Germans knew something of this, and bombed these centers specifically. (Churchill described one at Uxbridge near London, fifty feet underground!)

Only one source mentions bombings of RAF factories — and indicates this presented some problems, but nothing big.

The most effective Luftwaffe program in this period was the bombing of the RAF airfields (coupled with taking on the planes in the air).

Churchill says August 15 was the "largest air battle of this period of the war." Another source says, "the peak of the operation came on 15 August" *(Dictionary)*. (It classifies this period as attacks on harbors, etc. — and puts attacks on airfields mainly in the next wave of German assaults. But it recognizes some kind of definite peak August 15). Another source says, "Eagle Day [of August 15] helped turn the tide against Germany" *(Almanac).*

Since *The Hardest Day* made its specific documentation of the days most closely surrounding August 15, we now realize "August 15" was both the day of heaviest attacks (1,786 Luftwaffe sorties), and part of a *group* of days, including the 12th, 13th, 14th, 16th (1,720 sorties), and the final crack out of that first gun, the 18th (1,000 sorties).

The 18th was the most hard-fought day, with the highest losses. It was probably the "August 15" of some historical accounts.

What evidence did the Germans give that they had changed their minds — and that, indeed, a classic turnaround had occurred?

When they returned to the ferocious attack — which was so soon, and so ruggedly executed, and so prolonged that we virtually forgot the August period prior to the 18th — they no longer had, as top priority, destruction of Fighter Command to clear the way for the invasion.

They had retained the concept of destruction of the RAF, but only for purposes of clearing the way for their new (temporary) top priority — bombing deeper industrial, port, and rail targets than would be useful to aid an invasion.

The invasion campaign had been dropped from the German mind — but Nazi troops standing in the ports had not been notified.

Poor Biggin Hill airfield — just southeast of London — was important both to the old invasion bombings and to the new priorities! It caught hell in both campaigns.

The first of the new raids hit London's docks and rail areas (and one source says a raid hit Portsmouth, which was a port bombed under the old invasion priority). In any event, the main effort went to London. Fighter Command fields in the path of the new priority were also hit.

Some analysts cite the very heavy continuing pressure of RAF fields as proof that the Germans were still trying to wipe out Fighter Command so they could invade. However, if one looks deeper, the airfields now being hit were those having a direct bearing on the new pattern of raids. The former attacks on the RAF were on a very broad, 500-mile front *(Churchill)*, hitting airfields and drawing the British planes into combat. The new attacks were not primarily on the RAF but on London and other targets, while striking the RAF fields on a much *narrower* front relating to those raids. *(Churchill).* The Germans were not trying to kill the entire RAF now — only the planes which would interfere with their present raids.

(The *Hardest Day* has interesting maps which show the four main group sectors in England, plus a closeup of No. 11 Group, which defended Southeastern England. On August 17, Fighter Command had 918 serviceable fighters! That's a formidable armada! *However,* only 343 were in Group 11! The others were needed elsewhere. Group 11 flew some 600 sorties on the 18th, therefore, the twenty-three squadrons flew twice — not unusual, because Sir Winston says some individual squadrons in those fateful weeks flew three times in one day. With Ultra and radar, and the command networks fifty feet underground, the British *could scramble some planes from the Group 12 north of London,* and the Group 10 west of the city. No source draws any conclusions — but from my perspective, I would tend to believe that, as the Germans began to realize that the battered squadrons of Group 11 were being supported in the air, and replenished on the ground, by planes from *other sectors,* they just "flat gave up" on the concepts of eliminating the RAF and putting troops across the Channel. After the 18th, their time-frame had come and gone. Their moment in history had flickered — and flopped).

When Germany changed its top air priority from eliminating the RAF, did it go immediately to the policy of bombing civilian populations? No.

The chronology after August 18 was this: August 23 to about September 1 — industrial raids in London, and hammering RAF installations in the way of those; about September 1 — shift to hitting civilian populations as a distinct policy (hitting a lot of industrial areas, intermingled with civilian residential areas on the ground, and continuing, but with much less effort, to try to clear the RAF from the path of the bombers).

How did the shift to deliberate bombing of civilians ("to break British morale") come about? It was Hitler's intention from August 18 forward, in my opinion. However, various sources show the Fuehrer as a man who always wanted an "excuse" to attack — and would go to lengths to obtain one (even delaying offensives, to the frustration of his generals, until he had the "excuse" he psychologically needed).

He needed an excuse to bomb English civilians. Had he just started in fury after August 18, he would have been saying openly that the invasion plan was hopeless, and that now only slaughter of women and children was his revenge. This was the fact — but he didn't want this to be obvious. He didn't want to admit defeat of his air force — so he devised a heavier air attack scheme than ever before, and carried it out.

But, what was his excuse?

In the August 23-24 raid on London industrial areas, ten Nazi bombers went off target, and accidentally dropped their loads in purely civilian areas. August 25-26, the RAF Bomber Command retaliated with a raid on Berlin! Hitler waxed furious, pledging retaliation for Britain "indiscriminately [bombing] civilian residential quarters and farms and villages." *(Almanac)*. The speech was delivered September 4, and declared the Luftwaffe was now answering "night after night."

So the new policy was in the open — with an excuse — from about September 1. At the start, there was still some day raiding.

In the meantime, Hitler was requesting a "second opinion" about his defeated Sealion plan. Maybe Britain had no troops, and a landing — even if badly hit by the RAF — could succeed. This was in the realm of hope, not substance. He asked Admiral Canaris — head of one of his intelligence setups — to give a report. However, unknown to Hitler, Canaris worked against the Hitler regime, and often leaked information to the Allies. Britain in fact had twenty-nine weak divisions. Canaris reported thirty-seven at full strength — and as full of fighting spirit as the RAF fighter pilots! Based on this report, even Hitler's realm of hope collapsed, and, on September 2, he spoke of the continuing presence of Sealion troops as just a cover for his plans to go east. *(Bodyguard)*.

The *big* night raids on London began September 7. This severe raiding went on until spring of 1941. English civilian dead averaged nearly 5,000 a month, with injured about 7,000 a month, counting all cities. (By the end of March, some 30,000 were dead, 40,000 injured).

In all that bloodshed, it is easy to forget that there ever was an original objective of the destruction of the RAF Fighter Command as the prerequisite to invasion — and that the turn-around achieved there sent Germany to its doom. For many people, *the* Battle of Britain was — and quite understandably so — the bombings. This book will pick up Sir Winston's word, "civilization," and call the first phase prayer victory, the "Battle of Civilization." The next period, August 23 to the spring of 1941, it will call the "Battle of London" (a term others also use, though the dates may vary). And it will call the entire period beginning with Dunkirk and running into the spring of 1941, the "Battle of Britain."

September 7, 625 German bombers hit London. That was a very big raid for that day. London was bombed every single night without break until November 3, with an average of 200 bombers *(Churchill)*.

Because the *big* raids started September 7, many histories use that date to mark the change of German policy.

A change of policy is clearly recognized by all, but dates vary.

Sir Winston says the 7th marked a change of plan — and that Hitler made a "foolish mistake," because *"he could have won in the air"*! Think about that one.

One source speaks of a "crucial moment," but doesn't specify a date. It says, "At a crucial moment, their targets were shifted." *(Atlas)*.

In another summary, the above source says the Germans "allowed themselves to be deflected from their objectives."

This book sticks with its assertion that August 18th was the "crucial moment."

August 18th was the "prayer turnaround" of the entire War. The superior physical force — on the verge of victory — mentally quit; and turned its eyes towards Russia and self-destruction.

September 15 is a special day in the history books — and is celebrated annually. For a long time, people thought *it* was the most crucial day. As more and more information came in through the decades after the War, it could be seen that that specific date was not more meaningful than many other dates. However, there is nothing wrong with choosing it as a symbol of some other great days that summer.

September 15 was another "Eagle Day." (*Almanac,* directly quoting Hitler's order, calls August 15 "Eagle Day." *Bodyguard* calls September 15 "Eagle Day." *Atlas* (never strong on text — it makes its reputation with those wonderful maps! — ignores both dates, and doesn't mention Eagle Days. Churchill calls September 15 "Eagle Day," calls August 15 and September 15 dates of "supreme consequence," and doesn't refute August 15 as an "Eagle Day." The position of this book is that there were two Eagle Days — August 15 and September 15).

September 15 gained its prominence as the day on which all believed the greatest number of German aircraft were shot down. (Understandably, this type statistic was important — because it meant the possibility of relief from the bombings). However, in the decades after the War, the original British claim of 183 downed German aircraft dwindled to fifty-six, while the tally for August 18 climbed to sixty-nine. Therefore, August 18 was the day on which the greatest number of German aircraft were shot down.

September 15's raids have been billed in history books as a sort of ultimate attempt to "crush the RAF." In fact, though, the main effort consisted of a daylight bombing raid on London. Therefore, a little propaganda got mixed into the facts.

There was no breather after September 15. The raids continued unbated. Therefore, it is difficult to say that September 15 had any effect on the pattern of German raiding.

The raid was in *daylight*. Night raiding had begun near the first of September. Therefore, this raid was unusual. It was the *last* big daylight raid. This is the one unique thing that can positively be credited to September 15 — the final daylight raid.

Some have said that there was "linkage" between September 15 and a message decoded on September 17, in which the German General Staff passed along Hitler's order to dismantle some paratroop loading equipment at Dutch airfields. At the time, that looked as if the invasion had been called off as a result of September 15!

Churchill called September 15 the "culminating date." Since that time, facts have taken away some of the things on which he might have been leaning. (He didn't lean heavily on statistics, or on the effect of the bombing of London, or on the change of invasion plans — saying only that September 15 "may" stand as the date affecting the invasion).

Therefore, removing those, what is the basis for his calling September 15 the "culminating date"?

Examination of this brings to light an area which might otherwise have gone unnoticed — a special perspective of Churchill's.

Way back — on June 9, only a few days after Dunkirk (and fewer after his famous June 4, "We will fight them on the beaches," speech), when Britain was wide open to defeat — Sir Winston had spoken with Jan Smuts, the South African Prime Minister.

In that meeting, Churchill said he saw *only one way* Hitler could be turned back — that he should attack England and "break his air weapon."

Was the "air weapon" broken September 15?

No, but the Luftwaffe's original psychological strength — its insane Teutonic beliefs of invincibility, already wounded — was terminated.

In just ten weeks the Luftwaffe first had its mind or sense blown away — when it made the mental error of changing its course after August 18.

Next, its already injured blind certainty that the enemy would collapse if the Luftwaffe but put in an appearance — or that any given air strike could cause England to surrender — ended September 15. From that time forward, the illusions were gone, and the battle was just a hard job against a tough foe.

Surviving September 15 was much of the Luftwaffe's still awesome — but unguided and uninspired — merely brute strength. Germany punished England unmercifully — raining bombs until the spring of 1941.

Churchill knew something distinct had happened — some culmination — September 15. It was the defeat of the psychological thrust which had been igniting and sustaining the open German aggression.

The Luftwaffe had changed immensely in just ten weeks. Goering's original gang had sung and strutted with him — and defeated several nations. They believed they were a bunch of fantastic, unbeatable, men and machines. This bold, powerful organization had the physical ability to defeat England.

They campaigned hard between July 10 and August 18. They had painful losses of the original air crews, but the British were also hurting. In that period, they failed to destroy the RAF, but this was a mental failure. Speaking either of the August 18 (often called August 15) climax — or of no more than the next twenty days to September 7 (the accepted day of the beginning of the very big civilian raids, although smaller civilian raids began days earlier)— Churchill said they would have won if they had continued; *Hardest Day* said Goering made a "blunder" when he changed course; *Atlas* said the Luftwaffe changed at a "crucial moment"; and other key sources said similar things.

The Luftwaffe lost its sense August 18.

That, however, still left it with its psychological convictions and its brute physical strength.

The September 15 raid on London was simply an enraged, daylight, "We will clobber you," attack by a Luftwaffe which could still not believe it could not just show up and stomp England to death. It was a last, breast-beating assertion, by the Nazi air arm, of the mystical power it *knew* it possessed!

This was the last attack revealing the original psychology of the Luftwaffe. After losing September 15, the "psychological stuffing" went out of it.

The fantasy balloon was popped that day.

In just ten weeks, 1,000 elite crews — nearly half the Luftwaffe's operational crews — had been blown from the skies. The *numbers* could be rebuilt over the winter — but not the old illusions or camaraderie.

September 15 killed the already wounded vision. The dreams, the beliefs — already tottering — crashed in this final, enraged, arrogant, come-get-me, daylight boast.

Goering felt this. His men felt it.

And Churchill felt that the blind, motivating thrust had gone out of the "air weapon."

The thing which reached its "culmination" was the superioristic assertiveness of the enemy. Nothing more, nothing less. After this, there would be no more glory, no more walkovers — just hard work.

Was the "air weapon" *physically* shattered? No way. Germany then proceeded to pound English civilians in heavy night raids nonstop until the spring of 1941. Of the three elements of sense, psychology, and strength, only strength was left.

No one seriously expected the brutal attacks on civilians to defeat England — these were just cowardly punishments. The work was performed by just a capable — but no longer insanely inspired — Luftwaffe. The duty had become drudgery — a "trench warfare" in the skies.

Just Before Going to Press . . .

A QUICK BOOK REVIEW

Collier, Richard. *Eagle Day.* New York: Dutton, 1980 (original edition 1966).

Collier intensively examines the period August 6-September 15, 1940, which he regards as the most significant six weeks. (He points out that there are a variety of respectable opinions by others as to the most significant day or period — ranging from selecting days such as September 15 or August 15, to campaigns with beginnings such as July 10, August 8, August 11, and with endings such as September 15, October 5, October 31 — or as late as May of 1941).

Hitler ordered the attack in Directive 16, Collier says, with the purpose to eliminate the RAF to an extent that it would not be able to oppose the invading German troops. The "Eagle Day" was August 13. However, not all went well that day, and only a few planes got over England. The attack continued, however, on the 14th, and then — with fair weather — the biggie came on August 15th.

Goering had earlier expected to put the RAF out of action in *four days.* That optimism backfired when the going turned out to be tough, protracted, and unsuccessful. Also, the Luftwaffe greatly prized its aircrews, and even the loss of a few was felt.

Raids prior to August 7 had actually cleared the Channel of shipping and naval units. A convoy of twenty-five vessels leaving London on the 8th (for up the coast), was destroyed by the Luftwaffe.

On the 8th, the pressure shifted to the airfields — to RAF fields. However, the pounding went to the "Coastal Command" (not the main Fighter Command) fighter fields close to the shore, on a wide front relating especially to the invasion. (At the time, British fighter production was 496 units a month, but the shortage of trained pilots was acute).

On the 13th, Goering hit the radar stations, causing interruption for some critical hours of the raiding. The raids moved inland from the coastal bases into "Fighter Command" territory. The Germans, from leadership to aircrews, were disappointed in the high cost of their results.

On the night of August 15, after "watching" the battle from a plotting and control center, Churchill told Ismay the famous, "Never in the field of human conflict was so much owed by so many to so few." Thus, a great crisis was in the process of breaking up around that date — and this was further signified when the Prime Minister delivered those lines in Parliament August 20.

Collier does not make much of the important break August 18-24, nor does he relate this to a fundamental change in the invasion prospect. He focuses tightly on the air action itself. Likewise, he does not make any mention of the August 24 accidental bombing of civilian areas of London, and consequent five small British retaliation raids on Berlin, except as almost an afterthought, well out of the otherwise chronological narrative. This is due to his tight focus on just, for Britain's part, the Fighter Commands — including Coastal Command — and mainly the day, though some night fighter, activity.

The book suffers a bit from having been written in 1966. It was revised for 1980 republication. It has difficulty finding the exact point at which the invasion psychology on the German side changed. Once August 18 is passed in the chronology, the sought-after turning point becomes quicksilver, and besides, the remarkable combat documentation retains its dominant focus.

Both the British population and its military forces expected an invasion well into September — coastal inhabitants "reporting" landings, coastal defenses going on alerts, and the Air Ministry itself issuing an outright H-Hour alert early in that month. But all these were just the prevailing state of mind on the British side of the Channel — not on the other.

The book quotes Goering telling Gen. Student (C. of airborne troops for the invasion), on September 2, that Hitler had decided not to invade Britain. It also states that the decision to shift to hammering London was made September 3.

Writings immediately after the War focused (quite naturally) on what is really the "Battle of London" — the terrible bombings of that and other British cities, reported to the U.S. by Edward R. Murrow (which made him famous). The more important — for "civilization" (I refer to Churchill's speech) — earlier battle of Luftwaffe vs. RAF to enable the invasion, gradually submerged from sight as an item totally distinct from the great civilian bombings. It merged, in public view, with the later scene.

German troops were not pulled out of the Channel ports until mid-October. At first, analysts tried to call that the "cancelling of the invasion," and further, to connect it with the state of the air war at that moment, to attempt to find a cause-and-effect relationship in October. Later, Churchill's book tried to call September 17 the cancellation date because Ultra had decoded Hitler ordering some paratroop transporters at Dutch airfields to stand down. Churchill couldn't mention the secret Ultra, so only wrote, "As we now know . . ." — a hidden reference to his "most secret source." Then he tried to show a cause-and-effect relationship between September 15 in the air war, and the "cancellation." However, he didn't press the point, and wound up saying only that September 15 "may" stand as an air war date affecting the invasion.

In the mind of this reviewer, the more that August is studied, the more it will reveal that the change took place after August 18.

Collier clashes with *History of the German General Staff* in a couple of important dates. Admiral Raeder had told Halder (and hence Hitler and Goering as well) that the Navy could not transport the thirteen divisions, and not on the two fronts planned, and could not get supplies and reinforcements across in the needed quantities — even if the RAF was destroyed. A decision was made by the Fuehrer himself to use one front, and do things on a reduced scale. Collier places these items at *August* 23 and August 27 respectively. However, *General Staff* puts them in *July* (where this reviewer believes they belong), with the final decision made *July 31*. Which month is correct?

Collier's notes (if he hasn't just got the months mixed up), may refer to a reiteration of the decisions — however, it is only logical that the transporting German Navy would not wait until late August to reveal that it couldn't carry out the invasion plan! Hitler decided on "Sea Lion" July 16. Thus, late in July, presented with the plans, the Navy would have said what it could and couldn't do — and the plan would have been tailored by July 31. That seems logical.

Even if there were any such discussions and decisions — or any reiterations — in late August, then the invasion was still alive at that time, though dying; and in any event it was definitely off by September 2.

Collier reveals a three-step pattern: first, raids on the coastal areas on a broad front to destroy RAF and other defenses, through August 18; then deeper raidings on RAF installations — but on a narrow front, with reference to bombing deep targets, but not to aid an invasion, through early September; and then the announced primary mission of bombing civilian London and other urban residential areas.

Have British fighter-production figures confused readers of reference books? Well, take heart — they confused no less a figure than Sir Winston himelf, who complained drily on more than one occaison of the "variety of figures" "always" given by the Air Ministry.

Collier's dozens of remarkable interviews with participants on both sides distinguish his book. One special insight is into Nazi aircrew fatigue and low morale after August 18. They had shot the wad of all their elan. Fighter pilots were flying up to three "protection" missions per day for bombers. And Goering rewarded them only by telling them to their faces that they were failures and worse.

☆   ☆   ☆

The bows in World War II go to prayer in the various "first phases" from the central turnaround to every individual's foxhole prayer victories. The central prayer turnaround victory of the entire War was August 15-18, 1940, when powerful physical forces were met by physical resistance that could not have put up an adequate defense one more day. The Germans suffered a mental defeat, and their then-addled leadership turned from clear-cut goals to goalless suicide in the east.

Myth Three

That The Maginot Line Should Appear In Discussions Of WWII

The German master stroke westward in 1940 was simply the shortest distance between Germany and the Channel opposite Britain. It had nothing whatsoever to do with the usual press preface, "Bypassing the Maginot Line."

The German drive to the sea May 10-20, 1940, was a thing in and of itself. It didn't "skirt the Maginot Line," or "take advantage of the fact that the Maginot Line terminated" to the south, where Luxembourg and Belgium meet the French border. The drive had nothing whatsoever to do with the Maginot Line. To persist in describing the German strategy as affected in any way by the Maginot Line is to fail to see several things: the brilliance of the German move (which we have yet to see); all the astonishing innovations they brought to warfare (which are discussed later in this chapter, and which we have yet to see in full); and hence the full depth of the unfortunate stupidity of the Allied positions and plans (which we have yet to see in full, but which the Germans saw clearly — and exploited totally). To top all this off, the Germans achieved surprise (although the war — so quiet it was called the "phony war" — had been in effect for some eight months since Poland; and although Norway had been invaded and conquered within the previous month (April); and although the German armored and motorized divisions and the bulk of their strike infantry was poised opposite Belgium and Luxembourg).

The number of Allied divisions (French, British, Belgian and Dutch), roughly equalled the number of German divisions. They were probably good fighters — after all, their forebears had withstood the Germans in WWI. We know that their armored forces were much smaller than the Germans'. The West learned too late that communications (enabling coordinated quick response) was bad between Allies, stemming from France's system which did not even provide centralized command in the modern sense.

But even with deficiencies, surely the Allies could have put up an adequate defense! The Allies themselves were certain of this. And that became another deficiency.

What, then, caused the sudden collapse?

For one thing, the Allies assumed that the big French Army (more than 100 of the approximately 140 Allied divisions), was properly positioned for the defense of the main land mass — France. (For another thing, the Allies thought there would be time after the battle was joined — time as there was in the First World War).

But the Allied border stretched from the Netherlands to Switzerland — and the French portion (with its Maginot Line), was only the lower one-third.

If Belgium was invaded, there was little to protect a couple of hundred miles of French border with Belgium.

The French had about fifty divisions (about half their forces) behind the Maginot Line. This was an overemphasis.

They realized the Germans might come through Belgium, so placed about thirty divisions, plus about ten British divisions, on that common border with Belgium. Thus they were aware that the Maginot Line protected only about one-third of the Allied borders with Germany, and that the Germans would be tempted to plunge into the long borders with the Lowlands, and thus reach the French border with Belgium as an invasion route to Paris.

Why, then — when obviously more than two-thirds of the problem of defense didn't involve the Maginot Line at all — did focus on that Line remain? It was just a hypnotic mystery. Not only was it the most heavily defended, but every newsreel of the buildup and battle in France, and every historical account, begins with pictures or text about . . . the Maginot Line.

As Germany prepared for battle, it lined up Rundstedt with seven armored and nearly fifty infantry divisions opposite Belgium, on a front about 100 miles in length.

To the south, opposite the Maginot Line, on a front nearly twice as long, it spread, thinly, only some twenty infantry divisions.

The direction of the attack became obvious.

Was the Allied intelligence so poor it did not have any sense of the enemy dispositions? If so, that might answer some questions. But in nations which are populated by the same stock, and which often speak each other's language, surely one would think there would have been an adequate spy network.

So again, we return to the strange — and unfounded — Maginot Line hypnosis.

Analysts have emphasized that the French were blindly self-assured, resting behind their Maginot Line. If this had been true — based in fact — then one might say, The French were fooled.

But the French were *not* blindly resting behind the Line. They could see the other options open to the Germans. They positioned some troops to defend against such eventualities.

So the French were *not* asleep — not totally.

But there was — and is — a "mystique" about that Maginot Line which lives to this day! And which shouldn't live a day longer.

Analysts have said that the Allies could not conceive of the Germans cutting through the difficult Ardennes. It's true the Allies might have perceived this forest and difficult terrain as a natural barrier, but if they overemphasized its value, then they were in another state of hypnosis similar to the Maginot Line. After all — they had just witnessed *Poland* only eight months previous. Didn't they learn anything from that?

It's true that some generals "fight the previous war." But the Allies weren't stupid. They weren't digging trenches. They knew it would be a fluid war.

One might say the Allies were halfway between the previous war and the one they were in. Their thought was still anchored to the concept of "barriers" — the Maginot, the Ardennes, etc. — and not yet appreciative (although they had seen a remarkable demonstration), of the new war style of *motion*.

Once we grasp all the points of the Blitzkrieg, this ends the mystique which still causes descriptions of the invasion to begin with, "The Maginot Line . . ."

We say today that we understand *Blitzkrieg*. But do we?

The British invented the tank, and first used it in combat in WWI. It was a mobile gun, it was protected from bullets, it scared the enemy, and — the big point — it was used in support of infantry.

WWI was static. Barriers and immobility and masses of slow infantry characterized it (plus heaps of artillery). The tank was a weapon used in support of this immobility.

Those early tank tactics developed from the use of the horse in battle in history. The horse (or some other animals, such as Hannibal's elephants!) were used to support the infantry. The center of battle was usually the big blocks of infantry. Later, units of cavalry were developed to sweep flanks and roll up the enemy from the sides and rear!

However, even in this most dashing use, the cavalry was oriented on *two things*. It was anchored to *two things*. These were, first, the infantry, and, second, the particular battle (the purpose was to win the day).

While the British developed their armor and tactics between

wars, Guderian lept so far ahead of the field that we *still don't see* fully what German Blitzkrieg was!

The German Blitz was designed to win the *war* — not the battle or the day — in one continuous rolling of the tank treads.

It centered the battle on the armor — not the infantry. It reversed the traditional role of mobility supporting immobility — and caused fast infantry to support the armor. It detached this armor in very large, main battle forces.

The term, "Blitzkrieg," means "lightning war." We have usually assumed that meant lightning prosecution of war — or lightning *warfare*. Not really. It means what it says — lightning *war*.

The detached, large, armored forces — as the center of the invading forces — were to move continuously until the *war* ended.

With this, the concept of fighting a battle, then having days to regroup, smoke pipes, have tea, send dispatches, think about adjustments, and so on — so *indigenous* to the British and French systems — vanished instantly and utterly. The French in 1940 were organized in large forces which each "had their instructions," so to speak, well in advance, covering every contingency except this type of war. Compounding their difficulty, once lightning, one-roll-of-the-treads war was upon them, was little provision for communication between units or with the High Command. Their entire expectation was that, after the Germans came, there would be *time* and battles, battles and *time*.

The Germans gave the world an illustration of their new one-piece warfare in Poland. In just weeks, the *war* there ended, before the armor ever stopped rolling.

The Germans again illustrated this for the world in France, which fell in weeks, and Belgium which fell in days, as did lesser targets of Luxembourg (just passing through), and Holland.

(Later, in Russia, Hitler himself goofed up the plans of the General Staff for the quick knockout of that country. Had he started on time, and had he not forced Guderian south to form the useless Kiev pocket, the Nazis would have been in Moscow in

October — and Russia west of the Urals would never have recovered).

Was German infantry left behind — as the armor dashed off?

No, but, after a *major change of concept,* two things happened. The major change of concept was this: that infantry would now support armor, instead of vice versa. The two things that followed were these: some high-speed infantry would move with the armor in immediate support; and the old foot-slogging mass would also, (though more slowly), come along behind, nailing everything down, mopping up resistance, establishing the military government, putting in the supply bases, and so forth. (As a German soldier from the Russian Front said, reinforcing the truism that a war cannot be won without the mass of infantry, "Someone has to dig that partisan with the gun out of that outhouse").

In France in 1940, the Germans supported their armored divisions with infantry. Let's study briefly the makeup of the German attack forces:

A panzer division (1944 table of organization), had two armored and four infantry units totaling nearly 15,000 men, with 160 to 180 tanks, and some 200 field guns! *(Almanac).* Obviously, this was a formidable force — designed and used in a detached way. Those infantry units were not foot-slogging, but motorized. They were designed to move and fight with the armor.

The Germans also had a "motorized infantry division." This again was fast-moving. Armor-supporting infantry got to the spearpoint, and stayed with it, in fast trucks, big open cars, half-tracks or other gun carriers, and on motorcycles — even bicycles! Many photos show German troops on bikes.

The ordinary infantry came along later — reduced from being the center of battle twenty-five years previous, to the fourth rank behind armor and two types of high-speed infantry.

What was the composition of German forces driving westward? Of 140 German divisions, the heaviest emphasis was on seven or eight armored divisions with the backup of maybe three motorized divisions. These did most of the work, and, in effect, won the war against France and the Low Countries.

The reason for their success was that they employed a style of warfare which is *still* not understood in all its points.

The minute we see all the points of the German Blitz, this at once breaks the "Maginot hypnosis" which *still* causes many to begin analyses of German 1940 westward expansion with "The Maginot Line . . ."

To accomplish its end in the quickest manner, and by the most direct route, the Germans simply punched the shortest route to the Channel opposite Britain.

This was designed, of course, to achieve other objectives. The main one was to immediately turn south and drop down upon Paris — less than 100 miles away — and thus quickly end that war!

In another strange aspect of the hypnosis and fogbank immobilizing Allied minds and forces at that time, the weakest point of communications (and lack of high, centralized, command) existed exactly in the path of the shortest route to the Channel, and the best route for opening the Paris flank!

(The route Germany took should have been obvious. Maybe it was, but the Allies just thought there would be time to react).

Many analysts say the Germans "split the British sector from the French." This really is not true at all. The Germans simply went for the Coast. This rolled through virtually undefended Luxembourg, through poorly defended southern Belgium, onto French soil. The offensive punched through some French defenders and zipped to the water at Abbeville (really Noyelles). There were several big, powerful, columns. Counterattacks on their flanks proved useless.

Many French soldiers were caught on the north side of the split, so there was no spot which the Germans hit which severed British from French. (Almost as many French were evacuated at Dunkirk as Tommies).

The true analysis is that the secondary result of the main

thrust was to *open the flanks*. The Germans poured north to Dunkirk, and south to Paris.

The offensive began May 10, reaching the Channel May 20, and Dunkirk before May 30 — where the evacuation was completed June 4. Paris fell June 14, and Petain surrendered June 22.

The continuous action war thus ended . . . in forty-two days!

And, oh yes! The Maginot Line! Did it figure in there anywhere? Nope.

Myth Four

That The Submarine War Was Won By Any Method Or Men Popularly Credited

The submarine war in the North Atlantic was won by not less than twenty interlocking methods, weapons, and detection systems with one KEY item. These were developed slowly and agonizingly in a prayer-filled sea of defeat until the turnaround of Mar-May 1943. The second phase included the six-months' annihilation of the German fleet, mainly in the Bay of Biscay — not in the North Atlantic or at the convoys — before the very shiny last eighteen months of the War.

The Early History

From the moment England declared war (September 1939 after the Nazis invaded Poland), Germany felt justified in attacking her merchant ships (and vessels of any nation which might be assisting her).

In the first ten days of September, 1939, the Germans sank, mainly in British waters, twenty-seven merchantmen. The German sub fleet at the time was not great — only about thirty subs capable of battle. In British waters, Nazis could also bring to bear planes, an occasional warship, and two types of mines (the old contact type and the new acoustic one. Later, a new magnetic mine was added — bagging its first victim November 19, followed by ten more victims in a few days. The British developed counter-measures for the magnetic mine).

In September 1939 (still eight months before the invasion of

France), the British instituted both coastal and ocean convoys. (The U.S. didn't institute ocean convoys until the spring of 1941, and coastal convoys in April of 1942).

To trace the development and ascendancy of sub warfare, it's necessary to first see what the Germans attempted to do with surface raiders — both disguised and undisguised warships.

In the fall of 1939, the German pocket battleship *Graf Spee* was assigned to raid merchant vessels in the middle of the Atlantic — far from Britain's shores, and well below the North Atlantic. It sank its first vessel in September, when the Polish war was still boiling, and added eight more in the South Atlantic before it was bottled up in the River Plate estuary in December by four British cruisers. On December 17, the German captain scuttled her, apparently fearing battle, and soon thereafter committed suicide.

The pocket battleship *Deutschland* was also bagging helpless merchant ships in 1939 in the Atlantic — a "contest" of major warship vs. cargo vessel.

What was the theory? That German *surface* ships could deny merchant ships access to England. The theory was obviously flawed, because Germany just didn't have (due to armaments limitations imposed after World War I) many surface combat ships. On the other hand, Britannia "ruled the waves."

But the German surface theory would be tested in 1939, 1940, and 1941. Such great warships as the pocket battleship *Admiral Scheer,* and fabled cruisers, *Scharnhorst* (one of the most beautiful warships ever built — it's a shame it had to be used for any purpose other than peace and upholding high standards), and *Gneisenau,* were pressed into this duty.

In addition, Germany had several surface "raiders" which were armed vessels disguised to resemble merchantmen. They could get close to merchant shipping before dropping some facade or other and showing guns. *Atlantis* bagged twenty-two ships before herself getting the deep six (courtesy of a British cruiser) in November of 1941 — close to the end of the surface effort. Other raiders also had excellent success.

To back up again to 1939, in November, big Russia invaded tiny Finland — and began there a long, very bloody (especially for the invading Russians) unsuccessful campaign. (A byproduct of this was the conviction by observing German officers that Russians were terrible soldiers!)

In April of 1940, the Germans knocked off Norway. Thus, with the raiders of that year, and the battleships, and the invasion of Norway, Germany was militarily very active in the period September 1939 (Poland) to April 1940. Where the term, "the phony war" — given by many to the period at that time — came from, I cannot imagine. (I also cannot imagine how Germany's invasion of France a month later came as a "surprise" to anyone).

From Dunkirk at the end of May, 1940, Germany was in full combat with England in deadly earnest.

Important to the history of submarine warfare was Germany's declaration August 8 of a "total blockade" of England.

The testing of the surface theory had been — to this point — a sort of dipping of the toe in the water. The German surface ships were staying far from British land (especially from British land-based aircraft!), and hitting mainly isolated ships in the South Atlantic — and, mystically, the Indian Ocean, and even the Far East. Of course, Britain had, at the time, a huge empire stretching into those areas. But, in practice, the sinkings were definitely a harassment to this point, not a blockade or even a real test of the feasibility of a blockade.

It was obvious from the moment of the "total blockade" order that the sub fleet was destined for expansion.

The Germans attempted a blockade with their limited sub fleet, mines, and aircraft. This coincided with the beginning of the heavy bombing of the British civilian populations in the fall of 1940.

It was the time of U.S. "Bundles for Britain." Our family, along with millions of others, sent clothing regularly. Much of this went to the bottom of the North Atlantic.

(Other items, such as *soap slivers* — which were used, apparently, in the making of explosives — were saved religiously by Americans, and pushed east across the Atlantic. In 1982, forty-two years later, I found myself nursing a soap sliver in my showerbath down to a tiny, unmanageable piece — and asking myself, "Why?" It then occurred that I had been trained between the tender years of ten and fifteen, that the world needed these to survive! The entire dictum, "Use it up, wear it out, make it do" — a slogan from the War — came under question. I laughed at my stupidity in retaining this so long after it no longer applied. But, a year later, in 1983, one of the famed British Redgrave sisters was on a well-known U.S. talk show. She said, "I was in England during the War, and I *still* cannot throw away a soap sliver!" Such was the life-or-death psychology of the early War years).

Somewhere less than half of the supplies shipped at that time never got to England. Some small convoys would be savaged going into England and coming back. But others would get through without terrible problems. Of course, we heard of the worst ones.

Boatloads of British refugee children had been arriving in the U.S. After the sinking of the *City of Benares* in August, 1940, this policy was modified to one of systematic evacuation of children from British cities to the countryside. However, many individuals and small groups continued to come to the U.S.

In September, 1940, the U.S. gave the British fifty older destroyers to aid with their convoy efforts. At this point in time, the merchant sea war had been a bloody reality for a solid year.

The colossal role of the U-boat was looming. But the sub fleet, by the end of 1940, was *small*. Due to battle losses totaling thirty-one U-boats, only twenty-two Nazi subs were in operation.

Germany began producing eighteen new U-boats a month — enabling it by summer of 1941 to keep 100 at sea.

U-boats — of the type used then — were very rudimentary and smallish by comparison to today's boats, and could be built quickly. (The movie, *Das Boot* — although it was about a time much later in the War — was documentary-perfect as to the small size and cramped quarters of U-boats. The book, *Iron Coffins,* by the German U-boat Commander Oskar Werner, also gave remarkable descriptions of the limited quarters, small torpedo capacity (fourteen on the standard VII or VIIc or "Atlantic" type U-boat), and other limited characteristics of the basic German war sub). (The so-called "new type" German sub — the type XXI — was not produced until the last months of the War, and then in small numbers, woefully bombed in their estuaries and mishandled by green crews. These did not see significant action. The schnorchel or "snorkel" was original equipment on the XXI, but some retrofit units were made as early as 1944 for VIIs. However, the early retrofit models were crude, and prone to jam — causing sometimes fatal flooding below! A hydraulic closer was an advance — but few saw action. Werner says he saw five snorkel unit assemblies on the ground at Brest in 1944).

Hoyt's book, *U-Boats Offshore,* shows nearly 900 U-boats constructed. The main battle vessel according to his figures was the Type VII, of which nearly 700 were built. (*Battle Of Atlantic* lists length of the VIIc at 220 feet. Living space would be less than half that). Hoyt also lists ten milch cows, and fifty "Type II" "North Sea Boats" — shorter than the VIIs, and carrying only six torpedoes. He shows another classification — the Type IX "Long Range Boat" — longer and heavier than the VII. One hundred and fifty of these were built, he states. (His figures would indicate that no XXIs ever reached the statistical stage).

The basic Nazi sub of 1940-45 was fast on the surface (about eighteen knots), but slower underwater (six to eight knots). (The XXIs were designed for eighteen knots submerged!) The VIIs were fuel-economical, and could patrol long distances. Their life (a surprise to many readers) was mainly *on the surface* — diving only to avoid attack or to become invisible. Their original *attack* mode was on the surface! Their bases were north European estuaries (where most were built), fjords, and progressively in the War, the French ports of Cherbourg, Brest, Lorient, and St. Nazaire — the latter three Bay of Biscay ports in particular.

(As a side note, the huge "submarine pens" with the twenty-foot-thick bomb-proof roofs, were built just as Germany was switching to a heavy buildup of submarines. The Todt Organization, which built the Autobahns, much of the Siegfried Line, and, later, the Atlantic Wall, constructed these, according to Albert Speer. Apparent in Speer's book, and also between the lines there, is the theme that Germany should have had a firm naval submarine policy before the War — calling for a much vaster fleet and deployment in the Atlantic).

(*Battle of the Atlantic* lists 782 German subs *sunk,* of a total of 1,133 commissioned).

Early in 1941, convoys were growing. Just how effective was the "total" blockade"? It wasn't total. The British could break out and in — though at a cost.

The Germans pondered attack strategy. Surface warships re-entered their thinking. Could big warships (of which they had so few), break out past fortress England, past Iceland, into the Atlantic? And there interdict and perhaps sink *entire convoys?* (I suppose the Germans also knew their warships were not of any use bottled up in fjords or elsewhere — so they might as well try the open sea).

Thus, in May, 1941, the famed *Bismarck* (a battleship with fifteen-inch guns), and the heavy cruiser *Prinz Eugen,* worked their way out of the Baltic first to Norway, and then north of Iceland. They turned south — heading down the Strait between Iceland and Greenland into the middle of the great convoy routes — especially the route from the Canadian port of Halifax. However, *Bismarck* was engaged by the British battleship *Hood.* Some popular reports say the *Hood* took "one shell down the stack," or "one shell into the magazine," and exploded. But a detailed report in *Almanac* speaks of twenty minutes of exchanges of big salvoes, at 26,000 yards (about fifteen miles), with "two or three" hits on the big *Hood,* before one shell found the after magazine; then she sank in four minutes with all hands but three.

The *Bismarck* was leaking oil from a hit by *Prince of Wales.* But it sufficiently damaged the *Prince* to enable the German to break off and head for the French coast.

We all know the story, but the point is that the British so quickly and determinedly dealt with the matter of German surface warships attempting to enter the shipping lanes of the

Atlantic. (Later, Hitler, angry about the impotence of the surface fleet, would virtually quarantine it for the rest of the War — except for use against Arctic convoys).

On its attempt to reach a French port for repairs, the *Bismarck* met an array of British surface and air weaponry. After a long-range recon plane spotted her, carrier planes from the *Ark Royal* hit her rudder with a torpedo. As a result, she could only go in circles. *Bismarck* was a tough old bird, though. The British battleships *Rodney* and *King George* moved in and used her for target practice. Then it was torpedo time again, with "fish" from the cruiser *Dorsetshire* finishing her off, with most hands.

After this, Germany didn't have any more questions about the possibilities of using surface warships to destroy convoys!

As a result, subs, already in doubled production from 1940, were given the green light which roughly doubled their production again to some twenty-three a month — a figure which, with some variations, held as an average until the very end of the War (according to a chart from a British Official History, appearing in *Battle of the Atlantic*). Against this, in 1941, the Allies were lucky to sink three in a month — and only a little more than twice that in 1942!

As the spring and summer of 1941 progressed, sub warfare against convoys between North America and Britain increased sharply. In June, Germany plunged into Russia.

There were now three colossal reasons to increase shipments to Britain: Britain's distress; Britain as the logical base for operations air, sea, and land against Hitler from the West (including the North African invasion); and the special category of Britain as the base for the huge buildup required for the Normandy landings.

But it was still 1941. And the U.S. was *not yet at war* with Germany!

People in Baltimore and New York would not believe that, however. Ships were streaming out of, and back into, those and other U.S. ports, with war and domestic supplies for Great Britain.

Daily, photographs appeared in U.S. newspapers showing oil-grimed seamen who had been rescued from a merchant or tanker sinking on the North Atlantic run. An electrifying percentage of those seamen returned to the hazardous duty. The throb of war could be felt in those ports.

The U.S. was helping escort convoys — but the U.S. warships were not supposed to fire upon the Germans. Of course, there was some firing. And the Germans fired — hitting the *Kearney* and sinking the *Reuben James* in October of 1941.

All this was before the U.S. was in the War (or before the coastal sinkings of eight months later, in the spring of 1942).

Arctic convoys began in August 1941. *(Almanac).*

In September, the submarine war had been going on for *two full years.*

The Throat Is Almost Cut

From September 1941 to May 1943, the supply line to Britain (despite a huge increase in its dimensions), was almost cut.

The incredible sacrifice by all merchant seamen is largely unsung, because it isn't pretty, glamorous, or anything with which anyone would want to identify. Those men were heroes — particularly because they were civilian volunteers who didn't have to ship out, but who did so doggedly. (I read accounts in the *New York Times* of men who had had several ships sunk under them, who signed on again). This was patriotism in the extreme. The sacrifices made by U.S. merchant seamen — especially prior to our entry into the War — were remarkable. But then, many of them were immigrants who still spoke with foreign accents, and hailed from conquered countries, or had family ties there.

The U.S. tends to glorify its proportional role, but the British and Commonwealth countries ran most convoys, provided most ships (even after the North Atlantic got its share of some 2,700 U.S.-built Liberty ships), and took most of the losses. (The British lost nearly 5,000 merchant vessels (some 21,000,000 tons, for an average of just over 4,000 tons), and lost some 35,000 merchant sailors killed or permanently missing; the U.S. lost nearly 600 merchant vessels (some 3,500,000 tons, for an average of about 6,000 tons), and about 5,600 merchant sailors killed or permanently missing. The above figures, from *Almanac,* are for all seas — but the main merchant action was between North America and the waters around the British Isles — including the Russian run). The U.S. provided incredible amounts of cargo materiel — including vast munitions for convoy defense.

In December, 1941, the U.S. entered the War "for real." But for the merchant seamen, the U.S. had been "at war for real" for more than two years at that point.⟩

To the dreadful toll of merchant ships and small tankers on the North Atlantic run was now added the sinkings of U.S. coastwise shipping. Doenitz called the U.S. East Coast the world's "most heavily travelled sea lanes." He bragged he would sink coastwise shipping "within sight of the bathers" on the beaches. The boast was real. I saw three ships which had been torpedoed. The campaign extended to the U.S. Gulf Coast — and also into the Caribbean and off South America. The hunting was big — some 500 ships went down in that campaign.

To support the very long 1942 cruises of their subs, the Germans were using a "milch cow" type of submarine — literally, a fat submarine fuel tanker. (The Allies didn't "topple" to this for a while, and weren't able to destroy them until the late summer of 1943). I remember when the FBI arrested a fisherman in Savannah, Georgia, for allegedly taking fuel to subs offshore. However, he was released. The Germans were not getting their fuel from the U.S., but from their "milch cows." (The long patrols in 1942 took their toll of the willingness of Germans to remain cooped up. Only a few miles from my home, on the deserted wilderness island of Wassaw, subs would surface at night as crews came ashore, even killed, roasted, and ate game, and returned to their black marauders before dawn. Populated Georgia and Florida beaches were protected with barbed wire and patrol dogs. Blackouts were enforced. The only light would be from a stricken tanker).

In April, the U.S. instituted some coastal convoys.

In the early months of 1942, the U.S. was losing on Luzon's

Bataan Peninsula. This filled our newspapers, crowding out much of the North Atlantic war (which some say diminished during the coastal campaign), but not the coastal sinkings. Also, the Russians were continuing to drive the Germans back from the approaches to Moscow. This too was news — but greatly obscured (understandably) on the U.S. Home Front by defeats in the Far East.

I was twelve, attending prep school above the Hudson River at Tarrytown, twenty miles above New York City, in April, 1942 (although home was Skidaway Island in Georgia — a few miles from the wilderness Wassaw Island Beach the Germans later used for the only "R and R" available to them). In the Hudson Gorge, I saw ships lining up progressively from the George Washington Bridge northward. From my window at school, I could see ships being added at Tarrytown to the twenty-mile string! This was something at which I still marvel. One could *feel* their presence. One night, in the depths of the blackout, the River cleared — again, something one could literally sense.

When big convoys went out, usually one or two ships would "get it" within sight of shore, and burn or sink as terrible inaugurals of the journey ahead.

The year 1942 was the worst — with November the worst month on record in the War. In that thirty-day period, 807,000 tons went to the bottom *(Kemp)* — about 180 ships of an average of 4,500 tons. That didn't mean there was a climax in November. There would be months of the same ahead.

In all of 1942, the subs got 1660 ships, totaling about 7,700,000 tons *(Kemp)*. That averages 138 vessels (of about 4,500 tons each), *per month* all year — nearly five per *day* — and nearly 650,000 tons sunk per month.

The Germans figured to sink 500,000 to 700,000 tons each month — thus offsetting what they believed would be the peak of Allied new production. Thus, in 1942, the Germans were ahead of the game. (The figures from *Encyclopedia Britannica* vary slightly from Kemp's — but include all theatres. These show 8,245,000 tons sunk, against an Allied production of 7,180,000 tons — three-quarters of which was U.S. production which had *quintupled* from the year previous).

In August of 1942, the U.S. Eighth Air Force started operations gainst the European Continent, under General Eaker — a type of second front in the air (or expansion of the British effort, which had been bombing the Continent since the spring of 1940).

Britain was desperate for supplies. First of all, she was a maritime nation on a scale the U.S. could not imagine — because the U.S. (at the time) could find everything it needed within its own borders. But Britain had to import nearly everything — including a lot of food and oil. It had indigenous coal. It exported manufactured goods. To assure raw materials, safe trade routes, and semicaptive markets, it had the world's largest empire. To maintain the flow on the seas, its merchant fleet included 9,488 vessels (21,215,261 tons — for an average little ship of some 2,200 tons). In all the War, the Commonwealth lost nearly 5,000 ships. *(Almanac)*. (Note: sources vary, mainly due to whether they include the Commonwealth under the terms, "Britain," or "U.K." Sources also vary as they try to differentiate North Atlantic losses from other losses, and whether they include "British waters" losses under North Atlantic convoy losses, and for other similar reasons of definition). The British Isles (if I understand my source correctly) built some 1,800 ships (about 8,000,000 tons with the more modern average of perhaps 4,500 tons). So how could Britain be in need of food in December, 1942 — just before its Admiralty informed its Government that the convoy system was a *failure* (a pronouncement which caused a game-winning reshuffling?)

The answers were numerous: Beginning with Britain's basic domestic needs, the nation needed all its peacetime ships just to stay even at home. But the needs in wartime at home were greater than in peacetime — and its ships (not all of which called at the Isles, but served other parts of the Empire) were fewer. Add to this the burden of Britain's *military* needs. These alone required huge numbers of ships big enough to bring all kinds of stuff from raw materials through semifinished goods or parts, and finished goods. But that wasn't all. There were the needs of the burgeoning *U.S.* military establishment in Great Britain. Hundreds of thousands at first, they were growing rapidly in numbers. They had their "domestic" needs — food, clothes, etc. They also had their everyday military offensive needs — bombs, fuel, spare parts for the regular (and expensive) daylight bombing campaign. Add to this the needs of "Bolero" — the buildup for the invasion of France!

So even though it might seem that Britain had huge numbers of ships — and was never in real danger of running *out* of ships — that was simply not so.

The public was not told of the great numbers of ships England (or the U.S., for that matter) had afloat. The Allies had many more than 10,000.

The public *was* told — in horrified terms — of the sinkings of one, three, ten. The public honestly felt that these were *nearly the last ships* the Allies possessed!

To return for a moment to discussion of Britain's 9,000-plus merchant ships, many of these were too small for even minimum North Atlantic convoy duty! They didn't have the bulk or the power to maintain course or even headway in some of the rough seas, and were too slow even in calm weather. Also, they didn't carry enough.

On the other side of the coin, the ships that *were* sunk in the North Atlantic indeed had a special element of tragedy: they were usually loaded with specifically needed items (because nothing was shipped that didn't have a high priority); and they were usually serviceable vessels (and progressively, newer vessels).

I am mentioning all this lest the loss of 138 vessels per month — when compared with 9,000 vessels on hand — not seem catastrophic.

I was shocked when I first studied the figures of Britain's available ships — and, knowing the talent of the British to "con" the U.S. a bit (and downright deceive enemies) — I thought perhaps the greatest expose of the War might be the fact that England was never in real danger of having its throat cut.

But put that to rest — unless you can controvert the information in this chapter.

Britain — and the Allied effort to make it an effective base — was in imminent danger from June 1942 to February 1943 of *having its throat cut.*

Why wasn't the critical state of the North Atlantic supply route publicized more widely? Some can answer that it indeed *was* publicized widely. The sinkings and the horror were publicized. The threat to our Ally and threat to our military effort was publicized. But the real danger was not — that is, the closeness to the "edge" was not known. The public felt that by just continuing the effort, we would win — when that was not so. Fatal flaws were involved — but were not discussed. (As we will see later in this chapter, only the pronouncement by the British Admiralty in February 1943 awakened the military planners!)

The people to whom physical danger was most personal — the volunteer, civilian merchant seamen — knew the score where their lives were concerned, and lined up to serve. As Peter Kemp put it, in praising them, no merchant ship was ever held back for want of a crew! Having lived in ports, I still cannot keep a dry eye when thinking about it.

As evidence of the problems of supply, Operation Bolero — which was supposed to build up the Allied forces in England for Operation Sledgehammer (a quick invasion of France then and there) — fell so woefully short of even its minimum needs that it was called off. Many big egos in the U.S. fell, and much diplomacy was required of big British military egos which had steadfastly opposed "Sledgehammer."

The decision was made to go into North Africa instead — and this was pulled off successfully. (As a side note, the landings there opened up smaller southern convoy routes. These were not as persecuted, because they were not under the "total blockade of England" order. Also as a side note, a very large southern aircraft ferry route was opened — with armadas lumbering directly over my island home every evening from then Hunter Field at Savannah).

NOT SUNG-ENOUGH HEROES —
BRITISH GENERAL SIR ALAN BROOKE

At the time WWII broke out, the "sun never set on the British Empire." To the British generals whose traditions went back so many centuries, the U.S. generals were upstarts! Churchill — knowing the value of the U.S. production, and knowing that he would only get it if the U.S. was involved militarily — tamed his generals: but only barely!

General Sir Alan Brooke — Churchill's Chief of the Imperial General Staff — gets one of our "Not-sung-enough Heroes" medals for just keeping his mouth shut (beyond a certain point) and not killing our generals. He gets a "cluster" for the great plan which is explained below — which saved hundreds of thousands of U.S. lives. And he gets another "cluster" for taking a back seat when so commanded at Quebec in August 1943, when he could have just quit.

Let's take these up in order below.

Our General Marshall wanted the British and Americans to invade France in 1942 in "Operation Sledgehammer." (Stalin, who was about to lose the war in Russia, wanted a second front, and therefore favored this). But Marshall simply believed — in the best "Teddy Roosevelt up San Juan Hill" tradition — that we only had to show up in France in order to put the Germans to rout.

The British had just come from Dunkirk and other bad experiences (and would experience Dieppe in August 1942), and had bad memories of Gallipoli in WWI. They would not even listen to Marshall's pet "Operation Sledgehammer." (Some say Churchill ordered Dieppe despite last-minute adverse intelligence, as a means of proving the fatal problems involved in landings — *Bodyguard.*) Even beyond the landing stage, the British had many fears. They remembered protracted, expensive land battles in WWI.

But how to tell the U.S. to jump in the lake — a U.S. which was headstrong, inexperienced, but at last involved in the War (albeit with the upfront attitude that the British would not have been in such a bad position had they known what they were doing!) It was difficult for the proud British generals to use diplomacy plus some really sharp verbal encounters to slow the Americans while not antagonizing them).

The British were right. The Germans in 1942 had some remarkable forces stationed in France. These would have eaten an ill-prepared, ill-supplied, Allied force landing piecemeal from merchant vessels and the like. (Amphibious landing vessels of the later types were not even available yet, and there was little quantity of any type. Too, most production was heading straight for the Pacific).

The 1942 decision was finally made. There would be no European landing, but instead, the Americans would command landings in North Africa. Remarkably, Brooke and Marshall remained on speaking terms, if barely.

The overall accomplishment of preventing "Sledgehammer" and at the same time remaining on speaking terms (even if quite arch), was Brooke's. For this he gets his basic medal.

And now for the first cluster to that medal:

Brooke sold his plan to force Germany to defend *all of its perimeter*. This concept would eventually save untold thousands of Western Allied lives. It was opposed by American planners, and even, once, by Roosevelt. It was opposed by many British planners — but it found a friend in Churchill.

By threatening Normandy, completing the African victories, putting air bases there, invading Sicily and Italy, threatening the Balkans, threatening Southern France, the Allies forced Hitler to *thin out* his forces. Hand in glove with this fundamental, Brooke's plan also included reducing the Luftwaffe strength and arousing more resistance in Germany, Italy, and occupied lands.

(The big debate of Russia vs. Allied delays in opening a Second Front — which debate has never been settled — included Russia's claim that Britain deliberately held back a Second Front in order to weaken Russia and make it less a threat to the British Empire after the War. American critics of Britain's Empire concepts partook of some of Russia's views, and added that England persisted in its preoccupation with the Mediterranean (Marshall called it the "dark hole of the Mediterranean" — *Bodyguard*), because it was central to the Mideast (oil, the Suez, the route to India, and Arabia, which last was Churchill's stated "beltbuckle" of the Empire). As I say, points on all facets of this debate can still be heard).

For purposes of this chapter, I wish to concentrate on Brooke's plan to require Germany to defend its entire perimeter, including the skies and the interior, before cross-Channel invasion — a brilliant plan in and of itself (and prone to be lost in other arguments, however valid they might be).

When the time finally came for the cross-Channel invasion, if Hitler could have concentrated all his non-Eastern Front forces opposite Britain, the invasion would have been thrown off the beaches. (Few argue against this, and many flatly say that (even after the perimeter defense), only the Calais feint ("Operation Fortitude" — which Bradley said held "twenty" enemy divisions in the Calais area for "months" after the invasion), preserved the invasion. But after forcing the Germans to defend *all their perimeter* (and giving the Russians another year and a half to clobber the Germans, and clearing the skies of Luftwaffe, and gaining for Americans the needed combat experience, and pulling off "Operation Fortitude" (more on this later), we were able to get ashore in France. Two weeks after the St. Lo-Avranches breakout, we also landed in Southern France, making the task of the great sweep across France duck soup against German forces scrambling out of entrapment to "safety" behind the Siegfried Line.

Brooke has already been *recognized* for much of this — but not sung enough, especially in the U.S. Part of the reason is obvious — his constant friction with Marshall and King. Also, he was later to say some bad things about Ike — possibly stemming from all those U.S. people being elevated above Brooke in command roles. (A study of the frictions between U.S. and British top officers reveals clearly why Roosevelt chose Ike. Ike's first priority was harmony. Marshall couldn't have been appointed Supreme Commander, because he was already battling with the British. Likewise, Brooke — who battled with Americans. But Ike's special characteristic was his ability to bring all together and keep 'em together).

But Brooke is not sung well in Britain either, because, for one reason, the British are too polite to offend the Americans — and to sing Brooke's full praises is to be pretty rough on some American positions, and even some American personalities. But the problem went deeper. Sir Alan also offended some Britishers — particularly, Churchill. And Churchill offended Brooke, apparently, because in his memoirs after the War, Brooke was so outspoken that it is said Churchill would not speak to Brooke or see him again (*Bodyguard*).

All this aside, it's time we awarded Sir Alan his well-deserved cluster for his great concept.

And now for the second cluster: General Brooke at Quebec (August 1943) had been told by Churchill that he would be appointed the Allied Supreme Commander for "Overlord" — the Normandy invasion. After all, he was the senior British officer. The Conference began, but Churchill had gone first to Hyde Park to meet Roosevelt. There, Roosevelt said the U.S. would do only two things: Overlord in 1944 and Marshall as Supreme Commander. The Mediterranean was to be dropped. Fine, said Churchill (who hadn't really given up on the Mediterranean).

At Quebec, Churchill found that Marshall had emphasized his points by backing them with the threat of the U.S. having to "review" its priorities in the War — that is to say, its decision to put the European War first, the Pacific second. The British "heard" that message clearly.

But just at that moment, the Italians sent the Allies a message agreeing to surrender (leading to their joining our side). This provided sudden justification for Brooke's ongoing but just "terminated" plan. The "termination" thus never got out of the conference room. Instead, it received a big boost. Overlord remained the main goal, but the invasion of Italy was immediately authorized. Germany announced that thirteen divisions would enter Italy — pulled from other duty. Marshall agreed to all this (and, I suppose, gained Roosevelt's blessing).

Brooke had one victory — a big one.

But he had not yet heard the other news — that he would not head Overlord as Allied Supreme Commander. The Prime Minister took him for a walk and informed him without any preliminaries. Also, the blow was not softened by statements about his being "needed" somewhere else (as Roosevelt later softened the blow for Marshall).

Brooke swallowed hard and stayed on to continue to render his enormous service to the Allied cause. Never was such a big ego swallowed, with the result that such a bigger man (denied most headlines), emerged.

We owe him a lot — and particularly that he be more "sung." Hence his second cluster of our "Not-sung-enough Heroes" medal.

God bless you, Sir Alan.

Incomprehensible is the fact that in 1942 — this terrible time — each North Atlantic convoy had an average of only *five* *escorts*. (In 1940, each convoy had only *one or two* escorts! Those were British convoys — the U.S. not convoying or aiding much until the spring of 1941).In early 1943, despite the War-threatening convoy losses of 1942, the average number of escorts grew to *only seven*. This for convoys which — from latter 1942 — averaged *sixty or more ships* covering six miles by two miles! *(Kemp)*.

No wonder so many ships went to the bottom!

Too, the escorts were ordered to remain *with* the ships at *all* times. Their job was to stay with the convoy, and work to keep it bunched up. They were underemployed — but necessarily so — as sheepdogs. Bad seas, poor visibility, and radio silence had a scattering effect on the heavily laden, pregnant, small (at that time in the War), "fat cows" (a German term) — and a straggler (or a scattered convoy) had little hope of survival!

At this time, the average vessel was small — having worked its way up from an average 3,500 tons per vessel sunk earliest in the War, to the 1942 average of 4,500 tons, reflecting new construction. The small vessels — many of them converted from coastwise use — had a difficult time maintaining position in the heavy, often stormy, North Atlantic seas. Later vessels — such as Liberty ships being built from August 1941 forward in the U.S. (that's the earliest date I have), and later in Canadian ports, were 10,000 tons each.

It was known — from experimentation — that if escorts could *leave* the ships and attack a suspected submarine (a process which could take hours if the sub lay silent and didn't take a hit or near miss), the possibility of a kill was *very high*.

However, with the very few available escorts, and the need to put the vital sheepherding and close defense work above leaving and hunting (even if a kill could be expected), the assigned duty was to *not* leave.

I'm sure that decision — although a necessary one — kept many senior theatre commanders awake nights.

The German attack mode was *on the surface,* broadside to the convoy, at night. The few escorts would position themselves on the convoy flanks to provide a defense which consisted in large part of forcing the subs to submerge and lose position, visibility, aim, etc. To defeat this inadequate defense, the Germans would submerge first, run at the convoy underwater, then suddenly surface and fire. The most daring tactic was to run submerged beneath the ships, then surface *inside* the convoy pattern, throwing terror into these hapless ships which could see the sub, or see the explosions and realize the sub was inside — and practically in a position to itself avoid being attacked.

The Germans tended to make heroes out of living men — submarine commanders, fighter pilots, etc. This gave the military a tremendous stimulus and esprit in the early goings. However, when heroes went to the bottom in "iron coffins," the resulting effect was negative. Some "great" German sub commanders were lost in 1942 — a bad omen for the Nazi elite sub force.

BRITISH FLATTERY OF THE U.S.

The British leadership made a conscious decision to play "second fiddle" to the U.S. — to flatter the U.S. big ego. England owned the world's biggest empire — and didn't get there by being stupid or weak — yet they played helpless. (Part of this was due to the somewhat popular "Anglophobia" of the period — plain dislike for the British). The only way the British could get the inflated "western gunslinger" ego of the U.S. into action was to play the role of fair maiden in distress. In *Bodyguard,* we read that in the fall of 1940, "Churchill knew that Hitler would not invade without aerial superiority, but he deliberately led the world to believe that Britain was in mortal peril in order to rally his own people to meet the threat and to enlist the support and sympathy of the United States."

When the U.S. finally got involved, Marshall insisted on "Operation Sledgehammer" — a real "western gunslinger" head-on shoot-out with the Germans by invading France immediately (1942 or

1943). The British gained a reputation for always agreeing, but then adding, "But . . . ," and dragging the decisions out for months more. The Americans had the feeling that they could never get the British to finally agree — although the British seemed to be agreeing all along! "Sledgehammer" finally was mercifully shelved, and the U.S. began to learn some of the real facts of life in its battles in North Africa. The British continued to play second fiddle and helpless with one hand, and present such formidable people as Montgomery in Africa on the other. The "public relations" Britain and the "real" Britain were different. (Monty thought himself superior to the U.S., able to whip the world — and that Americans were amateurs if not fools, and certainly should be playing second fiddle to the British!)

There were more shocks coming up for the Americans from the "helpless" British. The huge, rawboned, John Wayne type U.S. Army was building up rapidly in the Isles — but, by golly, the Americans were discovering, more and more, that the British had all the intelligence. If the Americans wanted to know anything about the enemy, they had to go to the British. This was because of the Ultra program, which had cracked the German Enigma system, and was so supersecret that the Americans didn't know about it. (Only the FBI in the U.S. proper knew of it — and not much at that). It was not declassified until 1975. So the Americans found that — whereas they thought they were "running" things — the British, who pretended the Americans were running things, were in full charge!

Also unknown (in true depth) until 1975 (connected closely with Ultra), was the fact that the British had what they considered to be a distinct war of deception. This was not ordinary battlefield deception, or ordinary intelligence deception, which usually would be handled by the military and governmental intelligence agencies. Instead, this was a not large, but elaborate and top-level, extremely hidden (behind layers, so that if an office or network was discovered, one would think that was it, whereas that was only one layer), multi-storied structure constructed and directed by Churchill. It can't be described in a few words, but the 800-page Bodyguard of Lies (without which I do not believe the War can be understood), lays it all out.

Was Churchill capable of presenting an entire picture to the United States that was tailored to produce certain results for the British and stimulate American support for England? After studying what his separate deception war did to the Nazis, one has to conclude that he could (but without the cynicism or malice) easily manipulate the U.S. at all levels. He led his friends into things which would benefit the Western Allied cause, and not harm the friends, but often protect them — but he did this by the stratagem of pretending to be doing other things.

If true, the United States was not misled (in the sense of harmful leadership), but was brilliantly led — but by deception. One of the deceptions was that we were leading.

The British convoyed most of the North Atlantic ships, and lost five times more ships and merchant seamen. Yet they stood by and let the American convoy effort get the glory. Their inventions of radar, and the further development of centimetric radar from their magnetron (which German submarine "fuzz-busters" couldn't detect), and their HF/DF supersecret sub-pinpointer, working on an unused electronics principle, and their magnetic anomaly detector (MAD), which detected submerged subs, won the submarine war, making Western Allied land victories possible. Their people accounted for 500 of the 793 Nazi subs sunk or captured at sea in the entire war.

The overall war-winning Western plan came from the British — the plan to force Germany to defend all of its perimeter. And the British had to use all of their "con" and flattery to get the Americans to go along. The British did more fighting than we did, and took more military casualties (and of course, a lot more civilian casualties). The British landed more men on D-Day than the Americans did (more than seventy thousand to our more than fifty thousand). But in all actions, their top leadership let us believe we were doing it all and winning it all. (Monty as usual, refused to go along!)

They absolutely achieved their number one goal — to obtain the massive U.S. production. In fact, the utter volume of this surprised even the Americans. (The U.S. supplied the Pacific War as well as the Western Allies — and also shipped untold amounts of materiel through the underbelly of Iran into Russia!) Production was the U.S.'s crowning achievement in the War — and the Allies who took it were willing to pay the price of flattering the U.S. that its fighting won the War.

☆   ☆   ☆

Twenty Methods — Interlocked — With One KEY Item, Producing Victory

Below we'll look at twenty tactics, detection devices, and weapons, each absolutely vital — and their agonized, trial and error, increment-by-increment development to a position of superiority over the enemy — which *interlock*. These were *all used together* in their finally-superior forms in the remarkable dark-to-dawn turnaround victory over the U-boats, in March to May, 1943, and the annihilation of the front-line German U-boat fleet in the six months following.

The submarine war was not won by one or two dashing, confident, clean weapons or humans. The concept of their dominance came from the last eighteen months of War, after the victory had been won. This does not impugn their bravery or effectiveness, but it magnifies the real victory.

The *victory system* came *terribly slowly* — a winning combination born in the blood, and on the backs, of the *early* players.

The press loved those who appeared many months after the great turnaround. It loved victories that were clean, not messy; quick, not agonizing; confident, not desperate, groping, or trial-and-error.

This wasn't the fault of the press. The victory-starved and often fantasizing home fronts loved the later victories. Military recruiters, leaders, and morale stimulators loved the later, fast, sure, hand.

And who wouldn't love a gallant, clean, young escort commander stepping from a flag-bedecked, shiny destroyer — rather than a gut-sickening, oil-begrimed, sea-soaked, half-dead, middle-aged, grizzled merchant seaman with a foreign accent from working class Baltimore or Manchester?

1. The Convoy System

In February, 1943 — in the deepest "pits" of the failure to adequately protect convoys (and three and one half years after convoys had begun) — the Prime Minister of England received a report from the British Admiralty that said the convoy system itself could *no longer be considered effective.* (Indeed, the sinkings and wreckings of these convoys should have made that obvious earlier).

As the North Atlantic convoys had progressively grown huge, the escort forces had remained, by comparison, pathetically small. Five escorts for sixty-five fat, slow, loaded merchant ships is absurd. And yet, amidst all of our military geniuses on the Allied side, none seemed to insist on a higher priority for decent protection of a vital route.

Meanwhile, the enemy sub fleet grew into the hundreds, so that, at any given time, seventy to 100 could be in the war zone against the convoys. (In 1942 and early 1943, the Germans were using the famous "wolf packs").

(So often, we picture the wolf packs as lying beneath the surface, waiting to fire torpedoes. I still picture them this way — even while knowing better. Grand Admiral Doenitz wrote at least two books. One is his famous diary, captured intact at the end of the War, and made into a popular book. The other was written in 1939. In that, he describes the use of submarines on the surface, speeding, much as "torpedo boats." The basic attack mode was on the surface at night. The surface allowed speed (seventeen knots in contrast to the convoy's six or eight), great visibility (Doenitz called a submerged sub "blind"), maneuverability, ease of obtaining good firing position, and ease of distributing the "fan shot" of three or four torpedoes. As the War progressed, Allied defenses concentrated on forcing the subs to submerge — an effective tactic when full destructive capability was not yet present).

How many subs could the Germans put into combat? Every source book I've read uses different terminologies, or has different meanings for the terminologies. The basic terminologies are "total fleet" (which means, to all, every sub, sick or well, afloat or dry, in action or at rest, on station or enroute, in every type of duty, in every theatre). One chart shows the total fleet averaging fifty-seven boats in 1939 and all of 1940. Then, in 1941, the average for the year is 163! (The figure is climbing). In 1942, the average jumps to 330! In 1943, the average reaches 418. The peak quarter is Jan-Mar 1944 — 445. Then it drops by quarter until the end, when 349 U-boats were in the fleet at surrender time. (From a British Official History chart appearing in *Battle Of The Atlantic*).

Unfortunately, such charts don't tell the real story — though the precise facts may be correct.

In 1941 (163 boats), and 1942 (330 boats), the Germans could concentrate their efforts in the North Atlantic — and the Allies were woefully underdefended there.

But after May of 1943, the Germans had to face an utterly murderous Allied defensive apparatus everywhere — in the Baltic, in the Bay of Biscay, in the Channel, in the North Atlantic, in the middle and South Atlantic (vs. U.S. convoys to Africa), and in every estuary, at every repair dock and new construction ways. Therefore, the effectiveness of any "total fleet" figure after May 1943 was only about one-third of what appeared on paper. The enemy could concentrate *nothing* after May 1943 (and, in many respects, was in a situation similar to the Nazi surface fleet after the *Bismarck* was sunk in May, 1941 — bottled up, unable to get into a combat position without being smashed).

Popular terminologies on which there is not universal agreement include "operational" subs, and subs "at sea." Also, "engaged."

Here are the problems: the standard VII sub carried fourteen torpedoes. Doenitz' standard teachings included firing one's full load when in contact with the convoys! Therefore, a sub could leave port, travel to its grid station in the Atlantic in a few days, wait or cruise a few days, and finally get a crack at a convoy — only to miss connections, wait a few more days, then get into a firing position at another convoy. Then, in one night, all torpedoes could be exhausted, and the sub would return to base. At base, there might be a ten-day delay due to rearming, refueling, repairs, etc. The entire round-trip procedure might take one month — all for one night's shooting.

Therefore, what is the *meaning* of "operational"? Or "at sea"? Or "engaged"?

For "operational," this book takes the simple meaning of subs which are afloat and either sailing or able to sail. Just as with "total fleet," this "operational" figure bears *little relationship* to combat per se.

"At sea" bears more relationship to combat per se — but could be just subs on routine patrols off Norway, or in the Mediterranean. However, with the "at sea" designation, an analyst is closer to the real truth of how many subs can be brought to bear on a given night against a convoy.

Kemp served in the British war room for the North Atlantic. He focuses on subs operational in the North Atlantic — *in* (not in port). He speaks of "100" Nazi subs as operational in the North Atlantic at the peak, November 1942 to March 1943. If half of these were enroute to or from port, and half constituting actual "gun pressure" available to punish convoys on a given night, that would translate to a *combat figure*.

For the worst five months of the North Atlantic war, I am going to present my assumption from a study of all figures, of *fifty combat-positioned* subs in the North Atlantic on any given night. Of course, not all of them saw action every night (thank goodness). (For a comparison, the chart from *Battle of the Atlantic* uses a column entitled, "Engaged In Atlantic." Exactly what does "engaged" mean? Does it mean "combat-positioned subs"? Let's say it does: If so, it shows an average of forty in October-December of 1942, *fifty* for January-March of 1943, and a rapid drop thereafter.

Therefore, in January 1943 (in the peak months), with a total fleet of just over 400, Germany could bring to *combat position* in the North Atlantic, *fifty*. From Kemp's analysis, another fifty were chugging back and forth from the firing line. Possibly another twenty-five were dry-docked, (a dozen sunk, twenty-three built, and the total fleet increased by about ten).

What were the other 275 or so boats *doing?* About 100 were tied up in training. And the Germans had other combat areas —

the Baltic, Norway, the Arctic convoy routes (where most sinkings were accomplished by airplanes from Norway, some by subs, and a few by surface warships), the Channel, the Mediterranean, the middle Atlantic and South Atlantic, some prowlings of the U.S. coast and Caribbean (after the big 1942 campaign was pulled out), and the Indian Ocean. Also, the Germans had heavy repairs — subs that had been badly damaged. And refittings with new armaments, engines, etc.

But one comes away from a study of the distribution of German subs with the feeling that most of the fleet was not in operations against the North Atlantic convoys!

The loss of trained crews was a crucial point. Usually, a sub went down with "all hands." That was a wipe-out of years of experience and training. Instead of taking some trained people routinely for new boats, trained crews generally stayed intact.

Possibly the French port facilities simply would not handle more subs — even though more may have been available for the North Atlantic operations. If so, this is a factor which should be mentioned in the lineup of methods by which the Allies wore down the enemy. (We all know that the big "sub pens" were hit often with the biggest explosives Allied planes could drop. The twenty-foot thick reinforced concrete roofs were not dented. However, any attempt by the Germans to *increase* sub facilities would be smashed. Anything not under these shelters would be smashed). Also, perhaps the spare parts situation was so limited that Doenitz could not "field" a larger sub fleet in the North Atlantic — even though he had available subs.

I tend to believe the loss of not just the trained crews, but the truly elite crews with reputations in the Reich, adversely affected the Germans beyond mere statistical analysis. The loss of 200 North Atlantic subs in the "turnaround and annihilation" period May-December 1943 *ended* the German ability to engage in effective combat — yet (and this is important in studying the entire matter) the "total fleet" *grew* to 445 boats in the period, by January 1944!

My opinion is that the 100 North Atlantic boats were the elite cream, and the next 100 combined with it comprised a 200-boat

German "front-line" fleet. It was this "front-line fleet" which was annihilated in the March-May 1943 "turnaround" and the May-December 1943 "annihilation" of the German fleet. The "total fleet" grew — but the combat effectiveness actually went into reverse. That is, they became the *hunted,* not the hunters. Their casualties ranged to 100% on patrols, and Doenitz was not willing to risk more than a few at a time.

But to return to the convoys before the turnaround, in March, 1943 — the very darkest hour of the convoy concept — U.S. Admiral King announced the desire to withdraw the U.S. from North Atlantic convoy assistance! Could the British and Canadians go it alone (they were doing most of it, anyhow)? The U.S. increased its commitments to South Atlantic runs (the U.S. had been convoying in support of its military effort in North Africa since November, 1942), and contributed *one support group* to the North Atlantic *(Kemp).*

The convoy system was in absolute crisis.

However, during March, April, and May of 1943, there occurred a massive turnaround in the submarine war — followed by the "annihilation" phase mentioned above, during which, and following, bigger convoys than ever came across the North Atlantic like trains, one after another, only days apart, nearly unmolested.

What had happened?

What had happened was not a victory for the convoy system.

However, it was a shattering defeat for the subs. The subs were not defeated at the convoys. In fact, the subs were not defeated in the North Atlantic.

All that is not romantic. And it doesn't fit the myth. But it's true.

The subs were destroyed in the Bay of Biscay and its approaches.

2. Breaking The Enemy Code

The British broke the German submarine Enigma code — which was different from the German High Command Enigma code (which the British had broken since before the War). The great Turing Engine (nicknamed the "Bomb") could read any Enigma messages (despite the fact that Enigma machines were rotor encoders with infinite possible settings, and that the Germans reset as often as every night). The capability lay in a complex but thorough understanding of the wiring system of the several types of Enigma encoders known to the British. The Turing Engine decoder "read" the electrical impulses in such a way that it could determine *what code keyings* were being used for the particular machine and message. Thus, the various users could develop code after code but the Turing Engine didn't have to have these "keyings." (In practical fact, possession of the keyings was very valuable, and — although not essential — sped up the process greatly.)

Doenitz, however, used an Enigma encoding machine that was a bit *different* from all others. This stymied the British for almost two years after the start of the submarine war.

Then, in early May of 1941, a U-boat was blown to the surface near Greenland. Starting to sink her, Commander Baker-Cresswell of the British destroyer *Bulldog* noticed that the crew was diving overboard. He ceased fire, boarded, and found a complete submarine model Enigma — plus "operating instructions, manuals, keying tables, and spare wheels." *(Bodyguard).* These were transferred to the *Bulldog*. The captured U-110 (which was Lemp's boat — the one that sank the *Athenia,* thus ending the chivalry period when subs would warn civilian passenger vessels) was taken in tow, but sank. An idea slowly formed in the British minds.

The transmission of the report of the capture had been on highest security. As it turned out, this was not intercepted (or, if intercepted, not decoded) by the Germans. In the meanwhile, the British decided to call the whole thing the sinking of a sub. The destroyer returned to port flying a sub-sunk flag. Nothing was said about the interim period of boarding the vessel — and certainly nothing was said about the capture of the code machine, keying, and books! The prisoners were carefully put in places from which they could never report what happened.

Ultra quickly began cracking the North Atlantic codes. However, there were to be some bad gaps ahead. For the time, though, they had the code broken.

(Kemp's story of all this "jibes" with *Bodyguard*. It was one of the great breaks of the War, which the British thoroughly exploited. The account remained utterly secret until at least 1958, and maybe 1966 (that date is of no consequence, and both dates could be correct if defining certain types of releases or declassifications). As a final point, Kemp says that sometimes German messages (not necessarily in this period) took days to crack — and thus, although it is easy to say that we had their messages, sometimes the battles would be over or the timeliness of the messages past, when the final crackings occurred).

The first submarine code was "Hydra." The British read the German messages steadily with few breaks for some eight months until February 1, 1942, when the Germans switched to a new code, "Triton," for North Atlantic submarines. Goodbye was said to the ability to read the Nazi messages. Despite all efforts, Triton remained an "enigma" through *most of 1942*. (And 1942 was the big disaster year for convoys).

Mini-Myth: ♪

THAT WE HAD THEIR CODES —
BUT THEY DIDN'T HAVE OURS

Alas, throughout all the worst of the convoy wars, until June 1943, *after* the big turnaround, the Germans could decrypt the *Allied convoy codes. (Kemp)*. But new codes instituted that month ended the German information source forever, and this became one factor in breaking up the German "wolf pack" tactic. (Although "wolf packs" were discontinued at the end of May, 1943, and any formations were being annihilated, Doenitz still needed to assemble groups in order to have effective attacks in the North or South Atlantic. The old "wolf pack" just positioned itself and waited for the convoy it knew would appear. Now any formation of subs had to hunt — because it didn't know where the convoy would come).

I was very disappointed to learn of the German break into our codes. For much of my youth, I lived under propaganda posters saying, "Loose Lips Sink Ships." We were blacked out every night for years. People were so careful not to spill the beans about their ship sailing, or their friend's or relative's ship sailing — and all the while, the Krauts knew when, where, and how many sailed; and even used the same designations for convoys as *we* did!

Even when we had broken the enemy's code, this did not assure the sinking of their subs. We got their assigned coordinates, number, intent, etc. These things were certainly useful, but often — especially at that time — could not prevent an attack or produce kills.

The first break in Triton was January, 1943 — eleven months after the compromised Hydra had ceased.

These eleven months were not a total wipeout for North Atlantic intelligence, because much information was read on regular German High Command ciphers on their way to Doenitz, or from him to them. Also, the British could piece together important information by reading the flow of orders to subs in the Mediterranean or other theatres, which were on the ordinary Enigmas and keying they knew or could break.

Triton yielded its fruit in January and February of 1943.

On March 8 — in the month of deepest convoy problems — the Germans added a fourth rotor to their sub Enigma encoder. That again ended British access to Triton.

Kemp states, "It is a matter of history now how close the Allies came to defeat in the Atlantic during the first three months of 1943."

In April, the British began to break into the four-rotor codings for Triton. This progressed — and for the remainder of the War, the convoy defenders read the German messages! (And, as mentioned, from June, 1943, forward, the Germans no longer could read Allied messages).

3. Convoy Speed

The earliest convoys of little 3,500 ton merchantmen and tankers — many of them designed for coastal or fair weather duty — were slow. Six knots was a good speed. Subs could do six knots *underwater*. Later convoys with eight-knots speeds and better defenses made more use of the tactic of forcing subs to submerge, where they often fell behind, and if there was air cover, couldn't catch up (which required surface running to positions ahead of the convoy) and would just have to wait for the next ships to come.

Speed equated to safety — while, conversely, slowness equated to great danger. Convoys never achieved much speed, but every bit helped. (It is worth mentioning here, as a side point regarding speed, that extremely high-speed ships travelled without convoy or escort. The greatest example of this was in the many trips of the great *Queen Mary,* carrying some 10,000 troops per voyage, at more than thirty knots (blacked out, in radio silence). A submarine — even if it had spotted the *Queen* — would have had a nearly impossible shooting position. To maneuver, the sub had, at best, a speed of eighteen knots on the surface. Even if torpedoes had been fired at close range, the *Queen,* with her huge bulk mastering the waves, could — assuming the torpedoes' phosphorescent wakes were spotted — suddenly change course with ease, and vanish as a feasible target. (A torpedo could travel for miles, or fizzle out, but its best accuracy was at close range, 1,000 meters or about a half mile — and even then in a four-shot fan shot). The concept (which one sees in the movies), of standing way off, at periscope depth, and firing at some gnat on the horizon, and hitting it, was just fiction (with the shred of truth of an occasional lucky hit under such circumstances). But the Germans were very economical with their torpedoes, because the trip back to France and return took them out of action. The same philosophy of speed equating to safety was employed in the trips of Churchill to North America and back, and of Roosevelt to and from great conferences. Most naval vessels could travel at thirty knots — and the last ones produced in the War, at forty).

4. Convoy Maneuver

As newer, faster, bigger ships came into the convoys, and the slowest and smallest tubs went to other duty, tactics of maneuvering developed — and were effective. The old, early convoys could barely make it straight ahead in a rough sea (much less execute sudden, unified shifts of direction at night in radio silence!) The later convoys could routinely throw off the best calculations of a well-positioned enemy attack by shifting direction of 100 ships at once. Werner, in *Iron Coffins,* tells of an occasion when he executed a perfect "fan shot" of four torpedoes (could have been half his load at the moment), only to have the entire convoy (which had *not* seen him or the oncoming torpedoes in the rough seas and poor night visibility), just suddenly execute a maneuver to the right, causing all torpedoes to miss.

5. Ship Size

The early merchantmen and tankers were in the 3,500 ton category. (One can imagine the unfairness of a *Scharnhorst* encountering a little tub and bottoming her). Submarines had a field day with the vessels. The little ships would *break in two* from one torpedo, and sink. (This is shown in countless newsreel and still photos). Through 1940, 1941, and 1942, it was a slaughter.

Also, smaller ships had more trouble maintaining convoy patterns. They required more "herding" by escorts. The little ships were gallant — but often dominated by the sea.

As one wades through the figures showing tonnages sunk and numbers of ships sunk, the average size ship gradually rises. The 1,660 Allied ships sunk in 1942, totaling some 7,800,000 tons, averaged about 4,700 tons per vessel. This was an increase from earlier years. (For a later example, in one U-boat onslaught on convoys in a portion of March, 1943, twenty-one ships totaling 141,000 tons went down — an average of *6,700* tons). The average size of convoy merchantmen was rapidly growing — due mainly to numerous deliveries of the 10,000 ton "Liberty ships" being turned out in U.S. yards.

The larger, faster (but still slow), more maneuverable, better equipped, vessels were much more able to take the rough North Atlantic seas.

6. *Stupendous Production*

The Germans, in planning to *win the blockade* by destroying more shipping than the Allies could build, did not calculate a high enough figure for U.S. yards, and did not figure on the "assembly line" ship. The German target was 500,000 to 700,000 tons sunk per month — 6,000,000 to 8,400,000 tons per year! At the time (1940 and 1941), England was producing less than 1,000,000 tons a year, and the U.S. less than that.

But then the U.S. "got cranking." In 1942, it alone produced more than 5,000,000 tons, which, added to Britain's increase to some 2,00,000 tons, came close to offsetting the record 8,000,000 tons sunk in that fateful year.

Then, in 1943 and 1944, the U.S. *alone averaged building 12,000,000 tons per year.* Combined with the British, that gave the Allies a surplus in 1943 of 10,000,000 tons over the 4,000,000 tons (half their goal) sunk by the Germans; and in 1944 a surplus of more than 12,000,000 tons over the less than 1,500,000 tons bottomed by the fading Germans.

Thus the plan by Germany to win the war by sinking some 8,000,000 tons of shipping per year, was defeated in part by the topic of these paragraphs: stupendous production.

Unbelieveable production.

The Liberty ship was approved by Roosevelt from a sheaf of plans presented by Admiral Emory Land, head of the War Shipping Administration. Roosevelt said it was an "ugly duckling," but would "carry a good load." Remarkably, the original design stemmed from that of a British tramp steamer planned in 1879! *(Battle Of The Atlantic).* The important points were size and simplicity. Simplicity was vital, because the ship was to be the first "standardized" ship — and one that could be built anywhere, without fancy equipment, and without a lot of training. Furthermore, as we all know, it was to be fabricated in sections ("pre-

more, as we all know, it was to be fabricated in sections fabricated") on site, and assembled in very short periods on the ways. What's more — it was to be welded. ⅄

Henry J. Kaiser, who had built Boulder Dam and the San Francisco-Oakland Bay Bridge, made a further reputation building these ships. A trusted industrialist who had the ear of Congress, the President, the bureaucracy, and the military — and who got things done in a fair-and-square manner without a lot of red tape — stayed in the headlines by setting new record after new record for speed in "building" (actually, assembling) ships. One record was less than five days — but of course, his yard had built the sections before the assembly. The press and the nation loved the records. Other yards built the ships (although one hardly realized this). A yard at Savannah, near my island home, launched one every Monday for years. (A new industrial revolution hit the southern depression $1-a-day farmhand with $75-a-week welding wages with overtime — and it was hard, after the War, to get anyone back to the farm after they'd seen the Savannah Shipyards!) Canadian yards also built the standardized win-the-war Liberty ship.

There were criticisms of the ship, but the smaller problems could be traced to defects in production — not in the concept. With any project that huge, under extreme pressures of time, there would certainly be some badly-performed work getting through.

The worst criticism, though, was that they "broke up" in heavy seas — a defect critics traced to "prefabrication," a term which many associated automatically with "shoddy." Some felt that the all-welded assembly method contained an inherent weakness. Neither of these criticisms was accurate.

Some ships — very few out of the 2,700 built in the U.S. — did break up at sea. I served in ship transportation for a while in the Korean crisis, and we were taught never to load heavy items in the bow and heavy items in the stern — leaving the middle light. A wave rising in the middle of a ship so loaded would snap it in two! We were also taught that analyses of ships which broke up in heavy seas in WWII revealed improper loading. In WWII — amidst the great pressuress in jammed, crammed, wartime ports, to get loaded and get out to sea — it is logical that some chances were taken, corners cut on occasion, expediencies placed above wisdom and hopes entertained that seas would not be too rough. And sometimes this produced fatal results.

Obliquely related to the role of "stupendous production" in defeating the submarines, is the "exchange rate" — one of Doenitz' measures of his Atlantic battles. This was more than the traditional military term, "acceptable casualties." Doenitz had approached the Atlantic war as one of attrition. He had a certain number of subs with which to sink a certain tonnage of Allied vessels a year — and thus wear the Allies down into surrender.

In 1940 and 1941, Doenitz sank well over 100,000 tons, or about *thirty-five* of that day's ships, for the loss of *each* sub! The Germans called this the "happy time." Happy because they were killing so many helpless people and ships. This type happiness must rank close to the happiness of the Stuka dive bomber pilot strafing Polish civilian refugees along roads in Poland in 1939.

In 1942, there was little change. Ships were somewhat bigger on average, and one report shows 1,660 ships sunk by submarines — at a loss of only eighty-five subs. That would be an "exchange rate" for all of 1942 of nearly twenty of the bigger ships and roughly 100,000 tons for each sub sunk. Doenitz was still smiling.

The year 1943 witnessed the turnaround, so we will have to grab at dates to examine the rapidly declining exchange rate. But things started out badly! In February, in convoy ON-166, German subs sank fourteen ships while losing only one sub. (This was only a small portion of a disastrous February which saw the British Admiralty informing the Prime Minister that the convoy concept was not working). In just one small portion of the following month, twenty-one ships were sunk from two convoys in one battle — with the loss again of only one sub! And the Germans were building a new sub every day and a half!

However, March, April, and May were the "great turn-around" months.

In May, according to his own diary, Doenitz wrote, "the ratio was one U-boat to 10,000 tons of enemy shipping, whereas a short time ago it was one . . . to 100,000 gross tons." Using a figure of perhaps 6,500 tons average at this time, May was costing the Nazis one sub for about one and one half merchant ship sinkings! He concluded, "The U-boat losses of May 1943 therefore reached unbearable heights."

For years, he had been successful with his designed war of attrition. Then he watched in disbelief (and even the Americans were surprised), as America's many new special yards pumped out Liberty ships far in excess of the high side of Doenitz' estimates.

Next, he saw his precious "exchange rate" collapse.

At the end of May, he issued his stunning order to *withdraw* from the Atlantic! He wrote in his diary (but certainly notified no one else!), "We had lost the Battle of the Atlantic."

This ended the "turnaround."

The turnaround months were March, April, and May of 1943. In these three months, seventy-one subs went to the bottom — almost as many as the eighty-five in the entire year of 1942. May was the stiffest month the Germans had ever faced — forty-one subs sunk. (Note: different sources vary slightly as to the precise totals for a given year, or for a given month. The charts in the back of *Iron Coffins* and *Battle of the Atlantic* seem to be the most detailed. Although they differ a bit, the final totals are the same. Kemp routinely gives figures in his text).

But Doenitz' agonies were not over yet. The next six months are what I call the "annihilation of the front-line fleet."

In fact, after May, Germany could never mount a concerted drive by subs again. We'll study why, later.

Germany could never get a dangerous group of subs assembled anywhere again. It tried — and as it tried, the subs were blown away.

The loss of seventy-one front-line Atlantic subs and crews in the turnaround period was bad enough — but in the ensuing six months, 133 *more* were bottomed. That completed the "annihilation of the front-line fleet."

The subs once had the potential of winning the War. At all times in the past, they had been an arm which could *change* the

War. After the May turnaround, they could no longer change the War — but they still had the potential to put a dent in the Allied effort *if* they could find a way to again mass at sea. However, after November — after the annihilation of the front-line fleet — they gave up any attempts to ever mass again, and the subs were (in terms of the total war picture) only a nuisance from that time on.

During the annihilation period, the subs were sent back to the North Atlantic in September — but with little success.

The Allies were now winning a war of attrition against the subs!

For the month of November, we have a "reverse exchange rate" figure — against twelve cargo ships lost for the entire month, twenty-three subs went to the bottom! That was a *reverse* ratio of two to one against Admiral Doenitz!

There is yet another measure of the Atlantic war that might fit at this point: the *percentage of convoyed ships sunk.* "Less than two percent," says one history. That figure does not honor "phase one" — the agonizing three and one-half years from September 1939 until May 1943.

Let's divide this discussion into our three North Atlantic segments: one, the first three years (including the turnaround); two, the annihilation period of six months June-November 1943; and three, the final eighteen months (which included the colossal buildup for Normandy, and the supply of the European campaign after the landings).

In the first period of three and one half years, there were two huge dangers; one, a very *high percentage* of ships sunk; and two, the special savaging of one convoy or another. With few ships (and fewer defenses), the Germans could put twenty or thirty subs against a convoy of only sixty ships in a given night — and then pursue it across the Atlantic!

It is known that some convoys lost as many as *sixty percent* of their ships — one losing forty percent going over, and twenty percent coming back.

But another convoy might go over with few losses.

Part of this was due to the *number of loaded convoys on the seas at one time.* It's some 3,500 miles from Halifax to England — and a little convoy chugging along at less than eight knots could take twenty days one way. With convoys a week or so apart, there would be maybe three on the high seas at one time. One or all could be picked out and badly beaten up. Later in the War, the convoys came like trains — and whereas one or two might get picked on, others just rolled by.

(Not as a digression, but one Arctic convoy, the PQ-17 in July of 1942, lost twenty-five of thirty-six ships — or just at seventy percent of the loaded vessels — on one run to Archangel, to subs and aircraft. This illustrates the danger of near wipeout to one convoy when conditions and breaks all favored the enemy. There were other convoys, however, where weather, defenses, etc., favored the Arctic shipments. For the full four years of such shipments (August 1941 forward), the losses were ninety-nine vessels out of 811 going *to* Russia (total 1,528 sailings). However, only fifty-eight were sunk, or about eight percent — the remainder turning back. I find it a little hard to believe that about half of all sinkings on the Arctic route were in PQ-17!)

From the same source, appears data that the loss rate on *North Atlantic* runs *to* Britain was nearly twenty-three percent — 654 ships sunk of 2,889 involved. (That had to be data for one year, not four years, and probably 1941). That would have indicated about 240 sailings per month *to* Britain across the Atlantic — with a twenty-three percent loss rate loaded. I can believe that. *(Almanac).*

Somewhere there are probably exact figures on ship sailings from and to each port, by weight, by month, etc.

From fragments assembled — and, like old pottery, with lots of pieces — I am going to do some extrapolating, and make the following educated guesses: In the first three and one half years, forty percent of all ships which would attempt the North Atlantic crossing to England in the entire War, sailed — and losses thereto were in the *twenty* percent range (with additional losses on the return trip).

That leaves the final two years in which sixty percent of all ships which would attempt the North Atlantic crossing to England in the entire War, sailed.

Finally, we need to break that final two years into two segments. The first is the six months "annihilation" period — roughly May-November, or June-December, 1943. Roughly one-quarter of the ships for the final two years sailed in this six months — and had a loss rate of about *four* percent. (I have assembled that figure from data on specific convoys, and also from occasional quotes in various texts). (This four percent applies, then, to fifteen percent of all ships which would attempt the North Atlantic crossing to England in the entire War).

The second segment is the final eighteen months, in which three-quarters of the ships for the final two years sailed — and had a loss rate of only about *one* percent. (Again, this data is assembled from losses in specific convoys, and from occasional quotations scattered in various texts). (This one percent applies, then, to forty-five percent of all ships which would attempt the North Atlantic crossing to England in the entire War).

(Note: Does percentage of cargo exactly match the percentages of ships sailing? No, because later ships lifted larger loads per ship).

(Figures do not count convoys in the middle or South Atlantic — the African convoys — but only North Atlantic ones, and only the leg bound into Great Britain. Below, we make an adjustment for losses on return trips).

(Researchers tackling precise figures should be aware of such terms as "sailings" and "crossings," and determine if the source refers to one-way legs (loaded), or two ways. The answer sharply affect calculations).

Therefore, what are my conclusions, by period?

The average loaded ship losses in North Atlantic convoys inward bound to British ports for the first two-thirds of the War, was *twenty* percent.

For the next six months of sea victory, four percent.

For the last eighteen, "shining," months, one percent.

For the full five and one half years of the submarine war, a little under two percent — which agrees with official statements of two percent losses. If a fraction is added for returning vessels, the figure rises to a little over two percent — still in agreement. (Why a small increment for returning vessels? The subs husbanded their torpedoes for loaded ships. That didn't mean they wouldn't sink an empty vessel or one loaded with nonessential export items — but they vastly preferred, and hunted, the inbound ships loaded with materials which would support the War).

Thus, the "two percent" concept disguises the harrowing early three and one half years including the turnaround — and does not give sufficient credit to this time. The two percent figure should *never be used* without showing the awesome twenty percent losses of the first three and one half years of the War! And it should never be used without showing that the turnaround victory was *won* by these suffering people; and that this alone made the final, nearly loss-free months — which then so heavily tilted the statistics — possible.

7. Sheer Numbers Of Convoys On The Seas At One Time

This point has been largely covered above. Kemp speaks of thirteen convoys on the seas at one time during one later period (which would imply about 800 loaded vessels in the North Atlantic on the way to England at one time). Counting twenty or less days for a crossing, this would fit nicely into the figures for 1,000 and 1,250 ship months in his book and other sources, for a period after June 1943, and later. (Incidentally, thirteen convoys at one time for a twenty-day crossing, would mean a convoy arriving about every day and a half!)

8. Long-range Reconnaissance Planes

From an early date, some long-range recon planes were assisting convoys. However, weather was a limiting factor, hampering both operation of the planes, and visibility. And, in the final analysis, surveillance alone wouldn't sink subs. But it furnished some intelligence data, and often forced subs to submerge, which changed their effectiveness, and no doubt showed up in the statistics somewhere, in a small way.

But long-range recon planes were only the beginning of a developing pattern of aerial coverage — the ideal goal of which was *warplane* coverage of entire convoys all the way! And any little bit helped.

From the earliest time there was the land-based "air gap" — the distance between land-based air coverages from North America, Iceland, and England. As the War progressed, this grew enticingly less as aircraft ranges grew longer, bases developed, and newer types of planes were produced and allocated to that duty.

The recon plane gradually became a recon-*warplane.*

American Liberators with special fuel tanks were ideal for very long range convoy surveillance — and also, could be fitted with a dozen or so depth bombs! Subs had been surprised as these and other "harmless recon" planes dropped explosives! The subs caught on quickly — but results proved that the concept functioned anyhow! Enemy subs were vulnerable to land-based recon-bombing planes. Bit by bit, the system was "debugged." However, there were only *eighteen* Liberators in operation! And — Africa needed Liberators! So did the Far East.

Only after the absolute crisis of February, 1943 — when it was plain that *any* buildup for Normandy was impossible without *winning* the Atlantic war — did something of a miracle occur.

9. Roosevelt's Decision

Roosevelt himself, in March 1943, cut through conflicting arguments and ordered *255* Liberators to augment the meagre eighteen. Kemp says trained crews had been available for this duty of flying and bombing over the expanses of the North Atlantic. (These planes also made their way to the Bay of Biscay, and also relieved other warplanes for duty over the Bay of Biscay).

This decision was a major change of policy.

Germans were later to credit the *land-based bomber* (U.S.

and British planes, but mainly British crews), as being the most destructive weapon used against the subs! (Aircraft of all types sank more subs than did surface vessels. Land-based planes bagged more than carrier-based. A British plane, the four-engined flying boat, the Short Sunderland, was one of the major combatants. Also bombing were twin-engined Wellingtons. U.S. planes included four-engined Liberators (plus a few Forts, Kemp says), and twin-engined Lockheed Hudsons. Both four-engined and twin-engined warplanes covered the Bay, while only the biggest planes had the "air gap" duty. Note: the U.S. Catalina PBY flying boat was used extensively for patrol, and was mainly a recon plane — however, one source shows a photo of one clearly dropping a bomb). /

To overemphasize one arm or method, though, is to overlook the point of this chapter — twenty interlocking elements.

The bombing planes worked by themselves in the Biscay Bay and at the convoys when escorts were not available. However, when detachable escorts *were* available, the planes would work, but also call the escorts to the scene! Woe to the subs below!

Roosevelt's Liberator decision coincided with the availability of vast numbers of new aircraft pouring out of U.S. factories. The various hungry "pipelines" of prior deficiencies (many since the beginning of British shortages in 1939, and ours in 1941) in all theatres worldwide, had now been filled. This provident fact enabled the President to make his vital decision.

In March or April of 1943, the land-based "air gap" in the North Atlantic was considered closed at last.

10. Close Support Air Cover

Close support air cover was mainly carrier-based. Since the U.S. could furnish no regular carriers (its battered few were desperately needed in the Pacific, and the British were in worse shape), there was no close-support air cover for a long time.

The first attempt (in this age before the helicopter) was a cargo-carrying merchant ship with a catapult and *one plane*. These "CAMs" had one opportunity, because the plane, after looking around, maybe forcing a sub or two to dive, maybe strafing a sub or bombing one with the one egg it carried, and generally making the convoy feel better, had no more aircraft. The pilots had to have more "balls" than Evel Knievel, because each flight inevitably ended in a ditching or other rude return such as parachute, and only a hopeful pickup in one piece.

The next advance was the "MAC" — Merchant Aircraft Carrier. This was a tiny carrier built on a (non-cargo carrying) merchant ship's hull. It certainly had some effectiveness. (This was *not* the later development — the escort carrier). The *Audacity,* with six aircraft, was a MAC *(Kemp)*. Weather limited operations. Day visibility was often bad. And of course, it was impossible to operate at night — when the Germans did almost all of their attacking! But — as mentioned elsewhere — sometimes causing a sub to submerge and stay submerged furnished a measurable degree of protection — less attacks, poorer attacks, etc.

The next advance was the escort carrier, such as the *Bogue.* These had weather and night problems too. At first, there was only the *Bogue,* and it was, naturally, not available for every convoy.

As with other escort vessels, the escort carrier had to follow the then science of escorting. It was not to leave the convoy. It was *at*tached, not *de*tached. (We'll discuss the roving groups later).

11. Leigh Lights

Subs attacked at night. From early in the War, the main means of lighting up the area was the traditional flare. These had varied effects. If the convoy defenses were poor, the flares might only serve to light up the target better for the attackers. But if the defenses were super, and there were enough flares up, the subs might dive — and thus avoid being attacked.

An invention called the Leigh Light was installed on attack aircraft. The point was to bag submarines *before* the flares lit up the skies. In the pitch darkness, the bomber, following its radar, would swoop at low level upon the surfaced submarine. In the last moments, it would flick on its Leigh Light — which was a blazing searchlight! Bombs and bullets followed instantly — to the demise or damage of many subs.

12. Shallow Depth Charges For Aircraft

When a U-boat was avoiding a surface escort, it usually had a few seconds more time to dive — and would dive deep. Therefore, depth charges were commonly set to go off at 100 feet or more. However, when a *plane* was making the attack (which became more frequent as the war progressed), the sub was usually *just starting* a panic dive! Many depth charges exploded far too deep to kill an easy target. Therefore, the shallow depth charge was developed. It could explode at twenty-five feet — thus increasing the kill by aircraft, and making the subs very wary of planes!

13. The "Hedgehog" (And "Squid")

Escorts liked to keep subs on sonar while they attacked them with depth bombs. However, with the old method of releasing the depth charges from the stern area, sonar contact would be *lost* as the ship and its engines passed over the sub. The "Hedgehog" was developed to *throw* a depth charge ahead of the escort, or far to one side — thus enabling continuous sonar contact. It proved very effective. Soon the "Squid" appeared — which would throw three depth charges.

14. That Amazing British Radar

We all know the British invented radar. In the North Atlantic, in its early forms, it was useful in pushing the enemy sub fleet underwater — which we have already seen was a type of victory in itself (adventure movies notwithstanding!)

Ordinary radar on ships or planes could spot the surface-running German subs at night, and at least make things warmer for them — if not actually hot.

The Germans *could tell* — on their wartime-model "fuzz-busters" — that they were *on radar*.

End of part one of radar.

15. Early Shortwave Radar — The 1.5 Meter

England invented something called the magnetron, which cut radar wavelengths from several meters to shorter wavelengths. By the end of 1941, a radar with 1.5 meter wavelength was in production. These were fitted to Coastal Command antisub aircraft. Detection of German subs was greatly increased.

But — most important of all — the German "fuzz-busters" *didn't register the 1.5 meter radar.* The Germans were "on scope" — but *didn't know it!*

Kemp says the Germans would suddenly find an aircraft diving at them or a destroyer coming at them full speed, without any warning having registered on their radar search receivers.

About mid-1942 *(Kemp)*, or some four months after the 1.5 radar became operational on a sub-killing basis, the Germans wised up, and installed a radar search receiver known as "Metox" *(Kemp)*. *(Battle of the Atlantic* places the first Metox units at about September, and connects this first use with the "Biscaykreuz" — the "Biscay Cross" written about by Werner in *Iron Coffins*. This reveals the experimental early period in the Bay of Biscay, when British Coastal Command was, in 1942, testing concepts which — when proven out and debugged — would be put into practice so successfully the following year, beginning in March).

The new German receivers detected the 1.5 meter radar — but the British still had the advantage of the improvement in detection offered by the shorter wave radar.

16. Radar Less Than One Meter Wavelength — "Centimetric"

By the end of 1942, new "10-centimeter" radar was being installed in antisub aircraft and surface vessels, with excellent effect. Again, German search receivers *could not detect* this newest radar — so again, the Allies had a super advantage. *(Iron Coffins* speaks of a radar in the "upper centimetric" range, as preceding radar in the "lower centimetric" range). Early in February, 1943, an RAF plane was shot down in the Netherlands. On board was a centimetric radar set. The Germans had not believed it was possible to build such a thing.

To counter, the Nazis set about building a detector. While struggling with the technology, a U-boat reported that its regular Metox gave a *visible* response — although not an audible one — to the new centimetric radar, provided it was fitted with a special device. Hoping they had found the answer, the Germans delayed development of a new receiver, while fitting old Metoxes with the special device — called "Magic Eye."

Magic Eye, though, turned out to be a big flop. Within a few months, the problem was back in the laps of German designers. (Much of the above intriguing information is from Kemp).

The lost months, though, were the "turnaround" and the beginning of the "annihilation" period. So the lack of a dependable radar receiver cost the Germans dearly.

(*Iron Coffins* does not mention "Magic Eye" in its glossary, but mentions test equipment and various rigs in the text. Perhaps the specific equipment never reached his boat).

The big Bay of Biscay campaign began in March, 1943. This book calls March, April, and May (seventy-one subs sunk — forty-one in May; and the decision by Doenitz at the end of May to "withdraw" from the North Atlantic), the "turnaround." This was the initial, or turnaround, victory.

It was also the victory ending phase one. The prayer involved had been protracted over a long, bloody, agonizing period, not just a climactic or dramatic time.

During this period, the British put the Bay of Biscay and its approaches under round-the-clock aerial surveillance by land-based bombers equipped with centimetric radar which could detect anything that moved on the surface — while the prospective victim *could not tell it was detected* until too late!

March had started darkly for the Allies. Werner says it was Germany's "greatest month" — sinking 1,000,000 tons (that figure is high, but it was a bad month). He adds, though, a prophetic reference to a "plague of aircraft." He refers to May as "that fateful month."

Iron Coffins' chapter, "Above Us, Hell," describes the Bay of Biscay campaign. We have broken the campaign into two parts — turnaround and annihilation. Werner's chapter considers it as one period — the destruction of the U-boat fleet!

Let us consider some huge points about the U-boat war as a whole: Unromantic as it may seem, it was *not* won in the North

Atlantic, *not* won at convoys, and *not* won by the escorts! All the methods, though, were incrementally gained and proven in blood and agony in the North Atlantic at the convoys! But even the *turnaround* itself was not accomplished there! That — plus the further *annihilation* of the front-line fleet — was accomplished in the Bay of Biscay and its approaches, nowhere near convoys, and by land-based aircraft!

How were things at the U-boat level after June 1, 1943?

Of May and June (fifty-eight U-boats sunk), Werner writes, "We lost forty percent of our active force." Of July 1, he wrote, "The British were throwing in planes in such huge numbers that scarcely a U-boat could traverse the Bay of Biscay undetected," and, "It had become widely known [in the German ranks] that the enemy was sinking three out of five of our boats as they made their runs through the Bay of Biscay. On June 24 alone, the Tommies had sent four U-boats to the bottom within sixteen hours." Of late July, he says that "ten of seventeen" boats trying to cross had been sunk!

It was annihilation time!

His reports for August were no sunnier for the Germans! He said the Metox had "not helped much" to detect enemy planes, and that they relied on their eyes. As one of the most experienced and wiliest of the commanders, with one of the best crews, he knew how to dive fast. Inexperienced commanders lost their boats quickly — and even good commanders, with inexperienced crews, were quickly sunk. August losses were another twenty-five! (This following a horrendous July loss of thirty-seven, and a June loss (in a supposedly "withdrawn" month), of seventeen). Further in August he reports, "Only one of seven of our boats is returning from patrol." Of the loss of 100 U-boats (120 May-August), he said, "sixty percent of the operating fleet" had been destroyed.

By November, he said he had seen the end of the once great Atlantic fleet. (This coincides with the end of our six-month "annihilation" period).

The Bay ports of Brest, Lorient, and St. Nazaire only lay

about 250 miles by air, on average, from, say, Portsmouth, in Southeast England. Thus, the concept of knocking the subs off as they approached or left their "pit stops" was an enticing one long before the big campaign. But priorities had not made enough equipment available — and some of the twenty interlocking elements making it possible (such as the undetectable centimetric radar) had not come into wide use.

Too, who could have foreseen that the Germans would not develop a countermeasure for centimetric radar? They were certainly trying hard. They had something called the Hagenuk receiver, but Kemp says it flopped. They developed a decoy balloon, which Kemp says also failed. Werner is very rough on the balloon — saying it almost fouled his attempts to crash dive on a couple of occasions, so he said to hell with it.

Werner also talks about the "Biscay Cross" as if it were a development in the summer of 1943 rather than a year earlier *(Battle of the Atlantic)*. Perhaps he first installed his in 1943. It was "bulky," he said — and obviously a jury-rigged thing, and had to be removed before crash-diving, unless one wanted to rebuild it when surfacing again! With Werner's expertise in crash diving (which saved his life and preserved an extraordinary view of history), I can imagine he didn't like the thing. He describes it as able to receive radar waves in the "upper centimeter range," so this would indicate late summer and fall of 1943 before the ten centimeter (or "lower centimeter") radar. However, I imagine the British kept using detectable types of radar which the Germans would "read," as a cover for the fact that unreadable lower waves were closing in on the victim!

Werner places "Metox" after the Biscay Cross — and says it was capable of detecting "radar waves in the ten centimeter range." Hmm. First of all, I am now certain there were at least two "Metox" units. The first countered the 1.5 meter, and, with the Biscaykreuz, maybe some "upper centimeter" radar as well. Then Magic Eye tried to turn the Metox into a reader of ten centimeter radar ("lower centimeter" waves) — and was followed by nicknamed items such as "bug" and "fly," (both of which Werner says he was using June 30), which were attempts to cure the lower centimeter problem. Did these fit the Metox? Or were they separate contraptions? The situation was obviously changing rapidly. Some boats were receiving experimental equipment, some not, while some rigged their own, etc. (In another reference, Werner says the Bug replaced Metox, apparently in August, 1943. This could have been an upgraded Bug from the one he was using June 30. Also, he says the Bug *worked*. If so, this would be an important piece of War history. However, after examining all of his references, and all references I can find on the subject of the centimetric radar in the submarine war, I believe the reference could only be to a very limited success).

An almost desperate scrambling to rig a dependable detector is hinted in Werner's glossary description of the "Bug," which he calls "A revised German radar warning device, the fourth of a series, which detected radar waves in the lower centimeter range." The giveaway words are "revised" and "fourth of a series."

Detection was desired, but, with the *speed* with which an airplane could place a bomb on a detected submarine, not detection, but *protection* was the big thing from May 1 forward! Thus, the entire concept of being able to detect that pesky radar — when detection meant only a few more seconds warning than human eyes and ears could provide — became less important in the overall scale of things.

(Kemp mentions a "nine centimeter radar." He also mentions a later, "three centimeter" radar. On detection capabilities of this last, he says "No Allied radar, not even the centimetric sets, could detect the top of a . . . periscope." Later, he wrote that the three-centimeter radar (mid-1944, during Normandy invasion time), *could* pick up the top of a *snorkel*. The disadvantage, he wrote, was that it also picked up floating junk).

The Germans continued for the War to try to offset the improved detection capabilities of the Allies — and also to try to always know when they were on scope. Kemp felt the Germans *never* solved the problems of detecting the progressively lower centimetric radars. Werner indicates the Germans had makeshift devices which worked — but not in a manner sufficient to give the

Krauts confidence! He speaks of the "Fly," which was a "much improved" radar warning device capable of detecting the "lowest centimeter range." This might have been something to offset the three-centimeter range — the lowest centimeter radar I can find mentioned anywhere in the antisub war. The "Fly" also had the feature of being able to indicate where the radar was coming from (but, with the fast-closing aircraft, that didn't make a great deal of difference).

All of which brings us to the "snorkel."

A sub in those days liked to run on the surface with diesel power — but this required air. Submerged, it ran on batteries. Surface also meant it could run to port and back at seventeen knots. So who needed snorkels?

But when anything on the surface — day or night — became instant fair game for many dozens of roving aircraft, running submerged became a *necessity of life.*

So why not just run on the batteries submerged? Because every so often, there had to be a long run on the diesels on the surface to *charge* them thar batteries. And *long runs on the surface* were, from April 1943 forward, plain unhealthy.

The snorkels certainly wouldn't help in the speed department — because submerged subs ran at seven knots or so — but might mean the difference between life and death.

Also, since it was no longer possible to sneak up on a convoy and attack on the surface, combat tactics became snorkel-oriented. The new attacks (if a sub could get anywhere near a convoy) would be from a submerged position!

The first problems were the snorkels themselves. Werner says he first heard of them in August of 1943 — when the sub war was effectively already lost. He didn't *see* one until he saw three assemblies arrive at Brest in April 1944 (just before the Normandy invasion).

What kind of snorkels were these? They were retrofit assemblies to go on type VII submarine models. Werner learned that seven subs so equipped were operating out of Brest. (A month later, he stated that he believed these were the only ones in the fleet anywhere).

His experience with the snorkel was bad. Apparently, the assemblies didn't work properly all of the time — and when they jammed, seawater came pouring *into* the sub! This sometimes had *fatal* results — sending the snorkel sub to the bottom! Werner's snorkel jammed, but (with his 999 lives) he managed to avoid disaster. After that, he wouldn't use it.

However, a hydraulic closer appeared on later retrofit models.

Early in June, 1944, the Allies landed in Normandy. The Channel — so close to the sub ports — was clogged with Allied vessels of all types. The Nazis told their subs to go into the heavily-guarded south flank of the Allied armada, fire their torpedoes, and then *ram* the enemy. The submariners read this as "suicide." Few if any followed those orders, and the higher-ups didn't pursue the matter.

But it was found that the snorkel boats could sneak along the coast into the Channel without detection at first. And thus — with the War less than a year from ending — the mere handful of snorkel subs suddenly became big news. Werner claims that in July (1944 — a full year after the bad July in the Bay), snorkel subs scored as follows: U-953 got three destroyers; U-984 sank three cargo vessels and one frigate; U-763 bottomed three cargo ships and one corvette. This would indeed have been possible in the crammed Channel only one month after the Normandy landings — where upwards of 6,000 vessels were active.

However, defenses became alert to the new threat. Two of the snorkel boats were sunk.

The new type XXI snorkel boat also got a lot of "ink" — but had practically no effect on the War. It was one of Hitler's secret weapons — and the hope of the submariners. (Werner reports finding one newly afloat near its way in late April, 1945 — a few days before the final surrender. He commented something to the effect that he was astounded and pleased to see that there was even *one* of these things. The upcoming new boats had been dangled before the weary submariners for so long they had given up — but, by golly, here was a real one, newly launched and being outfitted. Only a few were produced. Two sources say they never saw action. On the type XXI, the snorkel was built in as original equipment.

17. *MAD Could Detect Subs Even Submerged*

As mentioned throughout this book — the sub war was won by twenty interlocking elements! What could be a better weapon than a detection device that revealed the presence of subs when submerged?

So — snorkel or no snorkel, submerged or not submerged — the German fleet was "on scope" to the bombing planes!

By the middle of the turnaround month of May — and for the remainder of the War — the British had "MAD" (magnetic anomaly detector), which could detect a submerged sub's *magnetic field!* These were fitted to aircraft in the spring of 1943.

18. *Asdic — The Hotshot Sonar Of That Era*

Every account by U-boat skippers mentions "Asdic pings" when being attacked by ships.

What is sonar? Sound waves travel beautifully through water (whereas common radio waves won't). Sonar is "sound navigation ranging." Asdic is a sonar device (the name comes from "Anti-submarine Detection Investigation Committee." Gad!)

The long vigils by escorts (sometimes five, ten, or even twenty-four hours) interspersed by periods of furious depth-bombings, were in most cases not guesswork, but based on the absolute certainty that a sub was *there.*

Occasionally, a beleaguered sub commander would be given new life when an attacking escort finally decided the Asdic-located object was a rock, a sunken ship hulk, a whale taking a long nap, or something else.

19. *Detached, Large Groups To Hunt And Kill*

I am specifically avoiding the term, "hunter-killer," until we are clear what we are talking about.

There were "hunter-killers" from the *earliest* part of the War.

Even then it was clearly established that *if* an escort could detach from a convoy and *stay with* a submerged sub *long enough,* the possibility of a kill was very high.

However, it was also learned very early that convoy escorts (as discussed earlier) would have to remain with the convoy. Other than for experimental purposes, escorts were flatly and absolutely *ordered* to remain with the convoy and *not detach even temporarily.*

When the CAMs and MACs came along, the policy was rigidly the same. Carrier aircraft could fly out, but escort vessels were to remain close. This didn't prevent, of course, plenty of depth-bombing alongside the convoys (and some kills). But the escorts had to keep moving, and keep close.

Whereas the secret to killing by surface escort was in detaching and staying with the detected, submerged, sub — usually for hours.

When the *Bogue* came on duty, it was supported by from two to five destroyers. This made a little combat group or mini task force — on paper. In fact, though, *Bogue* and any supporting destroyers were assigned as regular, attached, convoy escorts.

However, a trend was appearing: more and more escort vessels, and more of the escort carriers in the "group" concept.

Also, another trend was appearing simultaneously: the destruction of the sub fleet in the Bay of Biscay and approaches. (For example, *Bogue* was assigned in the Atlantic in March 1943).

In other words, as the number and power of escorts increased sharply, the number of subs able to make it out where the escorts were located sharply decreased!

That didn't mean the escorts were no longer needed. Nonetheless, it is a fact that, by the time enough of them were on the scene, the need for them had sharply diminished.

Bogue and its supporting destroyers were the immediate forerunner of the "detached" group. (Kemp says that between March and May, *five* new "groups" were added in the Atlantic — based on two more carriers (a third carrier, scheduled, had blown up in an accident).

The concept of the separated, detached, roving sub-hunting *group* was appearing.

However, evidencing some caution (and some ambivalence), *Bogue* and others were given the routine orders as *attached* groups — attached to this or that convoy. *But,* the orders left open the matter of *detaching, staying with,* and even *hunting.*

So these were not fully detached. They were attached — with permission to detach.

About this time (the months of the turnaround), a new head of the British Coastal Command decided that the most submarines could be found always closest to the convoys. Thus he changed emphasis from extra wide ranging (of aircraft, mainly), to more patrols closer to convoys. The effect was this: that whereas a lot of escort groups were now getting ready to go far afield, the subs were probably close to the convoys anyhow, and besides, there were all those wonderful scout planes practically overhead, ready to guide them to a kill close to the convoys. So the new groups, at first, stayed close. They worked with the air cover, followed in quickly when a sub was spotted or an airplane began an attack.

In June 1943, the Allies realized their Atlantic codes had been broken for the War to date, and changed ciphers. Doenitz had already called off his North Atlantic wolfpacks (but had been desperately trying to assemble more than one sub at a time in the middle Atlantic and South Atlantic for attacks on American convoys. He could slip some subs out along the Spanish Coast).

The Allies probably realized that, with the Bay campaign such a success that Doenitz couldn't form wolfpacks — and with the added blow of the loss of the Allied convoy codes preventing Doenitz from forming any group to wait for compromised ships — the enemy Admiral was converted permanently to hunting, and with singular subs.

OK, thought the Allies — no groups of subs anymore, no need to keep all our protection right alongside the convoys anymore.

Therefore, at last, the thing so many people believe won the sub war — the detached, go-and-get-'em "hunter-killer" groups — roamed with numbers of ships which exceeded the number of subs at sea.

The U.S. had formed the Tenth Fleet in May, 1943, with groups openly called "Task Groups." These were based around two other escort carriers — *Core* and *Santee*. (Kemp mentions another carrier later in the year — *Card*). (As a side note, carrier planes includes *Wildcats* and *Avengers*).

Blimps were sometimes used at sea. (Blimps also played a role in U.S. coastal defense).

The sea was now teeming with groups which could be called "hunter-killer" groups *in the sense of the romantic legends.*

However, they were *still not fully detached.*

They were still attached — but now with such wide freedom as to be virtually detached. Or "de facto" detached.

In 1943, the score by hunter-killer groups was *low* — but they kept the subs scattered, and ran them till they had to return through the blazing Bay.

Also, still in 1943, there was an important piece of the sub war in which the "groups" definitely took part. It was this: the killing of the milch-cows. With the newly-cracked (in June) Triton Enigma cipher (plus the aid of the always-cracked German High Command Enigma ciphers), Allied planes went after the German submarine fuel tankers. *Bogue* got one, *Core* got one plus a sub coming to refuel. *Card* got two (that places *Card* in action in mid-summer 1943, according to *Battle of the Atlantic,* which does not disagree with Kemp).

Four more milch-cows were sunk — three by British planes in the Bay of Biscay, and one by an RCAF plane off Iceland.

Only *ten* milch-cows had been built — so this was a dramatic wipeout!

All that terminated Doenitz' system of supplying subs at sea — with the result that subs more frequently had to run the disastrous gauntlet of the big, bad, Bay!

Still in 1943, the British built a group around the carriers *Nairana* and *Activity.* Designed to "hunt to destruction" enemy subs, it would be assigned (as was the habit) to convoys, but in a sort of loose way.

To again point to the type of ambivalent orders for groups in the latter half of 1943, *Battle of the Atlantic* says the groups sinking the four milch cows had as a *primary* role convoy escorting *when needed.* That's a nicety — and an advance in freedom over the type orders for groups earlier in the year. When *not needed,* they could proceed in independent operation! This fits with the progressive pattern of detachment as the year proceeded.

When was the point of complete detachment reached? Early in 1944. *Battle of the Atlantic* says that about the first of the year, "Escort groups . . . had been freed from the requirement to race to the aid of threatened convoys in mid-ocean. Time could now be devoted to killing the enemy."

In February, 1944, the British 2nd Escort Group under the famed Captain Walker sank six submarines. Each took "an average of four hours and 106 depth charges." *(Battle of the Atlantic).* It took time, and a lot of ammunition.

The apparent record for time spent sinking one sub was thirty-eight hours.

The escort groups got more "ink" than subs sunk, but each bottomed sub which had managed somehow to get out into the Atlantic near ships, took an immediate ship-killing threat out of the picture.

A virtual "glut" of escort vessels flooded the Atlantic in 1944 and 1945 — far outnumbering the few subs which could get out of the air net. From late summer of 1944, the French ports were captured by the Allied ground troops. At this point, the huge number of escorts in the Atlantic became apparent. But how many were there? From the lean days, the escort fleet had grown to a point where Kemp states that, *prior* to the end of the War in Europe, some 300 were to be sent to the Pacific!

As Captain Walker's famous Group warred against the subs, we witnessed the last steps in an incredible revolution from the earliest days.

With his "ring" attack, he stationed warships in a large circle around one detected, submerged, sub. As the sub tried to break out of the ring, any of the encircling warships — each of which had the sub on its sonar — could fire depth charges from the Hedgehog or Squid cannons (called "mortars"), and force the target back into the center of the ring! In the center, a couple of escorts would move back and forth, putting down the depth charges intended to kill thc sub. *(Kemp)*.

Thus, we had gone full cycle from one or two escorts trying to protect a convoy from forty attacking submarines, to a *dozen or so detached warships* which could surround *one sub* until it killed it!

Captain Walker's Group sank twenty-seven subs in twenty-one months — a little more than one a month.

So now we know the whole story, don't we? No — we still haven't talked about the most important element of all — the KEY.

20. Something Called "Huff-Duff" — The KEY

The Germans had a way of blaming the British centimetric radar for their failures — because the Germans knew (after February, 1943) that it existed, but could never adequately defend against it! This helped cover up something else that was being done to the Germans — something that was the KEY to the sub killing, and the KEY piece in the interlocking with the other nineteen elements.

So what was this KEY to *submarine killing* — the KEY to which the enemy *never "toppled"* at all, and which helped all the other nineteen elements function so beautifully?

Huff-duff was the nickname for an apparatus which could *take a bearing on high-frequency radio signals.*

The Germans chattered among themselves in code, especially as they grouped up and prepared for an attack. They also sent long-distance signals to Doenitz, and received such signals, with regularity. Of course, these were in code. But whether we could *break the code or not* was not an issue for huff-duff. The only need was for a German sub to *send* a high-frequency radio signal!

Huff-duff turned every sub into a station sending the message, "Here I am — and at thus and such coordinates."

Kemp is so clear on HF/DF — the real name for huff-duff (High Frequency Direction Finder) — that I will paraphrase and quote from him following. The science of high frequency signals is that they bounce off the ionosphere back to earth — *but* 100 miles or more from the sender. *However,* a *ground wave* is emitted for about thirty miles *around* that sender — a direct wave, not one bounced up to the ionosphere and back to earth.

The British invented a direction finder which utilized the ground wave. This furnished a "very accurate bearing" on the unwitting sender of the ground wave! Since most of the sub hunting was done within thirty miles of the subs, this was ideal. Ships (early 1943) and planes (a couple of months after) were fitted with huff-duff — with excellent results.

Thus the role of what I call the KEY becomes obvious.

Kemp writes, "It is surprising that the Germans never suspected that the Allies were using it. U-boat logs . . . have frequent entries recording the sending of signals and the subsequent appearance of an escort ship steaming straight for them at high speed."

Kemp says the Germans *never connected* the two. They thought the centimetric radar was the cause of their plight — and kept on talking on the radio as they formed up and made their attacks!

He calls this one of the "most inexplicable features" of the War, adding that the "German authorities had several photographs of British escort vessels, taken with long-distance lenses from Spain [near Gibraltar], which clearly showed the HF/DF aerial array."

Kemp adds the point that HF/DF gave a longer range detection than the also-very-useful radars. He puzzles why this *alone* didn't tip the Germans off to a new detection system.

Huff-duff was the catalyst around which the other nineteen elements interlocked in a combination which could not be penetrated, and could not be defended against.

Werner reports an historic event. On patrol in the mid-Atlantic in August, 1943, he writes, "We received a message which had a greater impact on our lives than any since the beginning of the Allied [Bay] offensive. ALL U-BOATS.

ATTENTION. ALL U-BOATS. SHUT OFF METOX AT ONCE. ENEMY IS CAPABLE OF INTERCEPTING. KEEP RADIO SILENCE UNTIL FURTHER NOTICE. This warning reached [us] in time, but . . . too late for some 100 boats which had been sunk before the discovery . . . we had been sending out invitations to our own funeral.''

Werner's statement reveals that the Germans *did* learn that anything which sent a high-frequency signal (and the radar receiver, Metox, apparently did this), could be detected by the Allies, and in a manner which helped locate the U-boat.

As Werner's book also brings out, though, nothing stopped the slaughter of the U-boats. There had to be some radio communications. I am of the opinion that the Germans kept sending necessary messages, unaware of huff-duff *per se,* but quit using anything which sent a *continuous* signal, such as the Metox apparently did when turned on.

At this point — late summer 1943 — the Germans had a morale problem. It was not shown in the bravado and grit of the submarine sailors (sources say their morale was high, but I rather imagine this was an artificial or manic state), but it showed in their hearts. The way Werner reports the loss of boats and crews of which he knew, tips us off that the Germans were hurting inside. Such a concept ties in with the experience of another elite German arm, Goering's Luftwaffe in the early days over England. Those crews had been together for years. The officers were close. They believed they would live in the triumphant Reich. Then — suddenly — in a matter of weeks or so, they were blown away. What a shock. Of course, they kept on fighting — that is the German way (as with the *Volksturm* of German youth and aged people defending Berlin's rubble against Zhukov's hordes). But the old concept was long gone — the old dream, the old ideal.

The Germans never said, ''Look, we've had it.'' This was their greatest failing.

The submarine force never let it be widely known that the British had obtained overwhelming advantage. Werner says

Doenitz tried to keep *losses* as secret as possible — but word got around anyhow.

In fact, the rate of sub sinkings was so great that — although the sub fleet exceeded 400 in January 1944, and exceeded 300 in the months before the War's end — the subs were *not being sent out.*

That is, they were not being sent out in force. Werner says that in the first four months of 1944, fifty-five boats put to sea — and only eleven returned! Forty-four out of fifty-five were sunk — an eighty percent loss ratio! This just got worse and worse in the balance of 1944, and the early months of 1945.

(For readers who might want more depth, the following figures are assembled: Shore-based aircraft bagged 323 (245 at sea, 62 in port, plus credit for one-third of the 50 killed by cooperation between ships and planes). Thus, shore-based planes bagged the greatest number of subs — but, even more important, they bagged almost all of the subs sunk in the "turnaround" and "annihilation" periods, and afterwards. Ships sank 263 (246, plus credit for one-third of the 50 killed by cooperation between ships and planes). Ship-borne aircraft destroyed 60 (43 at sea, plus credit for one-third of the 50 killed by cooperation between ships and planes). Air-laid mines sank 16; ship-laid mines 9; "other" (whatever that is — possibly capture in ports on the Baltic by the advancing British prior to the end of the War), 29; other subs 21. That's 785. There were still another 300 or so in the "fleet" at the official end of the conflict, May 7, 1945. *Almanac* is the source for many of these figures).

Werner says that he and others personally believed (until nearly the absolute end — as late as May 2), that the new U-boats would come out of the Baltic (where he was then stationed, French ports having been freed), and proceed into the seas and win the War! (This despite the fact that they had been able to hear Russian guns for thirty days or more!)

From all the stories I have read thus far, I have come to this general conclusion: The Germans knew or thoroughly suspected, but didn't know for certain — and didn't want to learn the worst. They retreated mentally into hope and fantasies for secret weapons, and into suicide orders such as to ram the enemy (which very few followed), and into general substitution of blindness and fanaticism for looking squarely at the array of Allied weapons and people.

☆   ☆   ☆

Summary

So the sub war — which lasted five years and eight months, and which Kemp called "the most savage war in history" — was won not by flash and dash of person or weapon, not by anything new in the second or shining phase, but by an interlocked combination of at least twenty elements developed and proven agonizingly over time, and by blood, which could not be defensed. The initial proving was in the North Atlantic, but the final killing was in the Bay of Biscay and approaches. It was won by the British — who had suffered most of the merchant losses, run most of the North Atlantic convoys, and lost thirty thousand civilian merchant seamen. It was won by British air crews flying land-based aircraft. British invention and intelligence were amazing. The main U.S. contribution was stupendous production. The second phase was brave, and much shinier, but it was mop-up compared with the first. The second phase also appeared to be "U.S. all the way" — but wasn't. I don't want to take anything away from the second phase people, but I don't want anything taken away from the first phase people either. And when the two are set side by side in the North Atlantic panorama, the second has to doff its hat to the first — and often does.

Myth Five

That The Germany Army Was Mechanized

The Germany Army was, at best, about one-third mechanized in tanks and motor transport. Panzer division spearheads gave a false impression. Most German infantry moved on foot, and most motive power for support was by horse.

As tanks and motorized infantry tore through Poland, France, and the Lowlands, the electrified press and stunned world cooperated with German hopes that its army would be considered fully mechanized and "invincible." Weaknesses showed up in Russia — after that war could not be won in one continuous campaign. However, the major myth of German mechanization survived for decades after the last shot was fired — constantly facing down the facts.

Guderian's panzer concept (he was the father of it) would use the mobile striking force as the *main war form.* Motorized infantry (motorcycles and some truck transport, and a few half-tracks), were *in supplemental roles.* Air cover was supplemental — aiding the mobile striking unit or Panzer division. As evidenced in Poland, France, and the Lowlands (and by the very name "lightning war"), the *war* (not just a battle) was to be *won* (and fast, too), by the mobile striking force.

(The only thing to which this revolutionary concept could be compared was the other new concept of those times — that of "victory through airpower" used not in supplemental roles but in the belief that the mobile striking force of airpower *by itself* could win the *war*. This concept was pioneered by several people, including Alexander de Seversky, and, according to Churchill, Goering — who was a theorist in something similar called "absolute air power." The Allies utilized portions of the concept in bombing Europe. It was semiproven in the Pacific, where mere airpower delivered the coup de grace — although from forward bases hard-won by conventional means. The long-range missile is today's ultimate concept in a quick, mobile, striking force which wins the *war itself* in one blow or one battle instead of a series of battles with distinct pauses in between).

The Panzer division was supported by its own motorized infantry, and by Panzer "Grenadier" divisions of motorized infantry (with about 2,800 vehicles and 45 self-propelled guns, but no tanks *(Almanac)*. This division was designed to move large quantities of the best infantry at the fast pace of the surging armor.

This is what we saw in the news.

No one can really blame the news for featuring the amazing German armored forces and their supporting infantry.

We all came to believe that *this was the German Army.*

However, neither the armor nor its supporting infantry was representative of the great bulk of that army.

Going into France in May, 1940, Germany used some ninety-five divisions in the attack (about one and one half million men), of which only *ten* divisions were Panzers, and three "motorized"). So effective was this thunderbolt method that Guderian made the spectacular run from Sedan to the Channel, and then sharply north to Dunkirk, with only *three* Panzer divisions!

Going into Russia in June, 1941, Germany used some 136 divisions (about two million men), of which only *seventeen* divisions were armored, and some of the infantry divisions "motorized."

The German concept was so revolutionary, it could do most of its work with just a few divisions. But part of the key to success was that each enemy thought the entire remainder of the army was just like the front running Panzers!

(As side notes: There was one German mounted cavalry division at the start of the offensive into Russia — outnumbered, though, by no less than nine Russian mounted cavalry divisions! (But the horses we'll discuss in this chapter are not war horses, but supply and pulling horses). How accurate are accounts of German and Russian troop strength at the start of their fight? They are probably accurate in a general sense, but vary depending on whether the source included just invading divisions, or all at the "front," or all in the "war zone" (supply, reserves, etc.). The German front line numbered about 2,000,000 versus about 3,000,000 Russians on the line. The German war zone held about 3,000,000, compared to Russia's 5,000,000 (to a depth of about 100 miles). The rough rule of thumb of about 15,000 men per division holds up for most times and places of the War, on both sides, except for parts of the desperate phases of the Russian defense, when divisions were formed so rapidly that they sometimes had only 8,000 men, and for the last stages of the War, when German divisions were seriously depleted).

The special point about the German deployments at the start of the offensive in Russia, is that the Panzer divisions were only a small part of the total force. Yet, they got all the "ink" — that is, all the publicity.

Although we'll discuss this again later in this book, the German tank strength was not all that awesome. A Panzer division had only some 150 tanks. One study shows only about 3,000 German tanks going into Russia at the beginning — which would be accurate if the seventeen Panzer divisions had 150 tanks apiece, and there were other scattered tank units.

James Lucas, writing in *War on the Eastern Front,* declares, "the mass of the army which followed in the wake of the driving armored divisions moved *on foot* at the pace of the infantryman . . ." (italics added).

Almanac shows 3,000,000 troops and 600,000 vehicles entering Russia at the start. That would indicate a ratio of one vehicle for five people. That would be a very high mechanization rate.

(On D-Day, the Allies were to land 150,000 people and less than 20,000 vehicles of all types. By July 26, the Normandy Allies had 1,000,000 people and 200,000 vehicles ashore — about the five to one ratio claimed for the Germans). However, a high proportion of motorcycles would affect the German figure at the start of the Russian campaign. Also the inclusion of the back area troop count (inflating the size of the German force to 3,000,000), indicates to me that many of the vehicles in the count (if it is accurate), are trucks in the far rear. Also, statistics have an interesting way of including "vehicles" that are *horse-drawn*.

An interesting statistic appearing in *Bodyguard* is worth examining: On the German retreat across France from the Biscay region toward the Siegfried Line (made urgent by the landings in Southern France in 1944), one column contained 20,000 Germans, 500 trucks, 400 cars, and *1,000 horse-drawn vehicles.* The averages — about ten people per "vehicle" or about forty people per truck in the column — might be meaningless due to the condition of the army at that time, but the presence of something statistically called a "vehicle" but which was in fact a "horse-drawn vehicle" could reveal much about the Russian campaign. In short, it could go a long way towards adjusting the German "mechanization" myth down where it belongs.

For the start of the Russian campaign, I believe the mechanization of the German Army was at a level of about one-third that of the later Allied front in France.

Now let's talk *German horses.*

More horses than vehicles were involved in the initial thrust into Russia! (*Almanac* cites 750,000 horses and 600,000 vehicles, along with "more than 3,000,000 troops." We know this includes "war zone," not just "front." And I am surmising that of the 600,000 vehicles, many were horse-drawn, many were motorcycles, and only some 200,000 would qualify as "vehicles" in the same statistical sense the Allies use. Trucks behind the war zone, back in Germany in supply work, cannot be counted).

The 750,000 horses were not cavalry or fighting horses. They were motive-power.

Lucas writes, "The German leaders, anxious to impress the world with the degree of mechanization that [they] had achieved, displayed . . . on every possible occasion and thus convinced the world that their regiments were equipped with armored carriers and prime movers. The truth was completely the opposite; there was an absolute dependence upon the horse for *over eighty percent of the motive power.*" (Italics added).

Wow. That's worth reading again.

"There was an absolute dependence upon the horse for over eighty percent of the motive power." (James Lucas in *War On The Eastern Front*).

The 750,000 horses were just "for starters," as things turned out.

Lucas writes, "How great was the reliance of the German war machine upon horses can best be appreciated by the fact that *two and a half million beasts served on the Eastern Front . . .*"

And that ain't all.

Hold your breath for this one.

"The losses were enormous: *an average of one thousand horses died each day of the war with Russia . . .*"

The press may have been missing, but not the "press gangs" — for horses!

Lucas continues, "To obtain replacement horses a vast remount organization was established in German-occupied Europe and there were great . . . drives of horses . . ."

The "horse casualty" rate for nearly four years in Russia indicates somewhere near 1,500,000 horses lost in the campaign. How many battle deaths? How many from overwork, exposure, disease? No one knows. What? Statistics were kept?

Yep — seventy-five percent were *killed in battle.* And no one wrote Mom. Shellfire did a lot of them in. They were not good

foxhole diggers. And apparently Russian close support battlefield airplanes loved to shoot them up — accounting for a heavy
portion of the seventy-five percent battle deaths.

That's a hell of a lot of horses — 1,000 a *day,* with seven
hundred and fifty of those, on average, *battle* deaths.

Of the 1,000, seventeen percent died of heart failure from
towing guns or vehicles through the mud, according to Lucas.
Even motor-driven vehicles often had to be towed by the horses.
(The Russian roads — even at best — were barely hardsurfaced,
just waiting to be demolished by the weight of ordinary trucks,
not to mention horse-drawn artillery, and, worst of all, any
tanks. Where traffic couldn't simply go through fields, (as often
it could in the Ukraine), the result was an avenue of mud. This
mud — described by Lucas and other sources — wasn't ordinary
sloshy, wet, mud, but a gluey, clinging, unique variety). (An
important note can be added to the Russian-German war that not
only was Germany inadequately mechanized, its available mechanization was underutilized due to the eighteenth-century
peasant conditions in general, of which poor roads were one
factor. It was not like zipping through built-up, modern,
Belgium, for example).

The final eight percent of the horses fell to disease, cold, etc.

**"The mass of the army . . . in the
wake of the driving armored divisions moved on foot." (James Lucas
in *War On The Eastern Front*).**

A type of battlefield "mechanization" which should not be
overlooked is the close-support aircraft in two roles — facilitator
of armored advances, and major enemy of opposing armor.

At first, Germany had control of the battlefield air (which is
different from strategic bombing, and different also from deep

tactical strikes which go well behind the lines to knock out bridges, etc.). The Germans used the Stuka to terrorize enemies unaccustomed to its screaming dives and release of a bomb. However, in time, this plane was, by comparison to others, seen as slow, not all that maneuverable, and not the hottest plane the German pilots wanted to fly. One critic coldly says the plane was useful chiefly for attacking lines of civilian refugees along roads.

Be that as it may, the Stuka contributed to the German "mechanized" myth — and also to its "invincible" myth (especially after the Polish campaign, in which the Stuka was featured heavily).

The Russians wanted a tank-killing plane that could fly right down on the battlefield. It had to carry a little cannon with exploding shells, not just machine guns. (The fifty-calibre or half-inch machine gun bullet strikes, but doesn't explode). The Russians had 20 mm and 23 mm continuous-fire cannon, which were particularly effective against tanks, knocking off treads, penetrating the cooling grilles on the rear decks — where many hand-delivered "Molotov cocktails" also found success — and blowing up trucks, artillery, ammo supplies, etc.

The Russians developed the best ground-support aircraft in the world — epitomized by the Il-2m3 or most popular of several "Stormovik" planes by Illyushin.

These planes would not perform well as interceptors, but at their low-level work, and performance up to about 8,000 feet, nothing could match them.

The U.S. had a plane called the "Airacobra," which had the little cannon in the nose cone. Just aim the plane and fire. I remember these planes well. The U.S. supplied Russia with many, but a Russian general, interviewed by Burt Lancaster in *The Unknown War,* played down the aid as minimal. He implied that the numbers were small, the effort to pick them up in Alaska a nuisance, and the reason for going all that way to get them at all was only to sort of keep the U.S. from giving up on other supply efforts. But despite these comments, it is a documented fact that many Russian ace pilots swore by, not at, their Airacobras. The Airacobras and early Stormovik models were active in the Eastern Front's most desperate period.

The Russians were very interested in forcing the Germans to fight on foot (out of the machines, or stripped of the machines). They wanted action hand-to-hand — against their overwhelming Asiatic numbers. (The Russians, who also developed a reputation for being greatly mechanized, were very basically a foot army (we'll go into this in much greater detail later in the book), despite their flashing of extraordinary tanks; and accepted about a five-to-one combat loss ratio, in favor of the Nazis).

Particularly at Stalingrad, the Russians knew the Germans liked to stand a good distance off, send machines ahead of them into battle, and, fire automatic weapons! Therefore, the Russian commander deliberately worked to put "every German under a gun," force hand-to-hand combat, take away mechanization, and remove any special advantage of distance! *(Stalingrad).*

If German mechanization was not as great as its publicity, what, then, made the German Army tick?

The German soldier, including German gunners.

The legend of the German soldier is *not* myth. Along with the bravery of the British Spitfire and Hurricane pilots in 1940, and a few other true legends of the War, it is not myth — and perhaps could even be expanded.

The Nordic Viking elements, the Hun nature from the deep, black central forested Europe which Julius Caesar fought (and which was also encountered by Charlemagne later), (and perhaps even some of old Genghis and Kublai Khan's armies' blood), twice in a modern half-century tried to conquer the civilized world.

It was a shame to waste half a generation in 1914-18, and an entire generation in 1938-45, of intelligent, skilled, resourceful, never-say-die people.

But, misdirected, all this immense capability went into the abyss.

The German nation was small — only some 80,000,000 people. Even if one fighting person from the original European central forest *could* lick ten average blokes (which it couldn't), it was still *outnumbered.*

Hence the necessity of mechanization.

Thus, it was fatal that the German mechanization was comprised two-thirds of myth.

Had the mechanization lived up to the fighting qualities of the soldiers . . .

DID THE FUEHRER KNOW HE WAS OUTNUMBERED?

From somewhere, after the War, came the joke about the German soldier being treated for wounds at home between battles. He saw a huge map on the doctor's wall. He asked what it was, and the doctor told him it was a map of the world. "What is all this green over here?" asked the soldier. The doctor replied, "That is Russia." The soldier then asked about "all this yellow over there?" The doctor replied, "That is America." Finally, the soldier asked, "What is this little tiny red spot here?" "Why, that is our great big Reich," answered the doctor. The soldier was stunned, but recovered quickly and asked the doctor, in a whisper, "Does the Fuehrer know this?"

A lot of "future mechanization" — really, future technology — myths stimulated and sustained the Germans.

"Future" items — "miracle weapons" — included the A-bomb (on which Germany worked); the type XXI and other later submarines (of which a few were built); the V-1 and V-2 rockets (which did so much damage); and other items. (In rage about a month from the end of the War, der Fuehrer ordered some general to go out with five or so of the newest Tiger tanks and stop Zhukov. Even Hitler believed in some magic about his weapons!)

Many of the German people believed in the Fuehrer's promises that "secret weapons" were about to appear which would turn the tide of the War. Volksturm people fighting in the suburbs of Berlin believed this two weeks before the end of the War. Werner reports that U-boat commanders on estuaries cut off by the advancing Russians believed, as late as May 2, 1945, that the secret weapons would suddenly appear. The War officially ended on the 7th.

Therefore, blindness and magic were part of the whole syndrome.

Germany missed one colossal chance when it passed up the jet plane in 1939 (yes, jet — not rocket plane). Messerschmidt had just equipped the Luftwaffe, when he presented Hitler with plans for the jet plane. Hitler said he was just trying to sell a whole new generation of aircraft — and turned it down. This was all written up in the old *Saturday Evening Post* in the 1950s. When the jets were introduced late in the War, they were astonishingly effective, but it was too late for any safe manufacturing locations. The Germans had to stick with what they knew — and could scatter into small plants. The jets — introduced even a year or two earlier — could have prevented the bombing of Europe. Most people think the Germans only developed the plane late in the War — but it was actually flying in 1941, but still rejected, according to Albert Speer.

(As a side note, the P-51 Mustang was a U.S. design which the U.S. military turned down around 1941! The RAF picked it up and fitted it with a Rolls Royce engine. This model first flew in combat with the RAF in August, 1942. In that same month, the U.S. Eighth Air Force flew its first mission. Schweinfurt was a year away — and by that time, U.S. daylight bombing was being blown out of the air for lack of fighter cover. Spitfires had a range of only 180 miles for air cover. The light was dawning, though, and fighters became equipped with longer and longer range fuel tanks. Lo, by 1944, P-51 *Mustangs* finally gave all elements — the range beyond Berlin, the speed, the equality with Germany's best fighters. Makes one wonder).

An unsung piece of German mechanization which should be elevated to "true legend" status was the "SP" or self-propelled gun. (The U.S. called its similar equipment a "tank destroyer"). German SPs were mainly half-tracks with an 88mm cannon. The extraordinary saga of these appears in Lucas' book.

Why were these unsung before? I can only guess because they were not flashy, and were most often used in defense, rather than in the popular Panzer offense which grabbed the headlines and was the most photogenic.

On defense, these guns were devastating. Of course, the entire German Army was as tough on defense as it was on offense — reminding one of some NFL football teams which win contests once the defensive unit gets on the field!

Had Hitler not consistently issued those "no retreat" orders — which prevented the Nazis from retreating in their polished, devastating, way (meeting those predictable Russian tank columns and infantry masses with ambushes, screens, and other skilled maneuvers in withdrawal) — they might still be fighting somewhere around Kiev.

Whereas the Panzers nearly whipped the world, it was the SPs which — despite the impossible orders — kept the Russians from Germany's door for two years after the great offensive might collapsed.

Lucas' book makes "known" many stories of the "unknown front," including the realm of the SPs — all told firsthand by German Army survivors.

(The well-sung, famous German "88" — useful in SPs, regular artillery, antitank and antiaircraft roles — fully deserves its legend. Even the Allies concede it was the best cannon in the War. It was born to the field — to the rugged outdoors combat role — and it had few problems. Why was it so much better? In addition to the above, it could hurl a shell faster than sound. Wham — you were dead, and had not yet *heard the sound of the approaching shell.* This was unnerving. For close firing, the shell (at 4,800 feet per second muzzle velocity) covered a mile in just over a second, with a flat, unseen trajectory. According to one survey, U.S. Army enlisted personnel in North Africa rated the "88" as "Most Frightening" weapon (48%), and "Most Dangerous" weapon (62%). *(Almanac).* Years later, in 1951, I was in the U.S. Army, watching a demonstration of our newest tank gun. We were told it could — match the "88").

The Germans were mechanical wizards. Somehow, though, they didn't seem to have a spiritual or divine ethos behind their inventiveness. The Allies didn't *seem* to be as inventive or clever (or nearly as efficient), but actually outdid the Germans in electronics, code-breaking, and the A-bomb. I like to at least believe that this was due to our more prayerful stance, and, at the least, our use of what we had for "right" (even if no more than the right of self-defense), in contrast to the German use, which had a fundamental misdirection and diabolism at its very base.

Had the Germans been as fully mechanized as their myth — and less enchanted with the unarguable excellence of some of their products, and more willing to make systematic improvements instead of hoping for quantum leaps into miracle weapons which never materialized for them — the course of the War could have been much different.

☆   ☆   ☆

That the Germans were more than one-third mechanized, in the sense in which we perceive mechanization, is a myth.

Myth Six

That The German Generals Did (Or Did Not) Run The War

> The top staff generals planned (often against their will), and the top field commanders executed (often against their will), brilliantly — while Hitler periodically stepped in and altered ongoing operations, with disastrous results. Then the Fuehrer would reshuffle his staffs and commanders, and the process would be repeated. Thus the generals alternately ran the war and didn't run it.

There were more than 3,000 German generals, but we are mainly concerned with perhaps no more than 300 — and, if we wanted to tighten the picture further, no more than fifty.

Even to that small number, three major groupings apply (with a lot of overlapping, splinters, and going back and forth): the old Prussian General Staff; the military top "staff around Hitler"; and the very competent top field commanders.

The Prussian Old Guard planned the War campaigns — but the planning was *forced upon them.* Even before that, this Old Guard wanted Hitler out of power. Their traditions and family names went back for centuries. They wanted nothing — or little — to do with the trashy Hitler. According to *Bodyguard of Lies,* Chief of Staff Halder was active in several treasonous plots to overturn or kill Hitler *before* the War.

The "staff around Hitler" — also often called the General Staff, (but which was more politically oriented and more compatible with Hitler than the aristocratic, superioristic, and mentally remote old "keepers of the German militaristic faith") — was comprised at least in part of members of the Old Guard. The existence of two staffs (although these were, on the surface, one) meant that often what was attributed to the old line German General Staff was not the pure stuff. (Even at best, it wasn't the pure stuff, because the old Staff didn't agree with Hitler's aims). Near the beginning, the planning was more Old Guard than not — but was always something of a mosaic. Later, the final plans were a bastardization, and a mixing of iron and clay to make pots which would neither fire nor hold water. The progressive power of the more agreeable "staff around Hitler" (confusingly often called the General Staff, and confusingly also containing members of the Old Prussian Guard who rotated in and out between tantrums of der Fuehrer), spelled the effective end of the old Staff as an integral unit with the old special powers. Yet it continued to exist as a separate unit (as oil would not mix with water). Its imprint on the War, though, is but mixed in with the main imprint, which is that of the confused and changing "staff around Hitler."

As to field commanders, the brilliant ones included some old-line Prussians (for example, Rundstedt and Kleist), and some ordinary generals of great competence (for example, Guderian and Rommel). Often, field commanders would rotate into top staff planning positions — or vice versa. As to individuals, then, there were no boundaries. A Prussian Old Guard member could rotate into Hitler's inner staff, and might also serve at times in the field. Goering was on Hitler's inner staff, and was also a field commander (Luftwaffe) — but was no Prussian! He was primarily a political figure — a crony of Hitler's who rose with him in the formation of the Third Reich. He became a member of the Nazi Party inner circle, and also a Reichs Minister. His handling of the Luftwaffe wasted it, and showed he did not understand the limitations or uses of air power (Dunkirk, Battle of Britain, Stalingrad relief, etc.).

In the very beginning, the old line generals planned the War (although forced to plan what they didn't want to), and *ran the* war through the top field commanders. Thus, Hitler's original influence was confined to forcing the military to do what he, as head of state, wanted done. The military — in the traditional manner — then did the rest.

Hitler first began interfering with ongoing plans when he told Guderian to stop short of the Dunkirk beaches.

Thus began a pattern, outlined below, which was repeated many times by Hitler — and which contributed heavily to Germany's defeat.

Throughout the War, Hitler would — after setting the goals unwanted by the Old Staff — allow them to prepare the extraordinary military and logistical campaigns which have to be ranked as classics in the history of warfare.

He would allow the campaigns to *begin.*

Then he would start interfering drastically (and with awful results) in the *ongoing,* carefully-planned, military operations.

It is popularly believed that Hitler *"took over and ran the War."* That was not the case. He alternated — always in the same pattern.

His interferences slapped the generals in their faces, displayed confusing reversals of his former high regard for their planning efforts, forgot logistics, switched major objectives, weakened offensives at critical moments, prevented retreats and regroupings, and opened the German armies to effective counterattacks.

The results made the generals look bad. So he would fire some, or accept resignations. Then, months later, he would pull the disgraced ones out of exile in a reshuffling of staffs and field commands. He never, to my knowledge, had one killed for incompetency — probably realizing in a dim way that it was his own stupidity that was messing things up. The reshuffled generals would then put things in order — pending some new disorderly acts by Hitler.

Wasn't this "taking over"? Not in any permanent sense. It was catastrophic meddling — and it alternated back and forth.

The generals should have complained more — but didn't. Certainly they expected some changes — so they assuaged themselves with this. But mainly, they succumbed most often to some of Hitler's most traditional instruments for controlling the military — medals and elevations of rank! He had a true knack for bestowing those things at just the right times to those great officers who were on the brink of openly criticizing their Chief!

It is popularly believed that Hitler took over and ran the war. Instead, he alternated — always following the same catastrophic pattern.

The level at which Hitler interfered changed as the War progressed. At first, his changes went "down through channels" — from top staff to top field commanders. An example of this was his radical change in the ongoing "Barbarossa" invasion of Russia, when, with Guderian only 200 miles from Moscow, Hitler forced him south, to close the Kiev pocket in mid-September. He could have been in Moscow on the same date, but the delay was fatal to the campaign for Moscow, eating up essential time, inviting the change of seasons, and allowing the routed Reds to regroup.

Later in the War, Hitler began interfering by notifying Army Group commanders direct, of his confusing and disastrous changes. An example of this was in the Baku oilfields campaign in the summer of 1942. This campaign was zooming along, with its left flank protected along the Don River. Suddenly the Fuehrer put the flank-defenders onto the *offensive* — target, Stalingrad!

Later that year, Hitler was giving orders directly to Army commanders. As Russians encircled the Sixth Army at Stalingrad, Hitler instructed the commander, bypassing everyone else in the chain of command.

By late in the War, in France, Hitler was telephoning orders directly to *division* commanders — revisng campaigns and changing orders, to the dismay of all except the Allies!

☆   ☆   ☆

German expansion started with lack of exact targets — lack of specific goals. The vague goal was "lebensraum" — "living space." There were broad but undetailed general objectives such as: control of Europe; expansion into sparsely-populated Russian areas lying in Europe (Europe being defined as reaching to the Urals), including control of the grain-producing Ukraine and the oil-producing Caucasus; control of the oil-producing Middle East (via a pincers south from the Caucasus joining with another pincers moving across North Africa, through Egypt, into the Middle East); and other general, even diffuse, and multiple, goals.

In the beginning, there were specifics — exact goals, time-tables, and "jugulars" — as in Poland and France.

The defeat at England threw Hitler off balance and confused his mind. His sense of goals became more scattered and non-specific than ever before. Even lebensraum suffered a lowered priority, while Communism as an enemy moved to the top of the list. But if "Communism" was the enemy, what were the exact territorial goals? What was the timetable — and did it allow for a phased war instead of the quick knockouts as previous? Could Hitler's quick-gratification temperament adjust to the new realities? Could the physical makeup and mental gearing of *Blitzkrieg* adjust to war by a series of battles and campaigns over a period of time and enormous distances? And what was the "jugular"? And where?

The Hitlerian goals became just a determined, "Go East, young men!"

The old line General Staff (much against its will), prepared the very specific "Barbarossa" plans. These had too many military objectives — a North (to Leningrad), a Center (to Moscow), and a South (to the Ukraine) — imposed by Hitler. The front was too long (1,500 miles) for a concentrated, lightning-bolt type army.

But the greatest military campaign in the history of warfare was launched.

It met with incredible success in its first months.

But not even one month had passed before Hitler began his

total destruction of reason. In July, only weeks after the start, and with his tanks only 200 miles from the capital of Russia, he became undecided about taking Moscow! *(Atlas)*.

Psychobiographers who have depicted Hitler as suicidal — leading himself and his nation into death-traps — and unable to deliver the victory blow lest it interfere with the master plan for defeat, had plenty of ammunition from studying Hitler's fatal errors on the Russian Front.

When the generals were fully in charge of plans and operations, there would be victory. But when he interfered and took over, there would be defeat!

Hitler decided to *delay* the advance on Moscow, while ordering Guderian to turn *south* to close the Kiev pocket (closed in mid-September). The moment he gave his order, though, he lost the only possible shot he had at the quick knockout which his Blitz method required.

There was no guarantee that Moscow would be a "jugular" — but all hoped so. (As it turned out, Stalin stayed and made the city an example of "Holy Russia" — so it was, as all had thought, the nerve center, the toppling of which would have brought down the Russian Government.

Guderian could have been in Moscow in mid-September — in the same time it took him to go south. That general was later to write, "I could never have believed that a really brilliant military position could be so [bleeped] up in two months." *(Atlas)*.

Was there a method in Hitler's madness to turn his Moscow spearheads south? Yes — but misguided, mistimed, and against the advice of his generals.

He knew he had achieved huge encirclements of the Russian Army, and felt that if he wiped out these pockets, Russia would be finished. His generals argued that those enemies were surrounded, had no armor or mobility, and were not a real danger. Get them later, the generals argued — go for the principal cities now, as planned.

But Hitler (who was having spasms of indecision about which cities to capture, long after the plans had been set and the campaign launched!), knew he would have annihilated a Russian Army of 3,500,000 to 5,000,000 by the time the pockets were wiped out — and could not believe that this number (twice his fighting forces in Russia) didn't equate to the utter ruination of Russia, and thus immediate victory.

THE BARBAROSSA POCKETS ALONE
(July-November 1941)

Note: The figures given below are just for the very largest of many dozens of pockets of Russian troops encircled by Germans. The figures do not count the other battling of the campaign — just the pockets! The notation, "trapped," used once below, means that not all of those troops were killed or captured, but many escaped. The Smolensk and "east of Smolensk" pockets were areas where probably many more were taken than historians (except *Almanac*) dare to state. All Kiev figures probably include some "peoples' army" soldiers — but an army is an army; and as many regular troops probably blended into the landscape in civilian clothes, to fight again, as impressed civilians were killed or captured armed and in some semblance of uniform. One asterisk * means that, in the absence of a figure from the particular source, I applied a figure from at least four other sources. K: Killed; C: Captured; W: Wounded.

	Dictionary	Almanac	Atlas	War Maps	Enc. Brit.	Eastern Front
Minsk Jun 27	300,000 K,C	290,000 C Minsk-Vitebsk	300,000*	300,000	300,000	324,000
Smolensk Jul 16-Aug 6	100,000	600,000 trapped 300,000 east of Smolensk	(See notation below)	(See notation below)	200,000 C Smolensk pockets	310,000 Gomel: 84,000
Kiev Sept 26	600,000 K,C	665,000 Includes "Peoples' Army"	500,000	Four Soviet Armies 500,000*	600,000 C	665,000
Vyazma	600,000 K,C	663,000 includes Bryansk	600,000*	750,000 includes Bryansk	600,000 C	663,000
Uman			takes note	takes note		103,000
Odessa			takes note		60,000 Dniepr Bend	

Mogilev	takes note				84,000
Ninth Army Nr. Azov Sea		100,000 C			107,000
TOTALS	1,600,000 K,C	2,500,000 K,C	1,500,000 K,C plus Smolensk	1,550,000 K,C plus Smolensk	1,700,000 C only	2,400,000 Encircled

Hitler was right about only one thing: He had destroyed the Russian Army of 1941 — numbering somewhere between 3,500,000 and 5,000,000, along with most of its tanks, trucks, guns, planes, and ammunition. As *War Maps* says, "The Soviet war machine should have been shattered beyond recovery."

And Germany did this at the relatively low cost of 200,000 killed!

RUSSIAN AND GERMAN LOSSES FOR ALL BARBAROSSA
(June 21-December 7, 1941)
K: Killed   C: Captured   W: Wounded

	Dictionary	Almanac	Atlas	War Maps
RUSSIAN:	3,221,000 KCW (KW three times Germany's; plus 1,000,000 C).	—	—	"Millions of men . . . 15-20,000 tanks and 20-30,000 guns . . ."
	Author's note: Since all other sources indicate C to be much higher — up to 3,000,000 — I would put KCW at 4,000,000.			
GERMAN:	770,000 KCW	750,000 KCW	750,000 KCW includes 8,000 officers, 200,000 men K.	—

Hitler *had* destroyed the huge 1941 Russian Army — but, when he delayed his timetable in the autumn, to clear up pockets and crow at home about his great victory, enough Russians regrouped around Moscow to defeat his overextended center force forward elements there in December.

By 1942, Russia had raised a *new* army! Had Hitler followed the original plan, Russia west of the Urals would have been his — probably permanently.

"I could never have believed that a really brilliant military position could be so [bleeped] up in two months." (Gen. Heinz Guderian).

One of Hitler's mental mistakes was that he thought he had "till winter" before he could get into Napoleon's trouble in Russia! Winter officially begins December 21.

However, bad rains — very cold and persistent — begin in October! Apparently, no one convinced him of this. Even in October, the rains alternate with temporary heavy freezes.

Severe cold — worse than Germany's *winters,* begins in November. Worse, though, this cold still shifts back and forth with nasty, icy, rains. All this before official winter.

Hitler didn't permit winter clothing to go to the Front, because he was certain "the war would be over" before it was needed! The Krauts stole a lot of Russian clothes — including the popular felt boots!

Nonetheless, the Germans were in Moscow suburbs in late November.

Stalin had evacuated the government, but, as he saw Hitler become progressively bogged down, decided to personally remain. He had organized a Winter Army which was *unknown* to the Germans. He struck with surprise December 7 (give or take a day, and allow for the International Date difference from North America). The German retreat began almost at once.

In the U.S., we don't remember too much about the Russian

Winter Offensive, because, within hours before or after, the Japanese (in an unconnected move), attacked Pearl Harbor. This —- very naturally — took top priority in news in the U.S.

Mini Myth Exploded:

THAT HITLER'S MOSCOW DEFEAT WAS SIMILAR TO NAPOLEON'S

We popularly believe that Hitler's Moscow defeat was similar to Napoleon's — but that is mythology. Napoleon defeated Russia and captured Moscow, and occupied it. Hitler's forces could see the Kremlin, but never captured the capital. The French Emperor got into Russia on his timetable. The Nazi dictator lost his golden chances through three mistakes in his timetable: starting a month late after he delayed things for no reason; forcing Guderian south when he was in position in August to drive into Moscow in September; not realizing rains came in October and severe cold in late November: both still in "fall." Napoleon was in Moscow in real winter. Hitler's offensive was all in the fall. Napoleon led his own troops. Hitler was some 1,000 miles behind. Napoleon voluntarily evacuated Moscow after the Russians wouldn't pay him the homage his ego expected as emperor, etc. (and, disgusted, he pulled out). Hitler was driven from the gates of Moscow. Napoleon was savaged on his cold retreat — not before. Hitler, after being driven from the gates of Moscow, made Russia pay. Napoleon really met those two famous Russian generals, Janvier et Fevrier — resulting in a decisive defeat for the French. Hitler's men did not meet them in a decisive way at all (the Krauts in January and February were in a well-conducted defensive operation, all things considered. But things were very cold. Lucas says motor oil froze in the trucks, and had to be thawed out by setting small wood fires beneath the crankcases. Notable was the fact that, in this period, the Russians themselves were nearly immobilized, but as much by exhaustion and depletion as by their favorite weather).

Under the long-forgotten goals of lebensraum, the capture of western Russia would have been an ideal accomplishment. There must have been something of this still residing in the original Barbarossa plans — because Halder (then Chief of the Army General Staff) reckoned "eight to ten weeks" for the campaign *(Atlas).*

That campaign would have started in May (not June), and dashed about 1,000 miles — or 200 or 300 miles beyond Moscow — in three months.

Hitler apparently never looked at a complete map of Russia! But surely Halder did.

Hitler was changing goals thirty days after the greatest military offensive in history started rolling.

But surely the original plans had some concrete goals! We can surmise from what we know of the generals and lebensraum, that the main concept was to quickly wrest European Russia from the Reds.

This would be followed by peace — and the permanent partitioning of Russia.

Once the campaign opened, Stalin could see this coming. He evacuated his industry to east of the Ural Mountains barrier. Even if Russia had to give up its western one-quarter or one-third, it would survive.

Absolutely nothing in the German plans or capabilities provided for a drive more than 200 or 300 miles beyond Moscow.

How accurate was Halder's estimate of the time necessary for the job? Very accurate. After only eighteen *days,* the drive had progressed 400 miles — and was only 200 miles from Moscow!

There, the routed Reds *didn't* stop the onrushing Germans! They were stopped by old you-know-who!

Even figuring the late start (from May to June), Halder would have finished off the Russians and had a permanent partition in place before the winter.

But Hitler's colossal interference not only stopped the drive, but, incredibly, cost Germany the War. This was not immediately apparent, but, when the quick knockout failed, the odds shifted to the Russians.

The Germans could have sued for peace — and maybe kept a great piece of western Russia. But that wasn't in Hitler's nature. (After all, this was the man who, later, personally inspired the Volksturm of kids and old people to "fight" Zhukov in Berlin's rubble).

The net result was that Russia took on Germany in very

physical terms. It slaughtered the German Army — literally. In the three and one half years remaining, at a staggering cost of from three to five uniformed Russian dead for each Kraut soldier killed, it bashed the German Army to a pulp.

The generals designed Barbarossa to permanently partition Russia after three months of summer warfare. Hitler's interferences in that one campaign — after it started and was going so well — resulted in the annihilation of Germany.

What a genius!

German intelligence failed badly in Russia. Perhaps it had what it needed for the knockout campaign — and didn't think it would need more! (There are reports that, later in the War, German intelligence often warned of Russian capabilities, only to be "put down" by Hitler. One example was the big Russian counteroffensive at Stalingrad).

From the time Barbarossa began to stumble, gaps in intelligence became apparent. There had not been enough information about the Pripet marshes between Poland and Moscow, and other low-lying areas. Information about roads was inadequate — beginning with roads which were almost causeways through boggy or low areas, limiting maneuver. Germans didn't expect to find primitive roads. Even the best roads were quickly demolished by tracked vehicles. Of course, had the campaign been completed in summer, as planned . . .

With the advent of rains, the road problem became critical. With the advent of a protracted war, roads through low areas — where vehicles could not operate off to the sides — became bottlenecks vulnerable to weather and partisans!

The original campaign would have brought peace and partition before Russia recovered from her first colossal rout. But once Russia gained breathing space, her huge bowels beyond Moscow and the Volga could produce great numbers of new fighting men annually. Thus again, timing was all important — and Hitler personally destroyed this timing. His failure to look at the maps of Russia's enormous bulk was catastrophic.

Beyond Moscow and the Volga, Russia had most of its land, and more than 100,000,000 more people!

Beyond Moscow and the Volga, Russia had millions of low-grade, corn-fed, illiterate farm youths. These would get a few days' training, a rifle, and a trip west — to be fed to the efficient German slaughtering machine.

In the breathing time in 1941, Russia assembled a few new people and the formerly routed central forces, behind Moscow. German intelligence did not warn of this. In the surprise attack, Russia used pincers, and other advanced methods. The Winter Offensive could have done much more damage, but it was undermanned, tired, lacking in confidence, and green.

Greenness was a Russian problem from the beginning of Barbarossa, because Stalin had "purged" his officer corps not long previous! So the Red Army which was destroyed in 1941 had been inadequately led. (This problem was to continue throughout the War. The front line non-coms and company officers were blown away with such horrible regularity that experienced cadres didn't develop in the sense of Western Allied armies. However, at the higher levels, Russia developed some remarkable generals — names which still raise goosebumps on those remembering them today — such as Timoshenko, Rokossovsky, Malinovsky, Konev, and Zhukov).

The failure of Barbarossa did not result in a single finger being pointed at Hitler! Had one been pointed, the result would probably have been death by the slow garrote!

Hitler's top generals only reluctantly went along with the idea of the Russian invasion. (They didn't oppose knocking off Russia, but would have done it differently). After it became such a huge early success, many were swept along, and Hitler bragged of this.

When it soon became obvious that der Fuehrer was wrong — and that he himself had spoiled what might otherwise have succeeded — no one dared say so!

Reshuffling then developed — a pattern which would be seen throughout the remainder of the War.

To cover the errors, Hitler permitted resignations of commands (and, if one had a centuries-old warrior name, one could even resign in mild protest).

Hitler needed his top generals. Also, he couldn't truly offend them or have them shot, or the Army might fall apart. Generals refusing to resign were fired — but temporarily. After a time, exiled ones would reappear in reshuffled, but still top echelon, positions.

Absolute obedience was Hitler's usual requirement. However, with his top generals, he "flexed" a bit. Nonetheless, he required ritual resignations or firings as preludes to later resurrections.

> **Halder planned Barbarossa to finish European Russia in ten weeks. After eighteen days, it had progressed 400 miles — and was only 200 miles from Moscow. Hitler stopped the drive.**

Another example of Hitler's drastic interferences in successful campaigns was in the summer of 1942. This also ruined the ongoing campaign, and also resulted in a situation which changed history.

A vast German force was racing for Baku and the oilfields in the Caucasus. Its long left flank was defended by another force, which used the Don River as a natural barrier. After the campaign was successfully under way, Hitler decided to put his flank-defenders onto the *offensive* — to capture Stalingrad. To further compound the confusion, he weirdly diverted a Panzer army south to aid the forces approaching Baku!

Maybe the Russian Intelligence had put him on the payroll to mess things up for Germany.

To keep things lively (and remember, this was all in one short 1942 summer offensive), he ordered that same Panzer army *back north* — to aid the Sixth Army, which was approaching Stalingrad!

Meanwhile, the southernmost forces never got to Baku. They

captured Maikop, but were stopped short of the Caspian Sea — and far short of Baku.

Halder, the famed Chief of the Army General Staff, resigned in disgust at having been overridden and driven nuts with changes.

As most readers know, the Stalingrad drive eventually took most of the available German forces in the South, got stymied, was encircled by November, and was wiped out utterly by the first two days of February, 1943.

As the War progressed, Hitler gradually bent the will of the average general more to his liking. He "packed" the ranks with those who would "go along." This accelerated the Fuehrer's disastrous intervenings.

He was still careful to retain his old and new Prussians. However, he watered them down as a group, and eliminated many of their old powers. He retained them as *individuals,* and he retained their names as still active in his Army!

The "yes-man" type of general — always present in some degree in any military organization throughout history — became not just the occasional bootlicker, or favorite relative of some influential person, or young protege, or good card or tennis player for weekend socials, but a prevalent, even predominate, type, including some otherwise strong generals, exercising little individual influence, but reinforcing der Fuehrer's sense of being omnipotent.

Some normally independent generals "chameleoned" as the end came nearer (or as the end became obvious to anyone with good sense). This included some of the remarkable field commanders, who grew philosophical.

As a group, the field commanders were tougher than others in confrontations with Hitler. They only saw the dictator once in a while — and couldn't believe that the mentality they encountered on those occasions was standard. Those who were around Hitler all the time adjusted to him.

The field generals on occasional visits tended to be less patient, offer open criticisms, sometimes explode, and even carry on protracted arguments. Guderian, (shelved for a long time and then elevated to Chief of Staff), was famous for more than one direct clash with Hitler. Rommel had some less than polite exchanges. But none of this changed Hitler.

Rundstedt (who was Old Guard, and served in Staff and field positions, and whose name was needed by Hitler), remained independent to the very end. However, Hitler progressively rendered him impotent. Placing him in command in the West, he deprived him of forces. Further, by that time, Hitler had adopted his habit of telephoning orders direct to division commanders! Rundstedt was to comment that, "The only thing over which I have absolute authority is the changing of the guard in front of my office."

A point worth mentioning is that Hitler instinctively hated the "aristocratic" German anywhere — especially in the military. And yet, he needed both the brains and the names of the traditional German military families! As a man who had risen from prisons and gutters, who had murdered one entire arm which had helped him to power, and who was far — very far — from being "aryan" and glorious in appearance (as also were Goebbels and Himmler far afield from the Nordic superimage), he felt inferior around the aristocrats who went back hundreds of years and felt Germany was truly theirs!

In the end, Hitler showed his disdain for all land warriors — aristocratic or not — and appointed, for his very brief successor after his suicide, Admiral Doenitz of the vanquished sub fleet.

Hitler destroyed the defensive strategies of his generals as well as their offensive ones.

"No retreat" — if spoken at the Alamo, where there ain't no place to go nohow — is the stuff of gallantry.

But Hitler used the great words at the wrong times.

He handed his best battle soldiers — who had done the best job for him — to the enemy.

He started this policy in the suburbs of Moscow. Many Germans were cut off (Demyansk and Vyazma), but later relieved — however, only because the hastily-prepared Russian attack petered out.

In late October, 1942, Hitler was at it again — ordering "no retreat" at El Alamein. Rommel managed to ignore this.

Shortly thereafter, the Russians crushed the left flank of the Stalingrad salient in November, cutting off von Paulus' big Sixth Army. Hitler ordered "no retreat." Von Paulus *obeyed*. A relief offensive was organized, which battled up close to Paulus' perimeter. But — the Sixth Army was *not battling out!* Why? The commander was heeding Hitler's orders of "no retreat"! (For this, Hitler made him a Field Marshal — at the end of January, about two days before he surrendered!) (As a side note, the Russians were impressed with the capture of a Field Marshal. They have films of the surrender meeting. Also, they released this general long after the War — although many Sixth Army captives from this battle were marched east in long black lines, never to be seen again).

A year and a half after Stalingrad, as Russians poured back into Poland, Hitler again ordered "no retreat." This policy was carried out while the Russians ate into eastern Germany. Entire armies were cut off in so many pockets the war maps looked like Swiss cheese! Once-vaunted German mobility had turned to stone — at Hitler's command.

Was any of this the will of the generals? No — it was against their wills and their plans. It expressed only Hitler's incredible, destructive, interference in ongoing operations.

Hitler interfered with his generals on defense too. His "no retreat" edicts turned once-vaunted German mobility into easily-surrounded stones

---

Was Hitler the ultimate authority? Some have said his astrologer "outranked" him!

Hitler established the military governments in occupied lands in such a manner as to arouse ferocious opposition, tie down numerous combat divisions, and contribute to his downfall.

When Germany first went into peasant Russia, the frontline troops were often welcomed as liberators. Only a few years previous, Stalin (with Khrushchev as one of his main assistants), had "collectivized" the farms at the cost of several million resisting Russian farmers. The Wehrmacht looked like freedom from Russian governmental brutality. (Of course, the mythologizing Russian war historians will deny this. Also, not many of the original German frontline troops from the early months of Barbarossa survived to tell any stories). (Albert Speer deplored the SS government units, and wrote that the conquering Nazis could have made friends of occupied lands by letting the losers set up councils and do some governing). \

Not all frontline troops were gems, by any means. The slaughter of people in order to obtain cows, chickens, lodging, etc., was not frowned upon.

But whatever bad impressions the frontline troops left were still better than recollections of the Russian collectivists! The Germans looked good by comparison.

However, the combat troops passed through.

Then Hitler's *SS government troops* came to stay. These people terrorized the civilian population, shot hostages when they didn't get their way, and turned the populace *against* Hitler. (This guy Hitler had such a *way* about him!)

The results are legendary — in the true, solid sense:

In the central front area between Warsaw and Moscow (Byelorussia — White Russia), existed the most important roads in western Russia. They were very few, and many ran through low areas and the edges of the Pripet Marshes. Germans had to use the roads, which were often elevated a bit above the surrounding countryside, or often were the only paths through dense patches of forests.

The partisans — once ready to welcome der Fuehrer — loved to hide in the forests, marshes, and other natural cover, where Germans would not go on foot, and could not go by machine! They not only cut the supply lines with frequency, but would capture and occupy "islands" of high ground and defend them for days against Germans forced to move through "bad country" to recapture their road link.

(A Yugoslav national, who became a U.S. Army major, told me of his being wooed for a long time by the OSS to parachute back into Yugoslavia to aid *that* country's partisans. He declined this, choosing instead to battle across France and into Germany. But he told me that, in winter, in the earliest part of the War in Byelorussia, the partisans — lacking at that time the famous Russian white winter garb seen in most photos — would strip naked and crawl across the ice at night to attack the thin roads and the "islands" of high ground . . .

The top officers planned and executed brilliantly (although often against their will) — while Hitler periodically stepped in and disastrously changed ongoing operations. Next, he would reshuffle the top, and the entire process would be repeated. Thus the generals alternately ran the war and didn't run it.

Myth Seven

That There Is Any Real History Of The Eastern Front At All

The story of the greatest military conflict of all time has never been told in truth or with adequacy — nor will it ever be; because neither Russia nor Germany used real reporters, and both had propaganda ministries which originated, manufactured, and controlled most news to fit the State.

The German-Russian war was the greatest military conflict in all history. The Western Allied press didn't perceive this at the time, mainly due to preoccupation with the activities of its own people. Since 1945, though, the press and public has continued largely in the dark about the giant struggle, because detailed news continued to be absent.

The basics could not be hidden — the huge offensives, a couple of internal struggles such as Kursk, and the main perimeter battles such as Stalingrad, Moscow, and Leningrad. But, for the most part, the struggle and its details remained hidden.

With most nations, more *details* appeared after the War than ever before — many of them fascinating, personal, and insightful. Not so with the German-Russian conflict. Germany was destroyed after the War. Records had been annihilated. Prisoners were kept in Russia until some of the few survivors were released in the mid-1950s after Stalin's death. And few Western Allies, if any, wanted to listen to their former enemies.

The Western press, which had fallen into the easy mythology

that the *West* won the War, remained comfortably in that rut. Gradually, this concept became set in the cement of history books and file data on the War — to be repeated anytime anyone did a routine background search for information.

There was very little aggressive peering into the dark, misty abyss between Berlin and Moscow 1941-45. Why? Because, at first, no one thought that was necesary. And, later, researchers began to nervously realize that if the full, incredible size alone, of that conflict, were to gain access to general thought — regardless of most details which would probably remain obliterated forever — this full awareness of the size alone would mean a rewriting of our *entire* Western war history.

In fairness to the Western press, it would have reported the news from Germany and Russia, had there been any news. (And, after the War, it reported, but in low key, and on inner pages (to a nation accustomed to accepting only what was in blazing headlines) whatever opinions and information any person of news credibility had on that conflict).

How is it possible that there was just *no news* in the ordinary sense (other than the obvious) of the greatest war in the history of mankind?

The answer is simple: both combatants were totalitarian in the extreme. Russia had no press whatsoever in the Western sense (and this condition continues to this day — only one newspaper put out by the State propaganda ministry, and no book publishing industry as we know it). Germany had newspapers, but the war news they received and could print was all manufactured and released by Goebbel's ministry. (They could not interview a returning soldier, for example, and print the results!)

Let's examine the news problem step by step:

Russia had no news reporting whatsoever. (The only factual data from their side of the Front was their remarkable combat film footage. The *words* or captions were added later — and bore no more true relationship to the scenes than file footage would to an adventure movie).

The Russians *did* have written reports sent from the Front! With each military unit (down to as low as battalion in many cases), political *commissars* were attached. These had varying powers. (Khrushchev served as a very *high* level commissar attached to the Russian armies that encircled the German Sixth Army at Stalingrad. He had direct, powerful connections with the Kremlin dating back to his role in collectivizing Russian farms, where he supervised the murder of not less than one million peasants).

Most commissars in the military were just hacks. But, right away, we can see that there were two lines of power reaching down through the military structure almost to the bottom — one, the usual "*military* chain of command," and two, the direct *political* authority!

(Zhukov, who rose to be the number two man in the military structure, behind only Stalin the C-in-C, was the only officer to do his own political indoctrination. He did this all the way up — from commands before the War. No commissar was attached to him. During the War years, he was the only man who could argue with Stalin (a dangerous business, because Stalin had purged (murdered) thousands of officers in 1937, killing off most of the real and potential argumentative spirits); and Zhukov occasionally went into the Russian doghouse — but no further — for his arguing).

Russian commissars "reported" — but not just the "news"! The system ruled by fear. Most commissars were interested in covering their own behinds. If a military campaign went successfully, the report gave credit where credit was due — to the commissar and the glorious Party for having the sense to send the commissar down there! If a campaign failed, the fault was that of the stupid commanders, etc.

The fears had a basis. Many officers and men were shot in the battle areas for real or imagined insubordination, cowardice, and . . . failure!

No real reporting of war news *ever* came from the Russian side.

A central ministry somewhere — probably Moscow — wrote the "official history" of the struggle. Archival material and all records were wildly suspect immediately after the War. However, even this "data" was subjected to "revisionist" review after Stalin's death in the 1950s. (Stalin, as most readers know, fell from grace after his death, and all historical records had to be cleansed of any glorious references to the wartime Chief — these replaced with mere erasure or negative references. As a side note, statues of Stalin were torn down and the rubble thereof removed, and the people of the place thereof told to "forget" that said statues had ever been there! Even the name of the great city itself was changed from "Stalingrad" to "Volgograd").

Very little that the Russians say can be believed.

Couldn't ex-warriors give eye-witness accounts to the Allied press after the War?

Ha-ha.

So much for that.

Long after the War, a few high-ranking officers appeared in TV documentaries — but these were reading, in effect, scripts prepared for them by Russian bureaus. That is Soviet society. Truth-telling can get one sent away for a long time! (And can one imagine the problems involved in trying to talk about the Russian side without mentioning Stalin? It would be like a British person describing the War without mentioning Churchill, or a U.S. person without mentioning Roosevelt!) The net result was a Russian policy of just "keepink mouth shut"!

The greatest amount of truth — and some of the most brilliant fragments from which we can assemble logical further pieces — escaped from the outermost perimeters of the struggle: the Finnish War, heroic Leningrad, Moscow, Stalingrad, and battles along the Black and Azov Seas.

The more internalized titanic battles — such as visceral Kursk — were, although known, much more hidden. We knew of the battles, and knew they were big, (we could practically feel the earth shaking over here in the Western Hemisphere!) — but we had few details.

The Allied press just naturally assumed that — at some point during or after the War — the missing details would follow. But, as the decades later closed in, there were no more details forthcoming.

The declassification of Ultra, and other, intelligence documents in the 1960s and 1970s provided more information than the total since the end of the War — but still not enough to satisfy normal curiosity.

The Russians had a lot of things they plainly wished to hide: the killing of many German prisoners; the Siberian work camps from which so many prisoners never returned (although some were released after Stalin's death); the sheer brutality by which they so often controlled their own untrained infantry in battle (the officer's pistol fire for those who turned back, or wouldn't go forward); their rape of their own land to feed their advancing hordes; their strengths and weaknesses in general; and on and on.

In the secret Russian soceity, there is a *reverse* of reporting — a suppression and hiding in order to maintain the secrecy.

In Russia, there is a reverse of reporting — the suppression and hiding in order to maintain the secret society.

The Russians were not keepers of battlefield records of any kind in the sense of Western armies — meticulous records of who went to what unit, when, and what supplies were moved here and there, who died, when, and the disposition of the body, who was wounded, where sent, etc.

The Front was in incredible turmoil. Both in the early retreats, and later in the advances, millions of uniformed men, and some women warriors in uniform (not counting many fighting civilians), were killed, wounded, or captured.

Not just companies, but battalions, regiments, divisions, and armies, were destroyed on occasion — their entire forces going into a record-less void. New troops were pushed in from the farm to the Front by the hundreds of thousands.

In such chaos, it was impossible to keep records.

Furthermore, most Russian youth were illiterate. So also were many of the non-commissioned and battlefield-commissioned officers — who had come up through the ranks in the fighting.

Many wounded died of their wounds where they fell. In winter, they froze where they fell — and weren't discovered until the spring thaw. There was very little official burial — much less record-keeping about it all.

Divisions were formed hastily, then changed, then amalgamated, then pushed into another part of the battlefront, then made into a new armies, and so on. One great genius of the Russian defenders was their willingness and ability to keep gathering up — to keep forming. Records were the first things to collapse in such circumstances. (To satisfy bureaucracies, though, many records were kept — written up sometime, somewhere; but these were not accurate, and sometimes not even educated guesses).

The official history from Moscow would make Hollywood blush. Any survivors who might have told all, if in a free society, are dying off today. We will never have the full, true story.

After the War, a grasp of the Russian-German conflict was aided greatly by new British, German, and even U.S. archives. In piecing things together, much can be learned from missing pieces. When six pieces of a puzzle fit, it's fairly easy to make accurate guesses as to the shape of the missing piece.

In the decades after the War, the general shape of the missing Russian piece could be guessed. But when the enormous *size* of the missing Russian piece was glimpsed, many turned away.

If the huge size of the Russian missing piece was to be admitted to general thought, then the other pieces would have to yield a lot of extra space. The time has now arrived for that new accommodation.

The German-Russian war is "unknown" — but the data now irrefutably reveals the size. And this size forces a restructuring of our concept of the entire war.

The TV documentary, *The Unknown War,* gives us little basic information, and also does not point to the crucial area of size.

(As explained in the Acknowledgements in the front of this book, I do not think highly of *The Unknown War* as historical truth. It was prepared in Russia, and was at the mercy of what the Russians wanted to tell us. To its credit is the amazing combat film footage — shot by Red camerapeople in the midst of the hot fighting. Many were killed on location. Also intriguing is the sense of inspiration of the "great patriotic war." Utterly fascinating are the many aerial views circling the great statue at Stalingrad. One did not have to be told that the woman with the sword raised not in gore but in glorious triumph and freedom, was located at Nostradamus' "city by the river" that would turn the tide in the great war).

The German-Russian war is still largely "unknown" — but some of the purposes of this book are to bring at least the *size* of it sharply into view. This will cause the remainder of the global conflict, with its many well-known pieces, to have to be refitted around the missing chunk — which will cause our entire perception of WWII to change.

> **Researchers shuddered and fled from the obvious conclusion — that accepting the size alone of the Russian-German conflict would mean restructuring our entire concept of the War.**

What about German reporting?

There was little, if any, real reporting as we would know it in the West, and few, if any, reporters. Reporting was "made to order" or the input scrapped and rewritten by the censors, or written as original material from scratch by Goebbels' offices. Goebbels, remember, was the papa of the "Big Lie" technique — tell a big whopper enough times, and it will be believed.

No publishing function was attached to the reporting. Whereas in the West, reports — even after censors and presenters got through with them — eventually got to a publishing entity (newspaper, broadcast, book, etc.), in Germany the final product was published by . . . one of Goebbels' offices!

News was a performance — an *act,* not a *fact.* But beyond that, it was designed not just to misinform — but to control the mind.

After the War, Germany's view of the Russian War was improved by press freedom, returning servicepeople, honest attempts to establish accurate archives — and, in the mid-1950s, by some prisoners allowed to return from Russia after Stalin's death. All that was the "first wave," so to speak.

Much later, in the 1960s and 1970s, (during and after Vietnam, Watergate, and the acceptance by the U.S. of some of its own acts which could be called atrocities), documentary makers in the West, book publishers, TV talk show hosts, movie makers, and others, began to accept relationships with former Nazis and Japs. Albert Speer — looking every inch the retired gentleman, and speaking clear English — filled in many important gaps. his book still sells well. The producers of *Tora! Tora!* — about the bombing of Pearl Harbor — invited actual Jap pilots who had participated in the raid, as advisors! America gulped — then took it in stride.

Oddly, discredited, defeated, German generals and officials who survived and were not considered war criminals, looked on TV like statesmen and car manufacturers. In the 1960s and 1970s, they became important sources of information — and of pieces of connecting information, and sometimes just mist-clearing insights — about actions in Russia.

There were other sources.

Suddenly, the West was willing to talk to anyone, dig into any story, question any formerly pedestalized authority, to get more information about the War.

Strangely, though, even then there was not a great deal of revelation about the Russian Front — although every bit helped.

One reason for the continuing lack stemmed from Hitler's "no retreat" policy, which had resulted in entire German armies being cut off — not to mention countless divisions and lower units. Although the German policy was to keep records as numerous as the U.S. keeps in battle, most of these went into oblivion, and never reached home.

And as to those which *did* reach home — what was there? Headquarters and repositories vanished in explosions — and, finally, the Government itself vanished!

Decades after the War, the West was suddenly willing to talk to former enemies, dig into any hallowed story, question any pedestalized authority, to get more War information.

In the mid-1960s, *Bodyguard of Lies* revealed in detail how the German codes had been compromised throughout the War. This *in itself* was a *rewriting of the War*. It brought to the surface many hidden facts about the German-Russian conflict — but not enough for a complete picture. The intelligence facts were finally in place, though.

What survived of the worm's-eye view — the trench view?

For the view from down-in-the-foxhole, or behind-the-self-propelled-gun, nothing beats the compilation of eye-witness accounts by German soldiers called *The War On The Eastern Front* (see Bibliography). I give it the highest possible recommendation. The compiler-editor-author is a British military man, who held a high post in the British War Museum. The book furnishes a missing dimension — the report from the battlefield. It displays the ferocity, flexibility and intelligence of the German fighter. It contrasts these with the clumsiness and quantity of the Russian untrained troops, going into battle by phases, on pre-timed rote signals, but accompanied by the bludgeoning power of Katyusha rockets landing all over the place and sometimes making defense, except by cleverly-hidden self-propelled guns (SPs), just impossible.

The book presents the bewilderment of the German dirt-soldier in an endless "eighteenth century" peasant land, with untopped roads and illiterate people. The countryside was a big, empty barnyard that kept growing wider, more engulfing, and more incomprehensible the deeper the Germans penetrated! It just kept going and kept going. There were no jugulars — no targets or goals. One didn't get closer to specifics as one advanced, but got farther from them! The few cities were important as centers for roads, railroads, and buildings. But even more, they were psychologically important as things Germans understood — mental touchstones to the modern world they progressively began to think they had left behind. The German machine and mentality was built for France. The invaders thought of Russia as an extension of Europe — of Germany, Austria, etc. Not so. Not far beyond Poland's Bug River in the center, and the Danube in the south, Russia turned into a weird experience for the Nazis.

A furloughed soldier tells in his own words of his trip back to Germany — through delousing and into someone else's retread but clean uniform, near German borders, before meeting the public. The German women were interested in their hair parlors and shopping. The general public had no idea of the war except from the aerial bombings from the West.

In part, there it is: The German public was told nothing of the great Russian hordes and huge armaments about to pour down upon them.

This was, after all, the super-developed country where Goebbels controlled not only the press but as much of the *minds* of the people as he could — and controlled them so well that he could raise a Volksturm army to "fight" Zhukov's 250 divisions in the rubble of Berlin! These people expected "secret weapons" were coming. Only people who had been fed a false structure for years could swallow such a disparity between obvious fact and press fiction.

From the "Volksturm" alone we can see that Germany had been told nothing of the Russian Front — nothing real; except that the Reds were here, and would harm them — and to go fight them.

What of the U.S. press, and its reporting of the German-Russian conflict?

U.S. reporters — who, in the main, were real reporters, and had unexcelled news integrity — were not permitted by the Russians onto their Front (and probably would not have gone anyhow, because there was plenty of frontline reporting to be done regarding U.S. actions).

The only true bias of U.S. reporters was their understandable focus upon what was happening to *U.S.* troops. This is natural.

However, a distortion of perspective and overall view was inadvertently produced by this. For example, one wounded U.S. soldier was bigger news than 500 dead soldiers of any other nations. This concept permeated reporting, censoring, presenting, and publishing!

Information about major German-Russian battles was not lacking, but *details* were missing.

The U.S. censors, monitoring all war reporting, hardly affected the German-Russian news, because there was so little of it beyond the absolute basics.

What of the "presenter" level?

The U.S. "presenters" were *very busy* regarding the Russians. The U.S. "Home Front" was fed all kinds of pap — including certain specific (and unquestioned) themes cranked out as "news" and "reality" for the length of the War. There was a little truth in some of the stories, to aid passage of the patent fiction.

The themes were these: (1) Russia was gallant, naked, and fighting for its life; (2) Russia needed our help to survive; (3) Russia was our ally; (4) "Uncle Joe" or "Papa Joe" Stalin was a good guy and our friend; (5) Our efforts in arms and ammunition were materially helping the Russians defeat the Germans; (6) If it wasn't for us, Russia would be defeated; (7) We were big, Russia was small — but we were too "big" to say such a thing, so we were to be silently patronizing to this almost illiterate country. And other items.

There were no offsetting statements to balance this material

— all of which came from high U.S. propaganda bureaus, in a coordinated effort.

(Every one of the above themes is rebutted, or adjusted, or put into perspective in this book).

The news "presenters" also told the West it won the War.

At the same time, England was flattering the U.S., saying — as the "hot button" that got the U.S. to produce more war goods — that the U.S. won the War. So the U.S. got a double dose of misconception of its role in the War — and loved it.

The U.S. presenters didn't *dare* tell the U.S. that its main role was production. And the press hasn't dared tell us since.

No Western government during or after the War has dared tell its people that even the entire West didn't win the War.

Therefore, the news about the German-Russian war was not just absent, tailored, and manufactured in a number of gaudy themes, but — progressively — excluded.

In summary, there is no established, complete, and true history of the German-Russian conflict — and never will be. And the true fragments reveal that if the irrefutable huge size alone is admitted, we must change our entire concept of the War.

Myth Eight

That The Western Allies, Including The U.S., Defeated The Germans

> **Russian *military* dead totaled 13,600,000. This compares to Western Allied (including French) on all fronts (including the Pacific war) of just over 900,000 — or *fifteen times* greater. The Russians defeated the Germans — and we need to know this if we are to ever meet the Russians in combat.**

Russian civilian casualties totaled another 7,720,000 (current estimates use a combined total dead of 25,000,000).

How did Germany fare? Military dead and permanently missing totaled only 3,300,000 for all fronts (plus some dead from occupied lands joining the Nazi forces; and plus more than a quarter-million Italian dead, most of whom were lost in southern regions, not against Russians, although some fought there). (Italy lost 17,400 military dead fighting *against* Germany after Italy's surrender, and these might be added to the Allied totals).

If the Western Allies exacted one German military death for every overall Allied military death in the War, that would mean the Russians killed only about 2,400,000 German military — for a ratio of about five and one half uniformed Russian warriors dead for every German counterpart.

Let's break down that Russian figure of 13,600,000 military dead and permanently missing. It includes 3,000,000 Russian captives who died (1,000,000 in occupied Russia; 1,000,000 in POW camps in Poland and Germany; 500,000 in transit; and 500,000 executed) *(Almanac). (World at War* "Red Star" segment, says 5,000,000 Russians were captured, only 2,000,000 of which were seen again — for a figure of dead of 3,000,000, which approximately agrees with the above). (Another source lists an estimate of 6,750,000 Russian military dead 1941-44, but does not attempt to estimate casualties for the remainder of the War, or to show prisoners who didn't return. *(Dictionary).* Assuming another million and a half Russians died between Russia's western border and Berlin, and adding 3,000,000 permanently missing prisoners, the figures would exceed 11,000,000 military dead — less than *Almanac's* figure, but still impressive).

(Author's note: In the rear of *Almanac* is a large section detailing many war statistics — production, casualties, ships sunk, etc. These are the most complete pages I've found anywhere. However, some other sources have more thorough specialized tables. *Almanac* has made a major effort to research and compile tables covering all aspects — and has the advantage of something of the "last word" (being published in 1981). Thus, it is a very valuable and dependable source, but I am not saying it is perfect. For researchers, another problem crops up in such areas as military dead: too many sourceworks do not attempt to state these figures at all, or may show something like "Russian casualties" — without differentiating between killed and wounded, civilian and military, prisoners who returned and those who didn't, or the precise period of time involved!)

Russian civilian dead of 7,720,000 were mainly from just being in the way of artillery, rockets, and other gunfire. Russian Katyusha rockets probably killed a lot of peasants. A lot of civilians were plain murdered by the Germans — for meanness, to teach "a lesson," to eliminate opposition in the rear, to steal eggs or lodging, and as hostages for reprisals for acts by partisans. Worse, 1,720,000 were Russian, Lithuanian, and Latvian Jews. Another large, identified group were the 1,000,000 dead in the 900-day siege of Leningrad *(Almanac).*

To ease the transition from mythology to reality, it should be remembered that the fighting abilities of the Western Allies are in no way impugned by any of the above. And, the Western Allies fell in no less great cause, and participated in no less great a victory than even the greatest of our Western Allied mythologies depicts. However, the myth that absolutely and permanently topples is the size or degree or proportion of the Western Allied contribution.

The figures for Western Allied military dead of 900,000 to 925,000 are comprised approximately as follows: British Commonwealth: 410,000 (which includes British 271,000; Canadian 39,319; Colonies 21,805; Australia 29,395; India 36,092; New Zealand 12,162; plus others); U.S.: 292,131; French: 205,707 (includes presurrender French and Free French).

These included the Pacific War (including CBI Theatre — China-Burma-India — not, though, Chiang Kai-shek's fight against the invading Japanese). (British losses against the Japs were 31,468 killed — *Dictionary*).

It was good for the Western Allies that the Russians bled the Germans white, destroyed their equipment, took everything they had in men and machines and left these strewn on the farms and in the forests of eastern Europe (which, as a continental definition, reaches to the Urals). The U.S. would not have wanted this wholesale encounter for itself; and the other Western Allies could not have assembled enough manpower to match the efficient Germans.

The Russians met the Germans in four years of continuous gut-to-gut, all-out struggle on a previously-unheard-of 1,500 mile front (often longer) *inside* their own country!

At most times, the Russians had at least 7,000,000 combatants in the war zone.

Hitler jumped Russia six months *before* Pearl Harbor — and by December 7th had killed or captured between 3,500,000 and 4,500,000 uniformed Russians (at a loss of less than 300,000 German dead).

In November of 1942, the highwater mark of Stalingrad had been reached, and the German Sixth Army was surrounded. That month Montgomery completed the rout of Rommel at El Alamein (important, but small scale), and the Americans landed in North Africa (leading to their first encounters with Rommel's collapsing rear, and their first taste of the European War — important, but small in scale, and three full years after it had begun).

In February, 1943, the Americans fought their first real battle, in the European War, at Kasserine, a few days *after* von Paulus surrendered at Stalingrad.

By March, the Russians had retaken Kursk, and were perched on the Donets, close to Kharkov. The Western Allies were fighting somewhere in Tunisia. In May, Tunisia fell. In July, the Germans attempted to pinch off the huge Kursk salient in the epic battle, beginning July 5. On July 9, the Western Allies landed in Sicily. In Russia, on the entire line, 3,000,000 Germans fought 5,700,000 Russians at the start of their third continuous year. The Western Allies were in Sicily with some ten divisions and 200,000 men, getting some practice. By July 15, the Russians were on the offensive again, and a temporary rout was on. By August 17, Sicily was ours. By August 23, Kharkov had fallen, and the Russians had one of the great offensives of all time rolling for the next four months, across the Dniepr River to take Kiev, and rolling within inches of Smolensk — the city taken in the first few weeks of "Barbarossa." Meanwhile, in September, the Western Allies had landed in Italy's toe, and at Salerno (where they avoided being thrown back into the sea only by the naval and air continuous, obliterative, close support bombardment. It was a "touch and go" situation for days, but the overwhelming advantage in guns and planes, plus unlimited ammunition, kept the Germans from adequately forming up and moving, and "blew them away." Also blowing them away was Monty coming up from the toe and joining forces about ten days after the hairy landing. The Allies were still learning). By November, the Western Allies were twenty or thirty miles south of the Gustav Line at Cassino.

By December, 1943, the Western Allies were in the beginnings of the battles for Cassino and Rome. Meanwhile, the Russians had paused for only a month, and were again on the move beyond Kiev Christmas Eve.

By April, 1944, Russia was more than 100 miles *inside Poland*

— and could throw a stone to the Bug River original starting line for "Barbarossa." The Red Bear was also nearly 100 miles *inside Rumania* — and could throw a stone to Hungary! Almost all of Russia had been cleared! Germany was defeated and the Western Allies had not yet landed in Normandy. Three months previous, the Western Alies had landed at painful Anzio, and in April, were still bogged down there. Also, they were, in that same April, in their fifth month in front of Monte Cassino.

Germany was defeated — and the Western Allies had not yet landed in Normandy.

Two months later on June 6, the Western Allies landed in Normandy (and please remember, I am not trying to take anything away from Normandy except the myth that the Western Allies' Second Front somehow won the War). On May 18, Cassino had fallen. On May 23, the U.S. had broken out of the Anzio beachhead. On June 4, Rome had fallen. As Western Allies landed in Normandy (and were still seven weeks from even the St. Lo Breakout, the Russians were only sixteen days away from their June 22-July-August campaign. While the Western Allies were consolidating inside Normandy, in preparation for the St. Lo Breakout, the Russians rolled *to the gates of Warsaw!* This historic offensive — which crossed the old Bug River Line and put Russia totally on new ground in the central area — had the Zhukov trademark stamped all over it. It quickly trapped and chewed up the remains of German Army Group Centre (under Busch) — killing 400,000 and capturing 158,000 (Russians say), or almost as many combat troops as the Western Allies had within the Normandy perimeter at the time.

Certainly 200 Russian combat division on that one portion of the Eastern Front, and probably 5,000,000 uniformed troops all told in position to be committed, had devoured the German armies. Busch totally lost *twenty-five division* in just a *couple of weeks.* That was an example of the Eastern Front at its most truly legendary — concentrated, vicious, and overwhelming.

From the Vistula near Warsaw, Berlin was only 300 miles away!

About 1,000,000 Western Allied troops, including British, Canadian, French and Americans, had completed their buildup, evened out their lines, but had not yet broken out at St. Lo. They were about 650 miles west of Berlin.

On July 24, following the first use of "carpet bombing," the U.S. First Army (under Bradley) with its U.S. VII Corps (under Collins), started the four or five days of battle which became known as the "St. Lo Breakout."

But then a great mystery occurred: With the most awesome land army ever assembled in the history of the world — bloodied only enough to have its appetite aroused, a shattered German Army in front of it, and Berlin practically visible 300 miles straight ahead — the *Russians stopped.*

And yet, it was perfect combat weather — August, with September and October coming up, in Central Europe.

Had the hordes continued on, Berlin would have fallen *by the end of September.* (General Tresckow, Chief of Staff of German Army Group Centre — which had just lost some twenty-seven divisions in a couple of weeks between June 23 and early July — reported to General Beck, former Chief of the German General Staff, on July 8, that "Russian tanks would be outside Berlin in ten days"!) *(Bodyguard).*

Russia could have taken all Germany, and entered France.

Had the hordes continued on, Berlin would have fallen by the end of September.

Does all this say something unusual — something different from our preconceived notions?

Yes. It says that the Russians stopped their forces from over-running territory too fast — lest political agreements about the division of Germany not be kept.

When in the entire history of the conflict to date had the Russians ever given the Germans "quarter"? Never — until this date, late July, 1944.

Then, they reined in their great machine with its overwhelming advantage in men and materiel, and let the Germans reorganize!

The world thoroughly expected the Russians to keep on going. So did the Polish partisans in Warsaw. On August 1, anti-Communist Home Army leader "General Bor" (General Tadeusz Komorovski) "began full-scale military operations against the Germans, anticipating the imminent arrival of the Russians, who were only a few miles outside the city." *(Almanac)*. Some say the Russians deliberately notified the Polish underground to rebel at that time. The Russians, though, knew they were going to occupy Poland permanently — and not set the nation free. They didn't want any Polish partisans in their rear. What better way to get rid of them than letting them kill Nazis? So the Russians encouraged the uprising — and sat there and did nothing, until the screams for help were silent as the grave. (And the Russians still did not move — not until *mid-January*).

THE UPRISING OF THE POLISH PARTISANS IN WARSAW — AUGUST 1944

One source shows the strength of the Poles under General Bor at 40,000, and the strength of the Germans under Governor-General Hans Frank at 100,000. So this was no small struggle.

This same source states that the Poles responded to calls made to them on Moscow radio. *(Dictionary)*.

The scenario was logical. The Russian Army was in Praga, on the Vistula, only a few miles outside the city. The partisans revolted, using small arms. They expected Russian relief. They were doing this to *aid* the Russians. Successful at first, food and ammo gave out, and the Germans opposed them with two SS divisions and air raids! The Russians made some feeble "attempts" to cross the Vistula (sources disagree on whether Russia made permanent crossings until much later). No aerial aid was sent by the Russians.

Witnessing this, both Roosevelt and Churchill asked Russia to fly in aid. Stalin *refused* — saying the Poles were "criminals." The Allies asked for landing rights, to fly supply drops to the Poles. *Russia refused.* The Allies flew about 100 sorties anyway — but lost about half the planes and had about half of the dropped supplies go astray.

It is obvious from all this that the Poles were sacrificed.

The battle was much larger than is believed. The dead were: 15,000 Polish resistance, 7,000 Germans — and 200,000 civilians (that figure seems high until the facts are examined: there were air raids, tanks gunning everything in the streets (every citizen "might" be a partisan), and the Germans razing the city). (Most of the above from *Dictionary*).

Another source also notes the beginning of hostilities by the Polish underground on August 1, expecting "imminent" Russian arrival. No more mention is made for August, but an entry for September shows the Moscow radio calling on Poles in Warsaw to rise up and fight. On September 18, an entry shows "U.S." planes flying supplies to Warsaw — and Stalin refusing further missions of this type. However, interestingly, it says "the Soviet air force also stopped airlifts to the Polish garrison . . . (but they were resumed three days later)." *The Soviets?* Hmm. I wonder if I believe that. Was this just tokenism? Well, on September 29, this source shows the Russians flying their "last" missions supplying the Polish garrison in Warsaw, stating that in ten days, "2,500" sorties had been flown and "50 tons" of munitions and food dropped! Well, those sorties must have been fighter plane sorties just scrapping with German planes on general principles. A good load for a short hop with a bomber would be five tons. The Russians weren't known for big bombers, but they had a hell of a lot of U.S. Dakotas. These would have carried two or so tons on a short hop. But "50 tons" for 2,500 sorties shows these were not *supply* sorties. Even 500 tons for 2,500 sorties would not be much. Besides, by late September, the situation was too far gone to even find large areas into which to drop supplies. My guess is the Reds were just flying fighter sorties, hacking at the German planes attacking the Poles. That was surely some help — but I would think that any such late help under circumstances of not allowing the British and Americans landing rights, would be motivated mainly by the opportunity to tangle with some German planes.

Fifty tons?

That same source goes on to show the end of the uprising October 2, after two months of fierce fighting that killed a "quarter-million" Poles. And here is a revealing fact: the Polish resistance was called the "anti-Communist Polish Home Army." Oh, oh. That alone — "anti-Communist" — would be enough to sign their death warrants. (All from *Almanac*).

Did the Russians mislead the Poles into hopeless battle? You bet.

Some say the Russian supply lines were so long the armies could not have gone forward to Berlin or even into Warsaw in August. That is just not true, in this writer's opinion. Supplies might have been thin, and lines stretched, but the offsetting factor was the disorganization of the German armies.

Some say the Germans in August were mauling Russian forward units *(Almanac)*. That is certainly possible, but the Germans were not mauling the main Red force. I do not believe anything the Germans did could have stopped the Reds. How could a few hundred thousand in chaos stop a few million thundering forward?

Some say the "oncoming winter" stopped the Russians. Nonsense. "Oncoming winter" when it was still *summer?* And fall weather would have been ideal. And even if it had been winter, the Russians loved the winter. (They proved this again by starting a big offensive the following January. Therefore, winter was not an argument for stopping).

Some say the Russians had to stop while the Baltic areas (to the north) and the Balkan areas (to the south) were cleared. But in fact, the Germans were so disorganized and defeated there was no military reason to stop and the *War was effectively over if the advance would just continue.*

(As a side note, the Baltic States area was cleared by October 15, or, at the latest, the end of October — at which time the Russians were in East Prussia, fifty miles or so from Konigsberg. In the Balkans, in the south, by mid-October, Rumania and Bulgaria had been cleared, Belgrade captured; and, in Hungary, the Russians were only sixty miles from Budapest.

The only possible *military* reason for stopping would be that the Germans had forced the Russian advance to its knees.

And that concept is a laugh.

Therefore, the reason the Russians stopped was a political one.

Westerners have often griped that the Western Allies should have raced forward and captured all or part of Berlin — instead of settling for the Elbe Line (with a partioned Berlin itself reached by a corridor). A mini myth is that this claim had substance behind it in any *military* context. (However, the concept as applied to Russia *did* have military substance. That is to say, the Russians could have had *all of Germany* just by going forward in late July, 1944).

In late July, the U.S. forces broke out at St. Lo and swung south, east, and north, pressing towards Paris, and forcing up the southern side of the Falaise Pocket (around August 15). The landings in southern France took place August 15, assuring very little German pressure on Patton's right flank. Paris fell in the third week of August.

NORMANDY'S LEFT FLANK PROTECTED BY — GERMANS!

Hitler knew that, given normal combat conditions, German forces could throw any Allied landing back into the sea. This would be accomplished by frontal attacks, and by sweeping down from the north on the Allied left flank. His forces were arranged in this manner.

The Allies — through deception — starved Rommel of the forces he needed for successful frontal attack, and simultaneously "froze" the flank attackers in position. The result was that neither the frontal attacks nor the flank attack ever materialized in enough force to push the Allies back.

Readers are no doubt familiar with the deception — which made the Germans believe the real invasion would come in the Pas de Calais area some miles north of the Normandy invasion beaches — and that the June 6th landings were a "feint."

However, until I read *Bodyguard*, I never realized the size or complexity of this deception — which Bradley said held *twenty divisions* out of battle in the Calais area!

The deception created a "paper" army of great size in Britain, and carefully leaked little bits and pieces of data to the enemy through codes known to be compromised, and through agents in occupied territories, etc., for a year prior to the invasion. Patton was the paper commander (though sources differ on whether he was very useful. Once he broke vital information to the press because he liked the attention. Fortunately, the Germans wrote that off as an attempt to mislead them!)

The operation was called "Fortitude" — actually, "Fortitude South." ("Fortitude North" pinned more German divisions in Norway against a landing there). Unknown to many, Fortitude South included an "invasion." Electronics trickery by ships under smokescreen and fog gave German radar screens pictures that appeared to be a full-scale fleet!

The deception plan continued for weeks after June 6th — until the enemy just finally quit believing. When Patton assumed command of the new Third Army after St. Lo, the jig was up — but by then, the Allies had ground superiority anyhow.

The author of *Bodyguard* indicated it should pass into history as the "greatest deception of any war."

General Bradley was later to write that Fortitude was responsible for "containing a minimum of twenty enemy divisions in the Pas de Calais during the first crucial months of the invasion."

When the American general public first began to learn of the deception, the information indicated something like two or three divisions. For years, I believed the enemy had withheld three divisions! But twenty divisions put the operation into a truly heavyweight class. Most of the details had remained secret along with all of the deception apparatus and most of the Ultra secrets.

When I opened these remarks, I said Hitler knew he could throw back the Allied invasion under normal combat conditions. Once we factor in "Ultra" — the compromising of all his command messages — and the multilayered Churchill-run deception war (which fitted in so well with Ultra), we certainly did not have "normal" conditions. Hitler was as compromised as if his generals had worked for the Allies! The deception plan was fitted into this to paralyze or, at the least, make continuously indecisive, the German defense! Only the innate gut instincts of first, Rommel (who wanted to use the Calais forces at once), and, second, that other wily true battlefield general, Rundstedt, said, by the feel of the ground and the sniff of the wind, that the battle must be made in the second week of June at the Normandy beaches — or "forget it" because the enemy would be *landed.*

There was another condition that was not *normal.* That was the ability by the Allies to pound areas as big as a mile square into quivering pulp by offshore naval gunfire day and night, and by less accurate but plentiful daylight close air support. The fact that Rommel had virtually no aircraft was another "not normal" factor — but let's roll this all up into that one super factor: the "rubout" ability of the naval cannon 'round the clock, and the close air support.

These things meant the Germans could not move equipment or men in large numbers without coming under continuous bombardment; could not mass men or equipment for attack without the same; and could not attack without virtually being blown away. This was the "Salerno factor" — multiplied many, many times.

I will give the Western Allies special credit for their particular problem in all their campaigns — they always had to start from an amphibious beginning. They learned this business well.

They also had the special problem of long and arduous supply lines involving an overwater transit. They mastered this well.

As we study the perimeter, we see that the Germans fought mainly a defensive battle. That was the only thing open to them. (And, as usual, they did this well).

Would the divisions at Calais have made the decisive difference? No. The main reason is the "Salerno factor" — the intense bombardment capability. (After the beachhead was firmly established, German defenders wanted to withdraw out of range of naval gunfire). In the first week, any large forces moving south from Calais would have been "creamed." The Allies were waiting for them over the rear areas, on the move, in the assembly, and in the attack.

Such a climactic battle in the first week had, in my opinion, less of a chance of dislodging the Allies as it had of blowing away the Germans. (Allied battle casualties would have been higher, yes — but after the crisis, there would not have been the terrible attrition losses of the nearly eight weeks of scary heavy fighting with little ground gained, while the Germans unleashed their V1s and dumped 2,000 of them on England).

Another factor to be considered was that Hitler had *no reserve* forces in the West in any conventional sense. The Calais divisions *were* his reserves — his entire Western Front reserves! (Monty's fighting reflected this fact. He tied down line divisions so they could not group up for more concentrated attacks. He made the Germans pay along every inch of his lines because he knew that their equipment, especially, could not last).

There was a definite hesitation on the part of the German High Command to commit *the* reserves to the naval gunfire and aerial grinding in the first week. Without those reserves, Germany was wide open.

The "window" was open only from June 6 to about June 13 — the first week. After that, there was the problem of digging out and dislodging an entrenched, well-equipped, well-supported, deep beachhead. The possibility of rout, and mixing with the Allied troops in such a way that the naval gunfire would be withheld, was permanently lost. Rommel knew this.

On June 23, the big, bad Reds were at it again — smashing up Busch's Army Group Centre, surrounding and eliminating twenty-five divisions (not to mention the rest of the front), clearing the remainder of Russia, and driving to the Vistula River at Warsaw in five weeks. You can bet that caused the Nazis in the West to constantly look back over their shoulders!

"Goodwood" was an attempt by the navy, air, and now heavily massed ground artillery and tanks, to pulverize a large area near Caan and break Monty out. This was in July. It failed only because the area was too large for total pulverization, and because the Germans had dug into seven defensive rings — of which the British penetrated six. The Germans outlasted them — but had it been the other way 'round, Montgomery would have been in Paris, and St. Lo only a gleam in papa's eye. But German equipment was down to a nub. *Bodyguard* (a Monty advocate) says the British had destroyed much of the German ability to fight, and also had tied down the Nazis. *Atlas* agrees.

July 25, at St. Lo, "carpet bombing" was employed for the first time. the principle was Salerno and Goodwood — but out of naval range. The area was small — about four miles wide by one and one half miles deep! By the 28th, the German infantry had had enough. There were no fresh divisions or lines of defense. Avranches fell on the 31st. Only now did Patton come into the picture. And for six days he often directed traffic, as seven divisions were rammed across the bridge at Pontaubault. (The rest of that swing is history).

August 15, the Reds were still ripping up ground in the East, but had basically halted July 31. However, no one knew this at the time. Also August 15, the Western Allies landed in Southern France — racing northward to meet Patton within thirty days. You can bet the Germans on the Biscay coast and west of the Rhone packed for home!

On August 17, Hitler secretly ordered evacuation of France. (It appears to me this applied to the Biscay Coast, etc. The obvious move for Hitler was to pull in behind his Siegfried Line and con-solidate. This was in effect in part).

The Falaise Pocket was closed about the 20th of August. Paris officially was liberated on the 25th.

The Russians kept poking at the Germans (and *Almanac* seems to believe they were trying to get an offensive going, but couldn't); however, my opinion from all sources I've read is that the Russians basically stopped about July 31, and then (as is normal), continued reconaissance in force, and set about tidying up their lines (which included some advances in the central area), and finishing up their business on the wide flanks — the Baltic and the Balkans. I can see no genuine evidence of anything else *except:* I also believe they did more than some of their poking about as a means of keeping the Germans off balance and guessing, taking pressure off the Western Allies, and freezing German forces which might otherwise be released for western duty. With 7,000,000 combatants, they could have eaten Germany to the Rhine in one gulp.

In September, the Germans had fifty-five divisions facing the Western Allies' combined ninety-six *(Almanac)*. "Operation Market Garden," made particularly famous in the accurate movie, "A Bridge Too Far," captured most of its objectives, but failed to take the last one, Arnhem, which would have permitted Monty's theory — turning the German flank and racing directly into the center of Germany — to operate. The next month, October, Western Allies were fighting on German soil at some points — Aachen falling October 13 to U.S. troops.

In mid-December, the Germans launched their famous counterattack in Belgium, concentrating about 300,000 men in bad weather (which prevented Allied air attacks), and succeeding in causing the most consternation since D-Day. The Western Allies lifted Bastogne's siege ten days later, on December 26 — but not until weeks later, (January 28), was the "Bulge" eliminated entirely.

As 1944 ended, the West was still entangled in the Bulge, and Stalin had now been sitting on the Vistula River for *five full months* plus a few July days.

Surely, someday Stalin planned to advance on Berlin!

In mid-January, Churchill called upon Stalin to start his winter offensive earlier than planned — in order to help take the pressure off the Western Allies! The West had twice the number of German divisions, and three times the combat personnel because the Nazis were understrength. Yet the West had become entangled in just one failed enemy offensive.

Stalin agreed to start.

What happened? Another classic Russian smasheroo campaign. The final one? No — amazingly. Follow the events: The Russians went through the Germans like the proverbial knife through hot butter. They could have done this in *July,* when the Germans were demolished — and not waited until the Germans had five months to reorganize and prepare positions! They could have certainly done this in November — against an enemy only partly reorganized! They didn't move, however, until January — and then only after prodding by the Western Allies.

And then, against the prepared Germans, they produced a slaughter.

The Russians — with 7,000,000 combatants in the war zone — put more than 1,000,000 into action on a short front between Warsaw and Berlin. It is universally agreed this was the most awesome military offensive ever concentrated in a relatively small space. "A total of 1,350,000 Russians went into action, attacking a German force one-sixth their size." *(Almanac).*

In only five weeks from January 12 to February 20, the Russians *again effectively ended the War.* But in an *even shorter time* — by January 31 (before the Western Allies had really gotten free of the overall problems of the Bulge) — Zhukov's forces stood on the Oder River, *only forty miles from Berlin!*

Think about that. January 31, the Reds were in Berlin's peripheral towns.

And then, again, the mystery.

Again, the Russians *stopped stock still* — while the Western Allies caught up!

In their short, fantastic offensive, the Russians achieved enormous destruction of German forces in mere days. They overwhelmingly outgunned the Germans — the subject of another chapter of this book — on the short 300-mile front. One source shows a three-to-one advantage in men (1,500,000 to less than 600,000); five-to-one in tanks (3,300 vs. 700); eight-to-one in aircraft (10,000 vs. 1,300); and more than three-to-one in heavy field guns (28,000 vs, 8,200). It can be assumed also that the ammo supply was heavily in favor of the Russians!

Could this plunging drive have continued the final *forty miles* into Berlin at that time — late January, 1945? Certainly — the Germans were shattered. And to the Rhine (which the Western Allies didn't reach until March)? Yes — it was just a matter of putting the tanks in forward gear.

So, again, why did they stop?

The *Germans* didn't stop them! That was obvious. They stopped themselves. And why?

The only reason the Russians stopped *outside Berlin in January* and waited, was the existence of high-level agreements apportioning the territory

Again, the Russians paused months.

On March 7, the U.S. got across the Rhine at Remagen. The War was only two months from ending. The Germans were in dis-array. Patton knifed ahead.

On April 16, more than two months after stopping on the Oder, and only twenty-one days before the War's official end, Zhukov (directly commanding 1 Belorussian Front — and also acting as Deputy Supreme Commander, second only to Stalin), and Konev (commanding 1 Ukrainian Front), put 2,500,000 combat troops, or about 160 divisions, into forward gear on a *very* short front of only about 120 miles! (Rokossovsky, com-manding 2 Belorussian Front, moved along the Baltic Coast, taking good care of this right flank). (Note: "Front," in this usage, means Field Army or Army Group — a group of armies — each with divisions).

In the very short center facing Berlin alone, Zhukov utilized about *twice* as many combat personnel as the Western Allies possessed in the *entire line* coming in from the West.

The Russians immediately drove the first forty miles plus forty miles beyond — leaving the German capital in a small pocket, totally surrounded. On the ninth day, April 25th, they linked up with the U.S. forces in the historic meeting on the Elbe.

From about the 18th, U.S. forces had been stopping along the

Elbe farther north. The Russians pulled up to most portions of their assigned line by about May 6. *(Atlas).*

In the meantime, Hitler committed suicide April 30. Successor Doenitz "commanded" for a few days. German soldiers had been laying down their arms to the Western Allies, where they felt they would get better treatment. These swelled western totals of captives (and swelled our heads, too).

Men were still dying. Resistance to the Russians inside Berlin was intense, mainly out of fear. Also, German General Schorner was fighting in Czechoslovakia. The official end came May 7. Schorner battled near Prague until May 11. (After that, there was some scattered guerrilla resistance mainly by young boys in Czechoslovakia. My former brother-in-law, who won a Silver Star for gallantry, was with the Fifth Ranger Battalion on the Third Army's spearhead from the Moselle on. He told of the action in Czechoslovakia after the official May 7th end, and of trying to keep from killing those kids of eleven and up. He was eighteen at the time).

The super myth was developed that the U.S. with its Western Allies were the powerful winners — while Russia was the weak assistant, staggering in rags and tatters.

The division of Germany was most generous to us. Russia could have eliminated Germany much earlier than May 7, but didn't. Twice Russia stopped giant offensives even though Germany didn't stop those drives; and even though such stops enabled Germany to reorganize — breaking a cardinal military rule when there was no overriding military need to do so.

As to Ike being criticized for setting the "Elbe" line — if he had anything to do with it, he should be praised; because, had the dividing line not been present, the War would have ended with the

Russians in France and the Western Allies little beyond Paris.

Ike told Monty in the late summer or fall of 1944 that Berlin was the "only goal." But in December, Monty was furious when he learned from Ike that the Western Allies were not going there. Montgomery spoke out about this after the War, and never forgave Ike. Ike kept his mouth shut, as a good soldier — but he obviously knew of a very high level deal that had been made.

Ike kept his mouth shut, as a good soldier — but he obviously knew of a very high level deal that had been made.

One of the smaller mini myths that has to be "popped" is that Ike somehow ran the whole show and didn't have a boss! Ike indeed ran — brilliantly — the part he was assigned (which included managing the diverse Western Allies in harmony). Marshall — honored by presidents, Congress, and our Allies — was Eisenhower's direct and total boss. This is known to all readers — yet somehow, a mystique rests on Ike that he was responsible for all decisions. Even Marshall was only the military Chief of Staff in a country under civilian rule. Congress had a direct say (including promotions!), and Roosevelt was Commander in Chief, and directly involved at the highest level in strategy and in selection of his chiefs. Ike was later to say, "No matter how high you get, you always have a boss."

The point is that Ike certainly *didn't* make the decision about the Elbe, although he was willing to say that he did.

He may have *agreed* with it. (If he did, he was agreeing with the best deal under the circumstances).

I rather imagine that the exact deal came about this way: Roosevelt, Churchill, and Stalin, at one of their meetings, decided there should be some line so that the various Allies would all have a logical prize for their efforts. The Russians very much wanted the West to have worthwhile prizes in Europe — because

Stalin had tried since Barbarossa to get the West into a second front.

The capture of Berlin itself was given to Russia for two reasons: one, Russia's huge blood toll earned it; and, two, the city is surprisingly far to the east in Germany itself. However — to pursue the theory of the "logical prize" — the city would be divided and occupied by the four major Allies, after the Russian capture. As with most top-level decisions, this one was probably "roughed out" and turned over to staff people to solve in detail later. The basic concept was not announced. Ike thought, as late as the fall of 1944, that the Western Allies were going to Berlin — and told Monty so. But, soon thereafter, the "word" came down.

There were at least three hidden reasons for the decision — and for not announcing it as a decision of the Allied leaders, and instead letting it appear that Ike made the decision himself (as he said).

The hidden things were these: first, the Western Allies knew that their forces did not have the physical numbers necessary to take Germany. (At the peak, the West had 100 divisions on the Western Front). A second factor was that no one thought Russia would beat the West to Germany by nearly a year! (By the fall of 1944, when Ike had to change the position he had expressed to Monty — and not be able to say anything except that it was his decision to stop short of Berlin — the Russians might have wished there was no deal!)

But there was a *third* — a giant — *hidden reason.*

This third — most hidden but biggest — reason was that the West feared, secretly (expressed by Churchill and others, but coming to light only well after the War), that *Russia might just keep on coming West.*

Hence, a deal had to be finalized about a line.

The closer Russia got to Germany, the more urgent the final delineation of the line became. The final decision was made in the fall of 1944, and Ike took the brunt of any criticism.

It looked as if we got the "short end of the stick."

In fact, we got a fantastically *good deal.*

Russia twice halted its juggernaut and waited for the West to

catch up. Of the final twelve months of the War, six and one half
— more than half the year — were spent by the Russians mainly
sitting and waiting. Does this sound like Russia?

This must have cost them plenty in terms of meeting a reorganized enemy each time the campaigns started again. (The
decision at Yalta to let Russia take Manchuria during the last
weeks of the Pacific War might have been a part of the package to
keep Russia *not interested* in overrunning Western Europe!)

**Of the final eight months of the War
— September 1 through April 30 —
six and one half were spent by the
Russians mainly sitting and waiting.**

Much of the Western Allied blood spilled from Normandy to
the Elbe could have been spared — if we didn't care how much of
Europe Russia took!

We knew instinctively that Russia would not respect the freedom of nations it conquered. Had Russia taken all of Germany,
we never would have gotten it back — any more than we have
been able to free East Germany.

If Russia had come on into France . . .

Churchill feared that, after fighting the War against the
Nazis, he would be simply looking at *Russians* directly across the
Channel!

Many U.S. roots are in the traditional Europe.

Therefore, a great deal of our effort in retaking France, the
Lowlands, and Germany, was not only to free these from the
Nazis, but *also* to *prevent* these from falling into Russian hands.

These were things that could not be announced to the press,
or given out as the results of some big conference with Stalin!
Obviously, these were decisions taken by the West — without
conferences with "Papa Joe."

Germany was already whipped by D-Day. Our job was to

finish her off *and also* to preventively take and be prepared to hold as much of Europe as we could. (We still maintain huge forces there — *against the Russians*. Only two years after the War ended, Russia was trying to force us out of Berlin. So the concept is valid).

Ike was often criticized for moving too slowly in the late fall of 1944. Monty wanted to race into Germany. War historians and analysts have often taken the position that the Western Allies could have finished off a demoralized, understrength, German western army in a hurry. Taking an opposite position, some others have argued that Ike's decision to take things slowly (which infuriated Monty), was justified in light of the strength the Germans showed, though briefly, in the Bulge.

But why did Ike move slowly? In simple fact, from early fall, he knew what the final line was going to be. And he knew that the Russians were going to do nothing from August until perhaps February, although only 300 miles from Berlin. His was the logical response to the hidden facts. He built up his supplies and supply lines. He opened the port of Antwerp.

And — again responding to hidden facts — he made his forces so strong the Russians would not want to tangle with them in case the Reds decided on betrayal.

He — and Monty knew this — could have knocked off Germany earlier. Analysts and historians can make very tight cases showing this. (But so could the Russians have toppled Germany, as early as late summer, 1944).

However, suppose the West — going for a quick victory — became overextended and undersupplied, although victorious? And suppose the *West's weakness tempted Russia?*

In light of the hidden reasons, Ike's actions were explainable. We can see that he was taking the defeat of Germany as a "given," and was basing his actions on *something else* — on making certain the Russians had *no temptation to come west.*

Analyses of the Western Front have overconcentrated on our offensive operations against Germany — usually assuming these were our only purpose for being there. These have overlooked our defensive operations against Russia.

Analyses of the Western Front have assumed that offensive operations were our only reason for being there — and have overlooked defensive operations against Russia.

Defensive operations against Russia were at least half our reason for being in Western Europe — not less than half, and maybe much more than half.

Russia could have defeated us if she had wanted to keep on coming west. On the central front alone — roughly the dimension of the German nation from north to south — she had three to five million combat and immediate support uniformed military people, and untold equipment to go with this. Behind that, available to come up from the Balkans through Czechoslovakia, for example, were millions more. Russia could field almost all of its military force of some 12,000,000 in uniform. To get right to the nitty-gritty, she could have put 3,000,000 in combat divisions right on the *short* front alone, in Germany against about 1,000,000 shocked Western Allied combat troops in the line.

Therefore, we come to one more factor behind Ike's slowness. He knew that (besides outright provocation such as maverick hero Patton was offering to Russia), the only circumstance under which Russia could be tempted would be *quick* victory. That is, even the powerful Red Bear could not remotivate its troops at the end of the "Great Patriotic War" for a hard new fight.

THE DANGER OF PATTON PROVOKING A WAR

This fear was reflected in the firing of Patton. Immediately after the German surrender, when Patton was so openly hostile to the Russians — and issuing inflammatory remarks to them — Ike handed the nation's top battlefield commander hero his walking papers.

On the surface, there was the obvious reason of diplomacy. However, under the surface, there was the even more compelling reason — the unseen factor of the possibility of a Russian attack. The West did not want to give the Russians *any excuse* for an attack.

Once that concept is factored into armchair analyses of decisions, the *reasons* for those decisions become very, very clear.

Patton was right — at least in part. He said we should be "fighting the Russians — instead of the Germans." The last part, "instead of the Germans," wasn't right — and was maybe just a slip of phraseology from Patton. However, Patton could see that we would be fighting the Russians in time. (The Cold War, which Russia would gladly have made hotter if it had not been for U.S. nuclear weapons, began right after the close of WWII).

But — most dangerously — Patton was willing to talk about hot war; and he was willing to provoke an incident! He felt we could whip the Russians — but our Chiefs knew the situation was overwhelmingly the opposite! Even a small incident at that time could have started a war — especially if the Russians were looking for an excuse!

Churchill had tried throughout the War to get the Western Allies to use Italy and/or the Balkans, Greece, etc., as the invasion route to conquer Germany. Why? He wanted to get into Germany *before* the Russians did. Why again? He feared the Russians sitting on the English Channel in place of the defeated Germans.

The U.S. press would not even speculate in print on the possibility of a Russian change of plans! It followed the Government position that we were all buddies, and "Uncle Joe" Stalin — one of the confirmed great mass murderers of his own people of all time — was a swell guy. This was deemed necessary to the War effort (and indeed may have been).

Furthermore, this Government-and-press cooperation built the super myth in the U.S. that America and the Western Allies were the powerful winners, while Russia was the weak assistant, barely staggering, in rags and tatters, into Berlin — and without the strength or mentality to keep coming.

In this climate, no one — during the War, or at the end, or for decades afterwards, for that matter — could say, "Hey, the top knew all along (and used as a major factor in decisionmaking), the twin facts that Russia might betray us, and that *we knew we didn't have the strength in Western Europe to stop 'em.*"

No one at the top could say it — but Ike, Marshall, Roosevelt, and a few others at the top had to *think* it.

No doubt the factor of preventively keeping Russia from overrunning all Europe was one reason the U.S. went along with the

Europe-first plan. Churchill talked us into this, even though the U.S.' main interest was the Pacific, where our great mood-changer and motivator had been the Japanese attack on Pearl Harbor.

By the time the War had ended, the myths of Russian niceness, raggedness, and our great military power and overwhelming contribution to the defeat of the Germans, were built into our thought to such a giant size that to challenge them with the truth would have brought upon the challenger not just the wrath of the myth-builders, but of all those whose sacrifices had become rationalized, and attached, through sublimation, to a redeeming myth.

As a footnote regarding our power, it was not until *after* the European War was over, that the U.S. completed and used the Bomb.

At that point, suddenly all the myths of our great power seemed confirmed.

We extended retroactively, in our minds, the astonishing Bomb power to reinforce our beliefs that we were indeed the great power on the European Continent, and the defeater of Germany.

☆   ☆   ☆

The Western Allies didn't defeat the Germans. The Russians beat the Germans to their knees — and would have done so without us. We do not realize that the German-Russian war was the greatest ever fought. Our lack of realizing this may cost us dearly in a future war.

Myth Nine

That Russian Tanks Defeated The Germans

It was heavy guns — of which tank guns were a surprisingly small part — that defeated the Germans.

The concept of "30,000 Russian tanks" at places like Kursk, Kharkov, and Byelorussia, is utter mythology. Three thousand would have been more like it. But the numbers of Russian heavy *guns* are impressive. In the last stages of the Russian victory — from Warsaw to the Oder — Zhukov had 28,000 heavy guns on just one relatively short (about 300-mile) front. This was the greatest assemblage of artillery in the history of war. Yet he had only 3,500 tanks.

The basic psychology of the Russian land warrior is artillery. The Russians believe in it more than anyone else.

At Warsaw, Zhukov's heavy guns outnumbered his tanks eight to one. To his heavy guns should be added his Katyusha multi-barreled, battlefield rockets, his self-propelled or "assault guns," and his mortars over five inches.

(Note: In the previous summer's campaign on a much broader front, driving to Warsaw, one source tells of 31,000 heavy guns including the big mortars (but Katyushas should be added to this), plus 5,200 mobile guns including tanks and SPs).

Tank guns, of course, are also artillery. The famed T-34s, some with 76 mm and some with 85 mm cannon, were formidable. However, in this chapter, I am trying to differentiate between other cannon and tanks per se, in order to explode the myth that tanks defeated the Germans, and to focus upon what really brought them down.

From November of 1942, when Stalingrad was encircled, forward to Berlin two and one half years later, a very high ratio of heavy guns to tanks per se is indicated.

Russia's T-34 tank (in several editions) was better than the Panzers. The German equivalents were the Panzer IVs and Vs, with 75 mm guns. (The 88s went on surprisingly few tanks — less than 2,000 Tiger I and Tiger II models). There were about as many Panzer IIIs (roughly 6,000) as IVs, but these carried only a 50 mm gun. The accolade of "best tank" was awarded by the Germans themselves. Complementing their tanks, the Russians developed a modified Blitzkrieg suited to their more staid armies, but still very bold, and well-executed.

Tank production furnishes some surprises. Russia alone built some 55,000 — of which some 40,000 were the basic T-34 models. Germany built only 19,900 — of which some 16,000 were Pz III, IV, and V. *(Almanac)*. (Another source shows 33,000 *(Atlas)*. The difference may be in SPs. Another source claims Germany produced "47,000 tanks" in the final two years, when production "doubled each year" to offset the crumbling fronts and Allied air attacks. This was simply a statement in a narration on a TV documentary. If it had any basis in fact, I would tend to believe it included any vehicle with armor plate and at least a machine-gun mount, such as a half-track, or a place for a gun, such as a gun carriage. The tables in *Almanac* are itemized, and I would accept them as the best source, subject to data to the contrary).

One thing is definite — Germany didn't have enough tanks. It had the war in the West, and in Italy. Also, through Brooke's policy of making Germany defend all around its perimeter, it was spread thin. To add to Germany's woes, the U.S. produced some 63,000 tanks, 49,000 of which were Shermans (which fought with many Allied forces, including Russian). The Sherman mounted a 76 mm. The British produced about 22,000 tanks.

It is no myth that Russian tanks beat German tanks.

However, it *is* a myth that Russian tanks defeated Germany. Neither tank superiority, tactics, or numbers defeated the

Germans. What defeated the Germans was overwhelming Russian use of heavy guns.

The Yom Kippur War (October 1973), brought out an astonishing fact revelent to our points in this chapter. There were *as many tanks employed* — and *more tanks destroyed* — in that tiny war as in the great tank battles of Russia (for example, Kursk in July, 1943!)

For many observers in 1973, the implication from this was that battles such as Kursk were of no greater magnitude than the Yom Kippur War.

In fact, Kursk was probably the biggest single land battle in history (as contrasted to a *campaign* such as Barbarossa). One source flatly states it was the "greatest land battle in history" *(Almanac)*. Another says it involved "over 2,000,000 men, 6,000 tanks, and 4,000 aircraft" — and calls it "the biggest tank battle ever fought" *(Atlas)*.

Kursk was the most visceral battle of the Eastern Front. It was raw power versus raw power in the center of Russia's contested lands. It would determine the continuity of the Russian tide back toward Berlin. It produced a major psychological effect on the German generals, who realized after that battle that they could not defeat the Russians at arms — without the Hitler-promised "miracle weapons."

Called "Kursk," the battle was really that of the great Kursk salient. The Russians, advancing steadily after Stalingrad, had captured Kursk and pushed well beyond it. This very big bulge had bypassed Orel on the north side, and Kharkov on the south. Hitler felt this bulge could be pinched off. The huge summer offensive (called "Citadel") was to attempt this, simultaneously driving from the north and the south, meeting at Kursk!

But Kursk itself never became involved. Through the "Lucy" spy ring in Switzerland, and the Enigma code breaks (although the Russians were never told about Ultra), the Russians were waiting in well-prepred positions for the giant attack! One source says eight concentric lines of defense had been built *(Atlas)*. Artillery in antitank positions picked off the German tanks. The

Nazis were halted in seven or eight days. The Russians immediately went to the offensive, driving the Germans back to the starting points within two more weeks. Next, the Russians kept on rolling for 200 more miles — along an 800-mile front, first taking Orel and Kharkov, and then going beyond Smolensk in the north, and to the gates of Kiev and the banks of the Dniepr River in the south. The whole affair was a German disaster.

But to return to our tank focus, wasn't Kursk a world-shaking *tank* battle? Don't we have mental views of thousands of tanks swirling and churning around in ironclad combat to the death, while the world — as the fair maiden might watch the knights in the lists — looked on? Yes, we have that view — but it was created by false reporting, or the glamorous fantasies of adventure stories or movies. The tanks were there — but not in the colossal numbers we believe. Also, the tank losses were not all that dramatic — and weren't the decisive factor (although German losses so depleted their stock that lack of this equipment was a deciding factor).

The Nazis lost 200 tanks in the north, and 350 in the south, in the first few days of the fighting *(Atlas)*. As usual, news from that front was sketchy, but one source reports a short (apparently one-day) big battle eight days after the start (July 12), writing, "the largest tank battle in history was fought near the village of Prochorovka [southern pincer under Manstein]. The Germans alone lost more than 400 tanks. About 3,000 tanks were deployed by the two sides in this vicious clash of armor" *(Almanac)*.

(Just after Stalingrad's surrender earlier that year, the Germans "had only 495 operational tanks left on the entire Russian front," and had "lost 7,800 tanks" [total] in Russia — *Almanac).* (Note: Apparently, new production must have raised that number to the estimated 2,000 or more available for the Kursk pincers alone by summer).

To return to a comparison to the Yom Kippur War, the desert struggle compared in no way — except, amazingly, in *tanks!*

About 5,000 were involved, as a total of both sides. On one side, Israel had about 1,700 tanks plus 350 self-propelled guns (SPs). Their enemy to the south, Egypt, had 1,850 tanks. Israel's enemy to the north, Syria, had 1,270 tanks plus 75 SPs, plus 1,000 armored personnel carriers (APCs). This produced totals of some

5,000 tanks, 425 SPs, and 1,000 APCs *(Dictionary)*.

The exact toll in tanks was never specified, because no one side wanted the world to know its precise losses. However, it is generally conceded that the losses were *higher than at Kursk's* bitter seven to ten days. Israel lost 200 tanks the first day it encountered the infantry-launched antitank missiles; and 200 more the second day. Israel had to abandon close air support along the Canal due to enemy infantry-launched ground-to-air missiles (Israel lost 100 planes to ground-to-air missiles, out of a total of 104 planes lost). The final victory took not tanks and planes but Israeli infantry with mortars to pick off the missile launchers and their ancillary apparatuses hidden behind the dunes. *(Dictionary)*.

There are three indicators pointing out the colossal losses of armor. The first was that armor was so depleted on each side in the first week of fighting that the major powers had to begin emergency supplying of equipment to their clients. The second was that press coverage (post-Vietnam style) from the fronts included photographs of the shattered armored vehicles in large numbers. The third was the world military analyses that followed the Yom Kippur War — giving general figures for the losses of armor, showed that the losses (of armor only) were greater than at Kursk, and specified that an "era" of battle had ended, that the "queen of battle," the tank, was dead, etc.

One authoritative source wrote, "Claims by either side of tanks and aircraft destroyed are . . . diverse . . . But, for certain, the Israeli-Egyptian tank battles were waged by more armored vehicles than were ever deployed in one battle [including] Russia, and the losses were proportionately higher . . ." *(Dictionary)*.

Russian big guns defeated the Germans. The Russians have always been dogged artillerymen, and also have always learned quickly from invading enemies. In WWII, the Russian mentality had "heavy artillery" written all over it. It might have appeared (as with the German armor), that the flash and dash of the tanks were the main factor. But Russian tanks were only an arm of the artillery-centered control of the battlefield.

The Russians modified the German Blitzkrieg, adapting it to fit their capabilities. They did not completely detach their armor with its own highly mobile infantry support — although on occasion, and for very short times, they did this (however, not for the main, knockout punch, as the Germans did). (The German fundamental method of one continuous, rolling forward of detached armor and mobile infantry, until the *war,* not the battle, was won, of course bogged down in December of 1941, in the vastness and lack of jugular in Russia, and was never seen again).

The Russians modified the Blitz to suit their own situation. For one thing, they thought in terms of *series* of battles — with profound (sometimes months) of breaks in between. This enabled the enemy to regroup — therefore, in a sense, this was foolish. However, their "clobbering" type Blitz tended to offset some of this, and get things rolling again when the Reds were ready!

The Russian Blitz was *artillery-centered.* Thus it was neither old-fashioned infantry-bloc-centered, nor German armor-centered.

The artillery was the heavy, central element. It was semi-mobile. First, there were such huge quantities that part could be moving up with the armor, while more than enough was firing in place. All the big pieces were at least wheeled, to be easily trailed. Second, the legendary Katyusha rockets were usually mounted on truck beds, or on tracked vehicles. At the least, they were wheeled, for quick trailing to forward positions.

The artillery and multiple-rocket launchers would "blow the enemy away." Many German soldiers reported the horror, stun — even plain admiration — of the shocking rain of projectiles exploding in massed patterns above or around them, wiping out whole companies, and clearing gaping holes in defensive positions.

The tanks never detached from the semi-mobile artillery mass (with a few exceptions).

How was the infantry used in the Russian type Blitz? *Basically,* the *hordes accompanied* the tanks. This was the basic mode — far from the German concept.

There was no motorized infantry as in Germany or the Western Allies.

Many Russian pictures show white-clad infantrymen riding T-34s! Thus, the concept of having *some* infantry up with the tanks was present. There was a difference, of course, between assault phases and breakthrough phases. In assault phases, large numbers of infantry on foot were right behind the tanks. In breakthroughs, only the most mobile infantry could stay with the tanks. However, *most* Russian operations kept the tanks close, and *hordes* of infantry right behind them.

Were the tanks in effect supporting the infantry? No — but hordes (not a selected, motorized few) supported the tanks. The Blitz had arrived, but in a modified form.

The Russian Blitz was uneconomical as to men. It wasted its own infantry in the Asiatic style — taking from three to five combat deaths for each German combat death.

Documented are uses of infantry *in front* of the tanks. Sometimes they were in front, sometimes to the sides, and usually in mass just behind.

Infantry sometimes went ahead of the tanks with mine-clearing devices. (In the last drive from Warsaw west, Stalin had demanded speed against an enemy which had had several months in which to dig in and lay minefields. Zhukov ordered the massed infantry ahead of the tanks — and cleared the minefields with legs! The men muttered — but blamed Stalin, not their hero Zhukov.

The Russians had a limited "play book." Their type of Blitz worked for an illiterate army without good communications, stultified by a top-heavy political bureaucracy whose representatives lived with the troops. A simple, "standard," operating procedure was the only thing that would function. *Without* the artillery, the concept would have failed — because the Germans *knew* exactly what to expect!

Another interesting point is that the Russian system worked as well on defense as offense, summer or winter, wet or dry — in low, medium, or high gear!

Thus, to summarize the Russian type modified Blitz, it was, first, artillery-centered (with semi-mobile artillery plus the multiple rockets), in enormous quantity, backed by endless ammunition; second, it utilized tanks on a short string, supported by two classes of infantry — riding and hordes on foot immediately behind; third, it had foot troops in overwhelming quantity — outnumbering the Germans probably three-to-one in most battle areas until near the end, when the proportions grew much higher; fourth, it used very basic, no frills, pincers; and fifth, it was willing to waste — squander — its own men.

(Before the War ended, another type of modified Blitz was to appear in the U.S. advance across France and Germany. To compare the American modified Blitz to the Russian, the U.S. was *very* economical in men. The U.S. believed in obliteration and starvation of the enemy side of the battlefield more thoroughly than the Russians! To artillery and close-support air, the U.S. added deep tactical air strikes, isolating the battlefield. U.S. communications were extraordinary. So was intelligence — courtesy of Britain's Ultra, which delivered every enemy battle move in advance except the Bulge (where Hitler had ordered a message blackout). The U.S. used deep-ranging, totally detached armored spearheads which even outdid the German concept. However, these were adapted to the situation, and could not have functioned well except at those times in the War (summer of 1944, when, with the "Anvil" landings moving up the Rhone from Southern France, the Germans were pulling back to their Siegfried Line, and late winter-early spring 1945, in Germany and Czechoslovakia, when the end was so near). Some of Patton's armor even left its close infantry support behind — and ranged so far in the enemy rear that it ran out of petrol (leading to the development of the rubber drop-bag for gasoline).

(Continuing with the comparison, the Americans were not geared for defense; were very literate; had a complex "play-book" and extreme flexibility within the centralized theatre-command; depended on the British for most intelligence; and depended on the British to provide the "hub" of the wheel in the north, while the U.S. rolled the rim of the wheel in the southern section of the line).

To return to the Russian Front, the German tank crews were superior to the Russian tank crews. The Germans were more skillful, unpredictable, and fierce on defense. But the combination of all elements of the Russian assaults was overwhelming.

Russian tanks did not defeat the Germans. The main element in the Russian battle mix — and the thing that made it go — was an overwhelming number, and unprecedented high ratio, of heavy guns and battlefield cluster rockets to tanks and SPs. The ratio of guns alone to tanks alone at Warsaw was eight to one. Adding rocket clusters, the radio might have been ten or twelve to one.

Even deeper than the heavy-artillery centered Russian mentality is their deepest mental concept of *control of the battlefield* — of the actual fighting area. The Russians understand this. It is in their guts. It is in their blood — because they are usually fighting on their own soil, defending their own land!

Before leaving artillery, we need to discuss a very light but powerful artillery — the Russian "tank-killer" or Stormovik series Illyushin Il-2, Il-2m3 (two-seater), and Il-10 (twin-engined) close-support planes. These mounted small, rapid-fire cannons pouring out continuous streams of exploding shells. (The Il-2m3 mounted 2 23 mm, the Il-10 3 20 mm). These were ideal for blowing treads off tanks, destroying trucks, ammo piles, artillery, fuel supplies, and the like. Some 42,000 Stormoviks were built. Armor-plated, they were an integral part of "control of the battlefield." The Il-2m3 was the best low-level ground support plane in the War.

(The Russians also starved the enemy battlefield by use of 150,000 *organized* partisans. Most partisans were not just hit or miss heroic bands, but were deliberately and methodically organized.

The Russians won through an overwhelming superiority in the battle areas. The *central factor* in this was *heavy guns,* and multi-barreled Katyusha rocket launchers. The Russians "blew the Germans away."

Myth Ten

That Rommel Had A Fighting Chance At El Alamein

The British advantage over the Germans was four to one in guns, five to one in tanks, and four to one in troops. Rommel was out of fuel, and burdened with Mussolini's troops which he deserted, taking their transport. El Alamein was a foregone conclusion — a planned victory with a blank check from Churchill, and all the time in the world. The real turnaround was at Alam Halfa Ridge — eight weeks earlier.

The Afrika Korps did not have a fighting chance at El Alamein.

It was October, 1942. The British had not had a victory about which they could really crow since the War began — while the Dunkirk disaster had been *more than two full years previous.*

Suddenly, at El Alamein, there was an absolutely decisive, tide-turning victory — followed (after a pause which some military historians have criticized), by a 1,000-mile chase of a defeated foe.

At El Alamein, Rommel was met by a British force *many times* his size.

Let's look at the "stats": In heavy guns, the British advantage was four to one — 2,311 to 644 (the proportion changing to two to one if Italian guns numbering 575 are included). In tanks, the British advantage was five to one — 1,029 to 211 (the proportion changing to two to one if 278 Italian tanks are added). In men, the

British advantage was four to one — 195,000 to 50,000 (the proportion changing to two to one if some 50,000 Italian troops are included). In serviceable aircraft, the British advantage was three to one — 530 to 150 (the proportion changing to two to one if about 200 serviceable Italian planes are included).

In fuel, the British advantage was total. The Afrika Korps was about out — and, as a result, could fight only a static and defensive battle. The British had developed a specialty of sinking tankers between Europe and North Africa — aided by Enigma breaks. The peak of this effort was the sinking of two desperately-needed, Fuehrer-ordered, special Afrika Korps tankers in Tobruk harbor, before they could unload, about the time of the El Alamein attack.

On the day of Monty's attack (October 24, 1942), Rommel was a sick man in Germany. He flew back to Africa on the 25th, taking over from von Stumme, who had suffered a fatal heart attack after the offensive had begun. He stepped into an impossible situation. The master of maneuver was forced to fight a nearly static battle.

The battle — and the absolute victory — had been carefully planned by Churchill. Supplies from the U.S. could reach Africa by crossing the Pacific and Indian Oceans without the submarine peril ships faced in the North Atlantic. Thus, a lot of supplies were flowing into the Mideast, making their way to Egypt (for the British), and to Russia. Sherman tanks fought with Monty.

Behind a heavy buildup, the British deliberately fashioned victory.

There had been several spectacular chases back and forth across North Africa, beginning in September 1940 when Italian General Graziani got to Mersa Matruh — well inside Egypt. The Italians had long occupied Libya, as part of their African wars. They had captured Ethiopia — which they would lose, for all purposes, early in 1941. (The Italians' heart never was in aggression, or in fighting against the English, or, later, the Americans; and their equipment was obsolete. Later mass surrenders of Italians in North Africa can be discounted as war victories. Later, after the Allies invaded Italy, the Facist Government fell, and the Italians fought the remainder of the War on the Allied side — very seriously and capably). ✓

The nature of the North African campaigns — which swung back and forth over 1,000 miles of terrain (more if the coastline, not the "crow" distance is measured) — had a special characteristic: the victor for the moment would go all-out until supplies were outrun. Then — like a compressed spring — the formerly vanquished would roar back . . . until his supplies ran out.

General Wavell ripped the Axis in late 1940 and early 1941, driving west to famed El Agheila (which soon became monotonous) in Libya — a good 500 miles by the "crow," and more by the coast.

Rommel arrived soon afterwards — in February, 1941. He immediately reversed the situation — driving all the way back (nearly) to Mersa Matruh, to Buq Buq — inside the Egyptian frontier. In this campaign, famed Tobruk (of the movie with Richard Burton, and countless other stories) was surrounded. The next months into December were taken up relieving the Tobruk garrison and mounting an end sweep to El Agheila again. Tobruk was relieved December 10, 1941, and El Agheila was reached January 6, 1942. (In the meantime, Wavell lost command to Auchinleck, with Cunningham taking the Eighth Army. Churchill was very much involved in selecting and pressuring generals).

Rommel was soon at it again — in fact, by January 21. By February 6 (1942), he was knocking near the gates of Tobruk — at Gazala, where the Afrika Korps rested. In late May, the Germans continued eastward, cutting off Tobruk again — this time taking it June 21. The Nazis passed Mersa Matruh for the deepest Axis penetration yet, and raced, by the end of June, to El Alamein, less than 100 miles from the Nile.

At El Alamein, Rommel continued on the attack, in the First Battle of El Alamein, in June and July, 1942.

Traditionally, the two foes had attacked the coastal towns, and then engineered wide "end run" sweeps down into the desert, to appear beyond the defenders and cause panic. As the battles entered deep into Egypt, the Quattara Depression — an old salt marsh not passable to armored vehicles — lay only about forty miles from the coast. Thus, big end sweeps were no longer possible.

Therefore, in the First Battle of El Alamein, Rommel came more or less frontally. The long Ruweisat Ridge lay ten miles below El Alamein, ten miles in length. It was a natural barrier from attacks from the south, but Rommel just came from west to east, passing on both sides of Ruweisat Ridge. The British (and by British, I include Australians, New Zealanders, Indians, South Africans, and any other Commonwealth soldiers present) fought along this Ridge, and the net result of fighting for most of July was to force Rommel to stand down.

Churchill demanded that his generals immediately go over to the offensive. Auchinleck wouldn't consider it until he had built up his forces, and gave mid-September as a date. Churchill relieved him, placing Alexander as Commander of the Mideast, and Montgomery as Commander of the Eighth Army. (Incidentally, this did not advance Churchill's timetable! Monty wouldn't move until he had built up a great superiority, and he was more of a bulldog in this matter than the previous generals!)

Rommel wasn't finished. The Battle of Alam Halfa Ridge came next. I call this the Second Battle of El Alamein — and the battle that turned the tide and should get the credit!

In August, Rommel — hurt from his frontal attacks — tried the traditional end sweep in the narrow corridor. He roared well south of Ruweisat Ridge, almost to the end of the Quattara Depression. He swept around the Ridge, and then — in the best North African tradition — turned up toward the coast.

About twelve miles lay between him and cutting off the British Army, leaving Egypt defenseless.

It was the deepest penetration yet into Egypt — and the most dangerous!

Between Rommel and the sea — well beyond El Alamein — lay Alam Halfa Ridge. There the British made a defense, using the Ridge, which paralleled the coast, as a natural defense. In the battles, Rommel ran short of fuel, and withdrew to defensive positions that set the stage for the final battle of El Alamein.

Monty fought the battle of Alam Halfa Ridge, but used Auchinleck's plan. *(Atlas)*.

I am a big touter of the Battle of Alam Halfa Ridge as the real turning point in the desert.

One source credits the *First* Battle of El Alamein as being "as decisive as the second, better recognized action" (meaning the final battle that got the fame). *(Dictionary)*. Personally, I can't see that the first battle was decisive at all — but I can certainly see that it was as decisive as the final one! To my analysis, neither one was *the* decisive one!

Alam Halfa Ridge was the decisive battle — the turning point, the deepest penetration, and the battle which forced the Germans onto the defensive. Even the above-quoted source says, "at Alam Halfa . . . the initiative passed to the British."

So why didn't Alam Halfa get the credit for being the turning point, and for withstanding the deepest point of penetration, and turning back the most danger?

The answer goes back to the considerations of the "Home Front."

"At Alam Halfa . . . the initiative passed to the British." *(Dictionary of Battles)*.

Churchill needed a victory that could be ballyhooed. The desert was the only place the British ground forces were engaging the Germans. Dunkirk had been more than two years previous. Of El Alamein, the Prime Minister would later say, "Before El Alamein we didn't have a victory, and after it we didn't have a defeat."

So the "turning point" that was sought was not just that of the desert war, but for the *War* itself, in the British sense — for British *involvement* in the War, for British *psychology* about the War.

And what was needed was a "peg" on which to hang the entire remainder of the British activity.

Alam Halfa simply wouldn't fit the framework preconstructed for the event, and — facts aside — had to be discarded from contention.

At El Alamein, not even Rommel knew the extent of the British buildup. But he knew his own impossible position. He had even been to Germany for a special audience with Hitler, to plead his case — but had been told to make do, because the main forces and supplies were going to the Eastern Front, then looking so promising (the Caucasus and the initial later summer approaches to Stalingrad).

The British were very clever at deception — both false intelligence and also the old desert game of rubber or canvas "tanks" and "guns" under camouflage strips. The traditional rule was to overstate or fake up a big force. Since Monty now had a big force he wished to hide, he made his *real* forces look like rubber ones. Also, by clever dust-raising, he made it appear that his real forces were too far from the lines to start anything without giving off plenty of warning. He also raised dust and erected the most realistic dummies in places in the line where he did not plan to attack. Meanwhile, he moved his real stuff up little by little, sweeping the desert behind the tracks (and making the real stuff look very obviously fake — to look like not even good canvas fakes!)

Churchill was awakened one morning about two a.m. to be asked if he wanted to set aside his absolute dictum that no action ever be taken as the result of an Enigma break *unless* that action could be attributed by the Germans to *another* source. (For example, if Enigma revealed that there were enemy ships at a certain point, although bombers would be prepared, they would not fly out and bomb until *first* an obvious-as-hell patrol plane went out to "spot" the ships — and be itself spotted!)

This particular morning, though, the issue was Axis tankers for Rommel, crossing the Mediterranean. Did Churchill want to break his rule in this case — since he was so adamant about nailing Rommel in the big, planned, victory?

Astoundingly, Churchill said yes — and the vessels were sunk.

British intelligence then had the big problem of how to cover up the fact that they might have obtained this information from a code break. (Rommel often suspected, and openly said, that there were code breaks).

The British had many codes which they knew the Germans had compromised — but which the Germans didn't know the British knew were compromised. When the British wanted the Germans to know a secret, they would transmit in one of these codes. (As a side note, when the British wanted to send a piece of information they wanted treated as *false,* they would transmit in a code which they knew the Germans knew the British knew was broken. Say that again??)

To solve their tanker problem, and deflect suspicion that they had busted into Enigma, they transmitted a message to a non-existent Italian underground group, "thanking" them for their "help" in detecting the sailings of the tankers! *(Bodyguard).*

The Germans accepted this as a genuine message, and, amazingly, within a day or so Enigma traffic carried messages saying that the source of the intelligence break had been spotted — Italian traitors.

(The Germans — though they sometimes suspected code breaks — always wound up attributing their intelligence leaks to traitors or Allied sympathizers. Many messages were sent by phone lines, and had to go through transmission points operated by conquered peoples in occupied countries. This opened the way for plenty of suspicion!) *(Bodyguard).*

We tend to think of the desert battles as being swirling, gallant, action-filled, Errol Flynn sorts of things.

But in fact, El Alamein — the most famous of them all — was the most nearly static of the desert battles.

The main feature was cutting through the German minefields — tedious work, done mainly at night by British and Aussie infantry, inching ahead on their knees in the dark, probing gingerly with bayonets in every square inch of sand, and laying a ribbon on each side to guide the tanks through.

The attack came at 9:30 p.m. on October 23 (1942). When the first daylight came, the tanks were *not* through the deep mine-fields. These were no ordinary minefields — being two and three miles deep.

Thus it was for ten days.

The British inched forward. Monty's tanks did most of their fighting from multiple lanes making up fat corridors. The toll was heavy, because the British were obvious, and the Germans were well dug in. This was no swirling tank battle.

About halfway through, the decision was made to continue the costly fight on an attrition basis. This was unheard of previously in the economical desert war. The British knew their overwhelming superiority in numbers, and were willing to trade loss for loss with the enemy for a few days. They knew Rommel couldn't stand *any* losses at all.

All the El Alamein movies with swirling tanks can be thrown away. Rommel (who mounted some counteroffensive activity) basically couldn't move, due to a lack of fuel and the omnipresent RAF. Meanwhile Monty was basically stuck in cleared areas in minefields, or between minefields. And the main battle phase was attrition.

Monty won, of course. Swirl and dash, cut and thrust? Nope — dull (and deadly) as hell: nine or ten days of slow, exposed going through four or five miles of enemy defenses before armor began to break through, and Rommel withdrew a bit (November 3 or 4).

Rommel hesitated. He had just been ordered by Hitler personally to not retreat ever, but stand and die. However, on November 4, as British X Corps began to break through in earnest, Rommel wisely fled.

In other words, by the time the armor got where it could do some of that swirling stuff, the battle was, for effective purposes, over.

The retreating Germans stole the Italian transport, abandoning Mussolini's men.

Part of the mythology created and perpetuated by El Alamein

was that of the romantic, tiny, ragged, defiant British force —
outnumbered, fighting valiantly, against huge and powerful
German armies such as those tearing into Russia at that moment.
The image maintained was that of the gallant little last-stand
British force with its Aussie hats and "Waltzing Matilda" wad-
dling tanks — the "desert rats" themselves, springing from the
sands, and rooted immovably, as at Tobruk in mid-1941. Even if
defeated, these stood like wraiths over the dune grasses — and
marched like "ghost riders in the sky" shepherding some fleshly
future force in indomitable combat.

But it was the Germans who were weak and ragged at El
Alamein.

German strength at El Alamein was mythology. Had the
truth been known at the time, sympathy would almost have gone
to the tattered Afrika Korps — beaten to where no more could be
asked, and fleeing finally from overwhelming odds!

However, El Alamein had been selected — and its image
would be tailored — to change world psychology about the War.
At the least, certainly to *change Western Allied war psychology*
— through its surrogate warriors, the British, in that faraway,
romantic desert . . .

And unquestionably, El Alamein — once it was packaged —
had the greatest psychological impact on Western thought of any
battle of the War.

Monty roared ahead.

Four days after his breakthrough, the British and U.S. came
ashore from Casablanca to Algiers in three widely separated
major landings. By November 12, some of these troops were only
about 100 miles from the city of Tunis at Tunisia's Cape Bon,
which stuck out in the Mediterranean toward Sicily. Thus, nearly
1,000 miles of North Africa *west* of Tunis came under Allied
military control in just a matter of days.

Monty roared ahead. He passed the old landmarks — Mersa
Matruh, Sidi Barrani, Bardia, Tobruk. He took Benghazi
November 19 (about the time the Russians were crunching the
flanks of the Stalingrad penetration, cutting off the Germans in a
vast area there).

The chase was an exhilarating time for the British people.

The advance covered 500 miles in fourteen days.

For the remainder of the year, the British pushed about 100 miles beyond the old stopping point — El Agheila. The western landing forces were still about 100 miles outside Tunis.

Montgomery was later to be criticized for not sweeping after Rommel in a manner to surround him and destroy the entire Afrika Korps. Indeed, at least "on paper," and with hindsight, he might have missed a giant opportunity. However, the El Alamein battle had been longer than expected, grueling, and costly.

Furthermore, to this writer, it seems that 500 miles of gain between the 4th and 19th — between the breakout and the capture of Benghazi — was doing everything that could have been done in that time!

Monty might have tried a deep dash across the bottom of the Cyrenaican bulge (as Rommel had done on his first drive from El Agheila to Tobruk) — to cut off Rommel in the Benghazi coastal bulge.

However, again I feel that this would have required planning, fresh troops, plentiful supplies — and Monty had been depleted not badly but beyond expectations.

When discussing this, another point becomes very important — a point we'll discuss in further depth later in this chapter, in examining Montgomery, the cool victor at El Alamein.

The jaunty commander was much more of a set-piece fighter than is generally imagined. He used maneuver *sparingly,* but extremely well within *his type* of planned battle.

After El Alamein, he preferred letting Rommel get away — and facing him again a few hundred miles away — to the alternative: letting the British and Commonwealth forces pursue in a manner which bespoke even a little disorder!

In his orderly, extremely rapid, chase, he stuck to the highways (which were on the coast), and hence to the coast. One group did cut across the bulge — but not *deep.*

In the opinion of this writer, the British, the Allies, and the world got more than they could have reasonably expected from El Alamein and its heroes — and should drop the argument about somehow trapping the Desert Fox at that Fox' own game!

Montgomery's victory at El Alamein brought into focus specific military characteristics of the man — characteristics which would not change throughout the War. They had a direct bearing on the victory at El Alamein (and Alam Halfa Ridge), and hence can be examined at this point.

The best way to pop Monty's specific and extraordinary characteristics into clear focus is to draw comparisons between him and the man to whom he is most often contrasted — Patton.

These two were soon to come on the world stage as Allies but competitors.

Patton began emerging in Tunisia — so first we'll look at the completion of the African wars.

Entering 1943, the great Allied conference was held in Casablanca (January 14-23). This had a way of saying, "Africa is ours," although Tunisia had not fallen. The British Eighth Army banged on toward the Tunisian border with Libya, taking Tripoli January 23, and pushing across the Tunisian border toward Rommel's dug-in defense line at Mareth. The western landing forces were still about 100 miles from Tunis.

Rommel left his main forces dug in at Mareth, and went north and west to punish the Americans at Kasserine. The plot was to drive through the American positions to the sea in Algeria — cutting off all the western landing troops in Tunisia. He nearly succeeded. This attack was February 14-22 (while Monty was pulling up to the Mareth Line about February 16). *(Atlas)*. The Americans made a poor showing. There were 10,000 casualties — 6,500 American (1,200 U.S. dead) to only 2,000 Axis casualties, for a sickening five to one ratio! It was the first "bloodying" of the Americans — but it had an effect upon the entire army, and they never again looked as bad. Eisenhower was in the field, and was badly shaken up by the battle. One of the net results was to move Patton up — to give some forward action to the American effort.

There were some other changes: The U.S. took over the northernmost sector, along the coast.

How was this structured? Ike was Supreme Commander of Allied forces in Africa (a result of the Casablanca Conference). This put the British *under* an American commander. This concept was Ike's (as given to Marshall when Ike was on Marshall's staff. Marshall had asked him for a concept of how the Allies might work together in battle. Ike had not put *his* name forth, but the paper produced the appointment for him in time). Ike's idea was that either a British or American could have top command, but the deputy was to be from the other Ally. (Thus, in Africa, it became Ike and Alexander; in Europe, Ike and Tedder). (Could a Britisher have commanded? From a practical and political point of view, America would not have gone along under those circumstances, so the British, reluctantly but heroically, played second fiddle). (As Churchill was to say when Pearl Harbor was bombed, "We have won the War," the British knew that whole-hearted American participation meant victory — and the impossibility of defeat).

General Alexander had all the combined armies under the Eighteenth Army Group. Monty, pulling up from the south, retained his Eighth Army (but this was now under the Eighteenth Army Group, and under Ike's supreme command — which must have galled the victor of El Alamein, who suddenly was not top dog in Africa). The only other *Army* was the First, under British General Anderson. The British were extremely capable and experienced soldiers. They just didn't get the press! The Americans served under the British First Army.

Monty defeated Rommel at Mareth in March, and drove up towards Tunis in April. (Monty hit the Mareth Line March 6. Rommel left Africa permanently March 9 *(Almanac),* leaving General Arnim in charge. Monty broke the Mareth Line March 24, and pushed on up to *within fifty miles of Tunis* by late April. (Yep, the western landing Allies were still — well, they were about fifty miles from Tunis now too!) So there ain't no flies on Monty!

When he rolls up an enemy, he rolls 'em up! That completed more than 1,500 miles of advance for him, while in western Tunisia — since those forces had moved within 100 miles of Tunis five months previous — little ground had been gained.

At the April perimeter around Tunis, Anderson's First Army covered everything except the short Eighth Army front (about twenty-five miles) along the coast south and east of Tunis. There were *four* corps in the First Army. Starting from Monty's western flank, these were the French Nineteenth (with about two divisions); (and, continuing left), the British Ninth Corps (with about two divisions, one of which I believe came from Monty); the British Fifth Corps (with about six divisions, directly opposite Tunis, and ready to bust things open); and, along the northern coast, the U.S. Second Corps! Well, the U.S. finally got in there!

Let's see how U.S. Second Corps was structured. It had fought at Kasserine. Two weeks later *(Dictionary),* March 6 *(Almanac),* Patton took command of it. He built it up to include 1st Armored, and 1st, 9th, and 34th Infantry Divisions *(Dictionary).* According to one source, there was some fighting for Second Corps under Patton in March *(Almanac),* in the center of the perimeter, before the move to the coast.

By April, Bradley appears as Commander of the U.S. Second Corps. The same four divisions are shown, and they have moved from the earlier placement near the old center near Kasserine, to the northernmost sector of the tight perimeter around Tunis.

Another source clears up the mystery — and the mystery of Patton's short (very short) combat reign as Second Corps Commander. Bradley had, by April, assumed command of Second Corps, and moved it into the northern sector. *(Dictionary).* Bradley took the Americans on in with the British to the finish of Tunisia in May (1943) *(Atlas).*

Where was Patton after his brief March appearance as Second Corps Commander? He was organizing the U.S. Seventh Army for the invasion of Sicily. *(Dictionary).*

Patton was under Bradley for part of Tunisia, then over Bradley for Sicily, then under Bradley again in France.

The British did almost all the work around Tunisia (including the counterattack which saved Kasserine). As for the Americans, Bradley did most of the Corps Commander work that succeeded.

But "Gen. Ink" — Patton — got most of the headlines. He was Gen. Excitement — but had little, very little, to show.

This might explain why he was almost manic when he hit Sicily.

The Sicilian invasion was commanded by British General Alexander with his Fifteenth Army Group. Under him, on his right, was Monty and the Eighth Army (landing about five divisions). Under him, on his left, was Patton and the newly-organized Seventh Army (which later became famous under Patch, landing in the south of France, and eventually taking a place in the Western Front near Switzerland). Under Patton was Second Corps commanded by Bradley. The Seventh Army landed about five divisions. (The exact division count on landings is difficult, because many units are brigades, Rangers, commandoes, and other special forces whose sizes are not specified).

Patton was under pressure to live up to his headlines, and he did. He did not follow the rules, and this antagonized Montgomery. He was at least partly in a battle for the spotlight — and for shouldering out Monty, which I feel was unnecessary. (After all, Montgomery was a proven hero, and not even Tunis fell until the lean man with the beret and the high espirit de corps pulled within fifty miles. I feel that should be recognized — not subjected to flamboyant competition). Patton was criticized for exposing his men to unnecessary casualties — but defended himself by saying that acting quickly saved lives in the long run.

The Sicilian conquest was wrapped up in August, but in the meantime, Patton had slapped not one but three soldiers — all of whom were in hospitals, and two of which were in bed! On the third, he pulled a pistol, and told him he should be "lined up and shot." All this cost Patton his job for the time being.

The British took advantage of Patton's image (although, on examination, there was little behind it!) Their deception apparatus took him under their wing and — without telling him much, because he was a great "leaker" of news to the press — made him highly visible in parts of the Isles where they were building their great "paper" invasion army — the one to land at Calais! The "invasion" army was called FUSAG, and was highly successful. But although Patton was commander, the entire non-entity was in the hands of the British deception people. Supposed to keep quiet, Patton went about with high visibility, giving "profane and bellicose" speeches, dressing in hand-made special uniforms, and generally endearing himself, in his own unique way, to British populace and Allied troops. *(Bodyguard).*

Patton knew little about FUSAG, and was supposed to keep a low profile while the British led the Germans to believe he was involved in preparing the great army. Since he went diametrically the other way and stayed in as much spotlight as he could manage, the British simply adjusted to this and used his visibility as proof that he was present to lead the great army.

The upshot of FUSAG was much, much bigger than the Allied press has ever generally accepted. In fact, the German High Command accepted that there were "eighty-five to ninety Allied divisions assembling in Britain, together with seven airborne divisions, instead of the thirty-five (including three airborne divisions) which was the reality." *(Bodyguard).*

That same source says Patton "despised" Montgomery.

The British in England — instead of "putting down" Patton as someone who had questionable credentials, was a braggart, etc., and someone who didn't like their national hero — contributed greatly to the Patton legend by elevating him for the purposes of making FUSAG look good. I mean, where else could they get an unemployed general whom they could pass off to the home fronts (which already believed it) and to the Germans, as one of the world's top generals?

But Patton had *one main characteristic in battle* which Monty specifically *did not have.*

A study of Monty's main features, and Patton's — and that the *leading characteristic of each* was something the *other did not have* — makes interesting reading.

Though Monty could have used Patton's special feature, he was a *complete general* without it.

However, Patton was not a complete general. In point of fact, he was a specialist.

The fortunes of war were such that Patton's specialty got more "ink" than the great qualities of all-round generalhood possessed by *many* men in the War. In a way, that shows the immaturity of the press and of (especially) the U.S. "home front" of that time.

But at the same time, the War at that time needed Patton's particular specialty.

Long after the War, Ike (who had a lot of experience with Monty in France), would tell Walter Cronkite (in the CBS D-Day plus Twenty Years feature), that the British General (about whom Ike was always carefully complimentary in public during the War), was a master of "set-piece" battle. This was mildly uncomplimentary, given the setting.

A plan had to be involved before, during, and after anything with which Monty was connected. In the absence of a carefully worked-out plan, one did nothing, of course.

Monty used maneuver, and used it well — as at Mareth — but it was a carefully-controlled, precise, and sparingly-used, capability.

In the accurate movie, *A Bridge Too Far,* British armor was held up — to the exasperation of the Americans — at a moment when an exploitation opportunity was clearly open. (Americans tend to have freedom within their plans, and to recognize goals in such as way as to take advantage of the "breaks").

Throughout his career, Montgomery tended to make the carrying out of the precise plan the *goal* — at any rate, putting it ahead of the breaks.

After El Alamein, Monty let the Desert Fox get away. At the very least, he had no plans to cut him off and finish him. He was criticized for not taking advantage of the breaks, but the British General did his type of orderly job — and did it superbly. This same type of careful work won for him in the earlier defensive role at Alam Halfa.

To have broken out from El Alamein in a big, unplanned, take-the-breaks chase of Rommel would have been, to Monty, disorderly.

Patton, on the other hand, was a "make-the-breaks" and "take-the-breaks" commander.

He like the disarray of breakthrough — and scorned those who didn't use it.

Patton was a genius at racing ahead, and at making remarkably good decisions in the field, day by day, hour by hour. Of course, had Patton fallen in combat, his army could have been jeopardized, for so much of the knowledge of dispositions and intents was in his head.

Was he like Guderian, Rommel, and a handful of other brilliant spearhead generals who rode with their men, were never far from the smoke and flame, led charmed lives, and were masters at exploiting breakthroughs? In some ways. But to be a top general (as Guderian, who fathered the Blitzkrieg, led armies, and finally served for a time in 1945 as Army Chief of Staff), or even a top field commander (as Rommel), a general must be a "generalist" as well as have several specialties!

Patton was a specialist — perhaps one of the five top armored exploiters of the War. As a "generalist" he lacked the patience, methodicalness, willingness to plan ahead, ability to work with other officers, and on and on. "Patton could seldom be bothered with details" *(Encyclopedia of World War II)*.

He was no "general" in the usual sense. And he often proved he could not be used as a regular general. Further, he, at the least, was patronizing toward real generals (such as Bradley), or scorned them (by the dozen), or "despised" them (such as Monty — a truly great one, in his classifications).

And Patton had negatives which were so uncharacteristic of a *soldier* that it is remarkable he kept any command — or even his uniform! He was wild, undisciplined — and disobedient. He would have been quickly removed in the German Army, and — unless he had a big Prussian name — met a firing squad. He "disobeyed Eisenhower's orders" *(Bodyguard)*. Patton had "almost total disregard of orders and of orthodox military methods" *(Encyclopedia of World War II)*.

For his genuine talent — exploitation of breakthroughs —

Patton should have been a division commander, or, at best a corps commander. In France, he was really a large corps commander — in the sense that whereas a corps might become detached, it is rare that an army would become detached. But he had corps under him, and enough men to constitute an army.

What made him a *general* of such stature that even the Germans considered him the number one commander to watch? The thing that brought him up from talented specialist, offset his negatives, and lifted him above division or corps functions, was *his amazing way with fighting men.* Even the Germans recognized this astonishing combat spirit that flowed through him, electrified his men, and caused even his enemies to admire him.

Let's proceed to France, and step for a few minutes into the shoes of the man who had to live with commanders of these diverse talents, and see how he used the capabilities of each. The plans were made in advance, but we'll follow the dates below.

By mid-July (1944), the Western Allies were still contained in their expanded Normandy perimeter — having taken only a fraction of the territory they had wanted by that time. The line was drawn from about Caen, west through St. Lo, and across the base of the Carentan Peninsula to the sea. Plans had been made for another attempt at breaking out.

Monty had the northern end of the line, and could not break out. But he was holding a number of enemy divisions fully engaged, and giving them fits, and requiring that more Germans be sent as reinforcements. All this was one part of his assignment.

Patton was officially still in England (ready to launch FUSAG against Calais), but was actually in Normandy, where he was briefed on what was to come. He then held a *news conference* and told the reporters things they shouldn't have heard — and also, by his acts, revealed his presence in Normandy, which could have blown the entire Calais program and brought at least several German divisions down upon the Normandy perimeter! *(Bodyguard).*

What commander could take the Allies out of the perimeter? Not Monty (who had tried); not Bradley (who had tried); *not*

Patton (who couldn't be fastidiously obedient in every detail, as was so necessary at this point).

The decision came to rest not with a special commander, but with a *plan* — an intense coordination by skilled, obedient professionals.

Previous efforts had used intense bombing and shelling ("Operation Goodword") and shown much promise. The Germans were just dug in too well against that effort by Monty. If Monty (who was technically, although not practically, the commander of all ground forces until September, when Ike came ashore and officially assumed this), had taken charge of the southern sector, he *could* have chopped through on the St. Lo plan. However, the problems no one likes to discuss — his friction with Ike, his refusals to come to staff meetings except when he felt like it, his dislike of serving under Ike — made placing him in charge of a *plan* which required such coordination, impossible. Also, Monty was not an exploitation man — and long-distance breakthrough was the *only* object. Could Monty be told this face-to-face — and would he relinquish charge of the breakthrough after he accomplished it? And would he relinquish it to that old rival George Patton? No to both questions.

But the "Goodwood" shelling and bombing program had shown that breakout *was* accomplishable where the Nazis were not as dug-in. So that was the plan — the most intense saturation of an area about four miles wide by about one and one half miles deep, using "carpet bombing" for the first time. Many U.S. troops were killed by accident. Unable to move the first day, the bombardment was repeated for two days — and on July 28, the Germans pulled out. The three U.S. corps which accomplished the task on the ground moved forward to Avranches by July 30.

Only then could Patton be given charge. Ike wanted an *exploitation* that would take advantage on the spot of every break — an almost uncontrolled exploitation. Thus *Ike used Patton in the only, and best, way Patton could be used.* This needed the permission of Bradley, Patton's immediate superior. Patton was "given his head," headlines — and even gasoline air-dropped to him in special rubber bags developed for him.

Montgomery was much more a general than was Patton, because he was an all-round "generalist" with several specialties.

Patton is especially interesting due to his extraordinary ability as an exploitation specialist, plus his ability to galvanize men, plus his remarkable field decisions. These things enabled him to rise way over his absence of "generalist" qualities — and his almost self-destructive negatives — to top command, plus a place in legend with the top generals of the War.

Comparison of the two men is interesting, because it pops Montgomery's qualities into sharp focus.

But especially interesting is the fact that the one (and only) really absent element in Monty's military makeup — exploitation with those hourly decisions — should be Patton's main (and nearly only, save for his gift with men), genuine top rank military qualification.

At El Alamein, Rommel didn't have a fighting chance.

Myth Eleven

That Patton Could Have, And Should Have, "Kept On Going"

After the War, many said — and believed — that "Patton should have kept on going" and defeated troublesome Russia. His Third Army, though, was only one-tenth of the ninety Western divisions, facing about 300 Russian divisions. Patton couldn't have gone five miles — but he could have caused Russia to "keep on coming."

Patton's Third Army was but one of *seven* armies on the Western Front! These were in three Army Groups. Montgomery's Twenty-first Army Group commanded the Canadian First Army, the British Second Army, and the U.S. Ninth Army. Bradley's Twelfth Army Group commanded the U.S. First Army and the U.S. Third Army. Dever's Sixth Army Group commanded the U.S. Seventh Army and the French First Army.

Patton didn't even command an Army Group.

The Third Army was picked and supported to do a certain job — and performed magnificently.

Near the Siegfried Line between September and November 1944, his command totaled only nine divisions in three corps, totaling (I imagine this would include support personnel) about 250,000 men *(Encyclopedia of World War II)*. Thus he commanded only about one-tenth of the ninety or so Western Front divisions.

The idea that Patton — no matter how mythologized — could have "kept on going," is fallacious.

Only the opposite picture contained any reality at all — the Allied fear that Patton might provoke the Russians and give *them* an excuse to "keep on coming."

Patton, soaked in headlines which the "home fronts" drank up avidly — ripped through weakened German forces. There were major phases.

First, the relatively easy run from Avranches after the breakout, turning the Falaise-Argentan flank, opening the way for the French to occupy Paris, racing eastward and joining with the "Anvil" invasion force from Southern France, and moving by September to the Siegfried Line.

Second, some tough battles in September, October, and November, along this line — where, for the first time since the breakout, the German forces were about equal in strength to the Western Allies (except in the air, where the Allies still had the colossal advantage of total supremacy).

Third, the setbacks in December (lasting into January), relating to the Bulge. And fourth, the move beyond the Rhine in March, when it was all over but the shouting.

These campaigns were not against the world's greatest military competition.

At the Rhine, the West had eighty-five divisions on the entire Western Front in March. One source writes, "The German forces were so depleted that though Field Marshal Albert Kesselring mustered sixty divisions to face the Allies, they were so understrength that only about twenty-six full-strength divisions could be made up of the decimated forces" *(Dictionary)*.

Patton was, of course, the spearhead. The West's eyes were upon the broken field runner, and ignored most of the rest of the team and organization.

Without the huge, self-effacing support of an immense, unheadlined, organization on the rest of the Western Front, and behind all of it, Patton's roman candle would have quickly fizzled. But a great deal of that organization, including other armies on his flanks, were committed to keeping his spearheads surging.

Patton had only one sector of the Western Front. Entering Germany, it was about 100 miles of about 400. A study of the various sectors reveals quickly that, had Patton not come along, the Western Front would still have progressed nicely. (However, without Patton's example and all-round excitement amounting to a type of battle inspiration, no doubt with less flair, in slower steps (not much, though), and with more casualties). At the Rhine in March, it was the U.S. First Army, also in Bradley's Army Group, that captured the Remagen Bridge. The First Army was also fast with spearheads. The Third Army crossed to the south, around Mainz, looped north to close a pocket with the First Army on its left, and then raced to the stopping line (the Elbe's tributary in that sector, the Mulde), then swung south along the Czech border, across the front of the Seventh Army sector, and across the front of the French First Army sector — as those armies turned south into Austria by design, or for something to do other than watching Big George.

Toward the end, hordes of German uniformed troops surrendered — tired of years of combat. They were beaten, ill-supplied, disorganized, and hopeful of surrendering to the Western Allies instead of to the Russians. Patton — having turned south all along the lower front — naturally took in many of these. Mystically, these huge numbers appear as "casualties" inflicted on the enemy (captured) — making the "stats" contribute to Patton's (and also to the U.S.') superman image.

From publicity, imagery, and mythology, one can get the impression that Patton commanded, or at least led — in the sense of being out in front of — the *entire* Western Allied forces. (One thing that has puzzled me from the last year of the War to the present, is the overlooking, by the press, of some of the amazing corps commanders, and division commanders — some of whom were in the St. Lo breakout before Patton reappeared, and who went all the way with the U.S. First Army or Patton to the final line).

Was there really no one to talk about except the superhero? What was this phenomenon?

It was years of pentup desire for signs of superiorism for the

U.S., plus nearly two months of terrific tension within the Normandy perimeter before the breakout.

The coincidence of Patton with the sudden release from the awful perimeter, and the quick "motoring" of the Third Army (won through the previous, but dull, and even horrible, attrition), created a shining blaze of glory fed by the realization that the end was near.

This angered Montgomery to no end. But the people wanted the brightly shining new knight. The press wanted this. The military effort wanted this.

And the "home front" wanted myths. People wanted to believe the flash, dash, and omnipotence.

The press fanned and fed the public appetite and psychic needs for a superhero — a hero who could stand above all heroes.

A hero who could go — *all the way through.*

Even if Patton had commanded *all* of the forces of the Western Allies (as so many believed anyhow) — and even if he had the full support of the Western nations to "keep on going" (a point in which he had absolutely no support, and instead an immediate desire to shut him up and remove him from command) — he could not have whipped the Russians.

The Western Allies at their best were spare, lean, well-mechanized and air-supported armies totaling some 2,000,000 men in the line, reserve, and support roles to a depth of about 100 miles (plus some more in the ports, etc.). (As an indication, the U.S. announced on May 10 (1945) that 3,100,000 U.S. troops would be withdrawn from Europe. That would presumably include Italy). *(Almanac).* They were facing some 7,000,000 Russians in the line, reserve, and support roles in the battle zones (plus another 5,000,000 under arms somewhere in the back, for a total under arms of some 12,000,000). (The U.S. also had 12,000,000 under arms, but most of these were in the U.S., many were in the Pacific War, and many were in the large Navy. Too, the U.S. maintained a far greater ratio of support to combat personnel than the Russians).

The Russian line divisions were less mechanized, but more

heavily equipped with artillery. They had battlefield air supremacy, with pilots who had wrested this (and much of the Western battlefield air freedom) away from the Germans, plane by plane. The Western Allied ground forces were capable fighters, but had done almost all of their fighting without significant challenge from the air.

Thus, tangling with the Reds would have produced two new "climates" — a two-to-one superiority in every ground department, plus plenty of close battlefield air opposition.

Comparing supply lines, the Russians were vastly more able to supply their hordes than the U.S. was able to get supplies to the Western Allies. Every pound of Western support involved a Channel crossing — and most of it an ocean crossing before that. Besides, at best, the Western effort was precisely tailored to do the exact job at hand — no more, no less.

The Russians were massively supplied — even over-supplied in departments such as ammunition — from their interior, overland routes. They were angry, and intended to keep the Eastern European countries they had captured as a permanent buffer to prevent any more invasions (two costly ones within twenty-five years, plus many previous), or other surprises from occurring. Mentally and physically, they had plenty of excess with which they could have punched on through the Western forces if desired.

To keep on coming, the Russians would not have to consult their population. But the U.S. — to "keep on going" — would have to consult populace, Congress, and the military.

In a pinch — and if the fight was not going to be too hard — the Russians could have motivated their troops with simple orders, backed up with customary junior officer's pistol. However, as discussed in an earlier chapter, Russia would not have risked a *hard* fight. It had a long history of troop rebellions passive and active. To plan to "keep on coming" for a hard fight, it would need a new emotional reason to replace the emotion released after Germany's collapse.

Patton's wishes and fantasies — and his inflammatory

remarks towards the Russians — never had the faintest support from any of the Western Allies. Quite the contrary, it made them very nervous — lest he give the Reds an emotional reason to keep on coming.

Russia's secret desires were unknown. The West sought to avoid any hidden "trigger."

Patton's ego was overextended at the War's end. His nature was unruly enough to have sent his divisions into the Russians on some pretext — regardless of support. Such an act would have done no more than dent the surprised Bear. But it could have started an unstoppable Russian forward march.

Neither Patton nor the entire Western Allies could have "kept on going" — but Patton could have given the Reds a reason to "keep on coming."

Myth Twelve

That MacArthur's Congressional Medal Of Honor Was Given For His Bravery

I am an admirer of General MacArthur. However, his Congressional Medal of Honor, given in Australia after leaving Corregidor, was not awarded for his bravery but by the U.S. Government to cover up its dishonorable and cold-blooded decision to write off Bataan and Corregidor. The real Medal of Honor for the valor of the force which fought and stayed there went, more than three years later, to General Wainwright, who accepted it for every member of the ill-fated force.

As an admirer of General MacArthur, I am not questioning his personal bravery, or his escape from Corregidor — he was ordered out by the President of the United States, and wisely so. I am focusing upon other circumstances in which the medal was bestowed, including the hidden motives of the bestowers, who had to cover their cowardly failure, and their cold-blooded decision, in writing off the Bataan and Corregidor contingents of U.S. and Filipino troops and nurses. A cover-up of dishonorable, deliberate, and hidden acts by people in high places in the U.S. Government was best accomplished by awarding Mac a Congressional Medal of Honor in Australia after leaving Corregidor. This redirected public thought away from the abandonment of all efforts to help our forces.

I am certain that — along with all other humans — MacArthur had some faults; and that, along with all other leaders in critical positions in world and national affairs, he could not have had a 100% batting average in decision-making. But I certainly rate him in the upper group of important world figures during his lifetime. He was an excellent leader and motivator; his staff work was the most thorough of the War; and he was number one in economical use of his men.

MacArthur's Congressional Medal of Honor could not have been offered to him for valor at that time, because his valor — although fine — did not exceed the valor of those he left behind.

Ostensibly, the Medal was for the purpose of making a valorous thing out of the entire Bataan-Corregidor situation. This was easy to do, because the situation was valorous in the highest degree. However, there were flaws in extending that real, valorous situation to Mac. One, the valorous battlers had not finished their battle, when Mac had left; and two, if anyone got a medal it should be someone there.

Nevertheless, one source speaks of, "the heroic stand on Luzon . . . where they were forced to capitulate during April and May 1942," and says, "For this gallant defense MacArthur was awarded the medal of honor" *(Encyclopedia Britannica)*.

Which leads us to question what was below the surface — what was not immediately apparent to the eye.

Below the surface, unseen to the public, the U.S. had made a cold-blooded decision to write off the Bataan-Corregidor situation and go on to the next war business at hand.

The brave battlers, however, were certain to the last that a U.S. naval force would appear over the horizon and relieve them. It was incomprehensible to them that the U.S. would not do everything in its power to save them. (Even before Mac left, "He was buoyed by the belief that the Navy would come and relieve [the Philippines] — but Washington misled him . . ." — *The Commanders*).

The Pacific situation was so bad in reality that the U.S., from one point of view, could almost be excused for not helping Bataan and Corregidor. The public knew that little could be done. However, the public believed that the Government was doing all that it *could* do.

Therefore, there were four hidden negatives practiced by the

Government: one, it had coldly decided to abandon the brave troops and nurses; two, it was not making any meaningful effort, nor was it making any plans, to aid, relieve, or remove the defenders; three, it deliberately conned the public that it was making an effort, was planning an effort, and had not written off the defenders; and, four, it took of the true fire of heroism and, at a place remote from the scene, fashioned a redeeming symbol which would hold the public's attention away from the facts for some forty years.

The Government felt that *any* expenditure of transport, man-power, or equipment would be — even if partly successful — a waste in the long run! It felt that anything available could be better used elsewhere. It felt that anything available should be husbanded in order to make a "real" effort later, in some other place.

Early in the situation, a few small supply vessels were sent from Cebu, elsewhere in the Philippines, but these "blockade runners" were sunk. One source lists these efforts in January, when "fifteen [vessels] totaling 40,000 tons, were sunk trying to carry supplies from Cebu" *(Almanac).* I can find no other references — including no references to any attempts at assistance from outside the Philippines. (One reference, in one source, to "reinforcements of 2,000 men" coming to Corregidor, was easily identified from other sources as being merely 2,000 troops trans-ferring over from the besieged Bataan!) That was it.

Mac came out March 11.

Wainwright moved his headquarters from Bataan March 21.

Bataan fell April 9.

Corregidor was invaded May 5.

The island fell May 6.

Effectively, for those final three months, a very high level decision unmatched in cold blood in the U.S. in the War had been made. It was, simply, to write off the Bataan-Corregidor battle, hope the screams of the dying hopefuls would soon end, and meanwhile go on to more pressing matters which had more of a long-range, strategic character.

FOUR GOVERNMENT NEGATIVES HIDDEN BY THE MEDAL

Under the Medal, the Government hid, first, its cold-blooded decision to abandon the warriors and nurses of Bataan and Corregidor. Second, it hid the fact that it was not making any meaningful effort to aid, relieve, or remove them — or any plans in that direction. Third, it hid its "con" of the public that it had not written off the defenders, and was making an effort, and had plans of some sort. And fourth, it stole some of the true fire of the heroism of that locale, and, at a remote place, fashioned a redeeming symbol which would hold the public's attention away from the facts for some forty years.

Was it right to order MacArthur out of the Philippines? Yes — most readers would have made a similar decision. He was a bit more than a general. He was a future asset of major stature in the struggle to retake the Pacific. He knew the area well, from his lifetime spent there. He knew the peoples well. Furthermore, the retaking of the Pacific would require the cooperation of Allies. MacArthur could command the necessary respect.

Was MacArthur's personal valor ever in question, anywhere? Yes, it was in question — but there was never any substance behind the question.

Did he spend too much time in Malinta Tunnel and truly earn the nickname "Dugout Doug"? I doubt it. I don't think he stayed in the tunnels any more than necessary. And I also don't believe he could have done any good if he had been topside — or over on the Peninsula. I say this for several reasons. One, he knew there was no hope for the defenders — so why go out and risk spreading that news from the top? If MacArthur had spent a lot of time with the battlefield commanders, in time his inner thoughts would have become obvious. Too, the battlefield was for the corps and division commanders, and for the regiments, battalions, and companies. He was an area commander — at that moment a "field marshal," so to speak, and soon to become Allied Supreme Commander in the Southwest Pacific. He didn't belong in the lines at that time. (In World War I, he was a battle-field officer, notorious for exposing himself leading his troops). If he had appeared, all eyes would have been on him — uselessly — and this would have detracted from the battlefield commanders, whose field and battle it was.

The worst criticisms of MacArthur I've heard have been from European Theatre personnel. The fewest criticisms have been from Pacific Theatre people.

The fiercest criticism of him I ever heard was a direct impugning of his courage — charging him with coming ashore at beaches days after the landings, while claiming in the press to have come ashore the day of the landings. One critic said public relations people caused "dead Japs" to be brought up and strewn about before the General walked ashore in the surf.

That particular criticism was exploded for me by a TV documentary of the 1970s, in which one of Mac's staff officers said simply that at Luzon (where most of the criticisms had emerged), there were several beaches. MacArthur came ashore on the first day at the first beach — but a day later at each of the others, making the fifth beach on the fifth day. The General himself was interested in having his picture taken on the first day, but the public relations machine he had encouraged covered him on all beaches on all days. Hence the troops on the later beaches assumed he was taking credit on, for example, the fifth day, for coming ashore on the first.

The General was theatrical, as all readers know. Ike, who was a major and a staff officer under Mac before the War, later said he "studied theatrics under him for years." (MacArthur had a dig of his own for Ike, saying he was the "best damn clerk I ever had"). So much for the roar of the heavy cannons! But each also had compliments for the other — including a salient point about Ike, that he "could see things from the standpoint of the top command" (a facility which, once pointed out, could be an unseen reason behind Ike's meteoric rise).

Part of MacArthur's wartime theatrics was deliberately created for, and aimed at, the "home front." After all, the Pacific was "second fiddle" to the European Theatre! He helped put the Pacific on the front pages in America, and obtained many special priorities. In all this, he had plenty of help from the U.S. Navy — which had a long tradition of knowing how to stay on the front pages (and which considered much of the Pacific War to be the Navy's war).

> **Part of Mac's theatrics was designed to put the Pacific War — which was "second fiddle" to Europe — in first place on U.S. front pages.**

To return to Mac's personal valor in WWII, I know at least three stories in which he and his staff were under direct fire near the lines on the shore. Everyone "hit the dirt" — except Mac! Some officers involved felt humiliated by him — and subjected him to criticism. I've heard more criticisms that showed his extraordinary courage than I've heard criticisms of the reverse. And, importantly, the incidents of his courage were eye-witnessed, while the negative comments on his valor were mere yappings from remote places. General Whitney, his chief of staff, has both written and been interviewed for film. He has expressed admiration — but embarrassment — at looking up from the dirt, after a shell exploded, or bullets flew by — to see Mac standing serenely, untouched.

Of course, those who "hit the dirt" were perfectly correct in doing so. And they were correct to train their men, and require them, to take cover. I'm not sure what point MacArthur was making by never hitting the dirt — because it went against the best rules of training. But he was making some point — probably the legend.

The real Bataan and Corregidor bravery medal — standing for the bravery of all the forces throughout the defeat, Death March, and years of further indignities (which included transport of some to Manchuria where germ experiments were carried out)

— was rightfully General Wainwright's, and was awarded at the end of the War.

(In the movie, "MacArthur," which was supposed to be accurate as to factual matters, Roosevelt was reported as asking MacArthur in 1942, if Wainwright should get a Congressional Medal of Honor that year — and MacArthur is reported as saying no. If this is true, then I think it was ungracious of Mac. However, within his ego-framework, this was predictable, because Mac had to stand out. That ego-framework, though, was not negative to the nation, but positive in nine points, to one point of negative items).

The real Bataan-Corregidor Congressional Medal of Honor finally came in 1945, after the Japanese surrender and Wainwright's release. It was awarded, I believe, by Mac himself to the emaciated general. If Wainwright had not survived the War, the Medal would surely have been awarded posthumously, because it was the true recognition of the valor of that entire command.

As so often happens with history, the action keeps our attention, while we don't see behind the scenes.

As to Bataan and the Rock, no one looked deeper — and no one wanted to look deeper.

But, after the War, the package became subject to unravelling.

On any deep examination, the write-off decision, with multiple misleadings of the public, becomes obvious.

As so often in history, the action keeps our attention, while we don't see behind the scenes.

In sum, General MacArthur's valor was never questionable. But the bestowal on him by our Government of a Congressional Medal of Honor for Bataan and Corregidor covered up an act of dishonor in high U.S. places — that of deliberately abandoning those contingents. The real Medal of Honor for those who stayed in the Manila Bay area went — though more than three years later — to General Wainwright, who accepted it for every member of the ill-fated force.

Myth Thirteen

That U.S. Armaments Were Vital To Russian Victory

U.S. arms were only a moral support for the Russians, but 500,000 trucks we sent them materially helped them win their war.

U.S. arms shipped to Russia gave that beleaguered nation evidence that there were real allies out there who could, and did, ship weapons of war, planes, ammunition, etc.

But the only times Russia has acknowledged that our armaments materially aided them have been occasions when such statements were "obligatory" — for example, state functions involving the U.S. and Russia (or, during the War itself, when more help was wanted).

Russia is incredibly vast. Its war was too huge for the trickle of American arms to have helped much in turning battle tides.

Also, Russia was a much larger producer of war goods than the West realizes! For example, it produced 106,230 fighter and attack planes, compared to U.S. production of a little more than 120,000 such planes. Of U.S. production, 7,300 Airacobras, Kingcobras, and Thunderbolts are statistically shown as "delivered" to Russia (but is this shipped and ferried, or received?). Thus, our contribution was only six or seven percent of the Russian fleet. (This is not intended to "play down" our part. Our contribution was there, and it was substantial — but it was small in the gigantic scale of things in that struggle. *(Almanac)*.

The Russians have often said that armaments help was there — but that it was not all that significant. When we study that war,

and get a glimpse of the colossal scale of things, the Russian statement becomes not a "put down," but the truth.

What about tanks? Again, Russia was a "world class"producer of its own tanks in enormous numbers. Tank statistics are
frequently conflicting, but when pure tanks are separated out,
those figures are lower, but concrete. For example, pure tank
numbers drop when separated from other tracked vehicles (such
as halftracks, gun carriages, and prime movers), and from
"armored vehicles" in general (such as personnel carriers on
tires, and light armored vehicles on tires — and even vehicles
carrying gun mounts).

Russia produced about 54,000 pure tanks — some 40,000
T-34s of two types alone. Germany produced less than 20,000
pure tanks. Very little more need be said. (The U.S. produced a
little more than 60,000, some 50,000 of which were Shermans).
Exactly how many Western Allied tanks were shipped to Russia,
and how many got there, is probably not known. But the number
was not tide-turning. The tide was turned in the tank department
by Russia's own two-to-one production superiority over
Germany.

As to tanks — and all armaments — Russia said, "thanks,"
but made it clear that these didn't help much.

I don't believe we shipped much artillery. The Russians had
enough artillery to blow away half the world.

Our armaments didn't help materially — but they helped in
the morale department, particularly in the early going. More on
that later below.

Though they were a peasant land, in their new industrial areas
back of the Urals, they understood *standardization*. They could
train peasant labor. They could be inefficient by Western
standards, but still pour out the standardized items which seldom
changed during the entire War.

Russia smashed Germany into the dust — and would have
done so without any U.S. arms aid.

The British used the Arctic Convoy Route to ship a lot of
armaments to the Russians. This was a most perilous route —

subject to such cruisers as the *Scharnhorst,* lying in some Norwegian fjord in the fog, or aerial attack from a number of bases also in the north of Norway.

The overall record of the Murmansk and Archangel runs was good — but, as with the North Atlantic, the tonnage that made the record look acceptable came late, after dedicated blood had stained a red carpet in the seas.

The "over the top" route was most famed for two things: one, in the winter of 1941-42, Russia was on the ropes (and the U.S. was occupied with Pearl Harbor and Bataan), and Churchill most feared that Russia would *seek a separate peace.* Therefore, the morale and support factor took precedence over the material benefit of the arms shipments. It is a fact that the convoys were maintained at all and any cost — even when the material benefit was questioned — in order to show dogged and even sacrificial support for the Reds if they would unwaveringly stand until the day grew brighter.

(I suspect some of the plain lies told to Stalin in 1942 — that we would have a second front in Europe that year (which story was later moved to 1943) — also had something to do with making certain that Russia stayed in the fight).

(One source declares that, much later, it was firmly decided that Stalin never intended making a separate peace under any circumstances. That is obviously just an opinion, because who could know the mind of Stalin when even Zhukov didn't? But if so, perhaps then "Uncle Joe" was engaging in a little "gamesmanship" of his own with the West — to see what scare tactics would produce in the way of assistance).

Personally, with Russians dropping dead in the streets of Leningrad that winter from starvation, Germans in the suburbs of Moscow, and several million armed Russians captured or killed or dead of wounds within six months of a surprise attack, I would believe that Russia was genuinely on the ropes, and playing no games with the West!

The other thing for which the Arctic Route was especially famous was Convoy PQ-17. This, in the summer of 1942, lost twenty-five of its thirty-six ships to enemy action on the way to

Russia. If the Russians didn't take the British effort as seriously as they might have, the Germans certainly did! (Were more ships lost coming back? I can find no record of the return trip).

Catastrophic losses such as those were not the rule, but the *danger* of such devastation was always present. Weather was the main ally, especially fog.

Of particular interest to readers of this chapter, is the distribution of types of cargo lost on PQ-17: tanks 430, aircraft 210 — and *vehicles* 3,350.

This illustrates the heavy proportion of transport to other items.

Trucks were Russia's desperate need.

The U.S. used mainly the Persian route for movement of supplies into Russia. The Pacific and Indian Oceans did not have the submarine danger of the North Atlantic. A very large base was built in Iran.

Whatever tanks the U.S. shipped direct came by this southern route. Russia has marvelous film footage of *its* tanks in action — but one never sees an American tank. I would guess that few came in — and that these were used in the southernmost portions of the front — the less important sectors, and closest to U.S. spare parts and ammunition coming up from once-friendly Iran.

(As a side note, most of the Arab and other Moslem peoples of that region during the War were in tribes. England often controlled several of the "nations" of the Mideast with a mere handful of troops. As a second side note, Russia today can come down the Caucasus or the east side of the Caspian, into Iran, just as supplies flowed up during the War).

An aircraft ferry route existed via Alaska to Siberia to the front. In the TV "documentary" *The Unknown War,* Burt Lancaster had an interview with a Russian general who had helped ferry Airacobras from Alaska! The general liked the plane, but said the numbers were insignificant — and implied that it was a nuisance, bother, and risk to go fetch them! He also said, in so many words, that all other U.S. help — though no one was going to say, "keep the stuff" — was not much help at all! He was ruder than the older line after the War — but smoother.

Whereas no U.S. tanks appeared in pictures of the Russian Front, the U.S. Airacobra has indeed appeared. The Russian pilots were proud of the plane. Apparently it performed as well as their Stormovik Il-2. The planes were very similar — both with small cannons firing exploding shells continuously, like a machine gun. But the Airacobra and Kingcobra each carried one 37 mm (in the nose) — which is about one and one half inches in diameter, while the Russian Il-2 carried 2 23 mm. (The Il-2m3 was a two-seater, and became the most popular close-support plane in the war. The later Il-10 was also a "Stormovik," but was twin-engined, and carried 3 20 mm).

Russia smashed Germany into the dust — and would have done so without any U.S. arms aid.

What about *transport* shipped in from the U.S.? Was this a material help to Russia in winning its war?

Definitely, yes. U.S. trucks greatly aided the Russians.

General John Eisenhower — interviewed by ABC's "Nightline" as he stood above the Normandy beaches on the Fortieth Anniversary of D-Day — said, "We sent a half-million deuce-and-a-half trucks to Russia during the War."

There it is.

Translated, that's 500,000 two-and-one-half-ton trucks — standard Army trucks.

A half-million is a big figure, compared to, say, 7,300 planes. (Again, this is not to belittle the effort in planes. It is to put things into their factual perspectives).

Is it possible, then, that a huge assistance to Russia was indeed rendered but hidden — hidden in truck figures?

The answer is, Yes.

Let's go deeper into this topic: At the start of the War, there was little motorized equipment in Russia.

Also, there were few roads other than the plainest dirt type. Most "good" roads were what we would call improved dirt roads — clay, gravel, perhaps elevated a bit, with ditches. There were very few surfaced roads — and those just covered with thin coatings waiting to break up in heavy usage. (*Atlas* says Russia lacked "metalled" roads — a British term for hard-surfaced roads).

The Russians knew how to make farm tractors of a crude sort. These would go on any terrain.

As the War started, they quickly learned how to build the world's best tanks, which could also go on nearly any terrain! These were crude and standard — and they became plentiful!

But they *didn't* know how to make trucks — at least, not really good trucks, and not in necessary quantities. This is a strange fact — but it tied in with their lack of what we would call roads.

As the Russian offensives began to move rapidly westward early in 1943, they could cover 400 miles between pauses. The logistics were stupendous (just the artillery ammunition consumed couldn't be calculated, not to mention food, petrol, rockets). Mere horses, mules, and hosts of backpacking infantry support troops could not marshal in rear areas, or transport to the front, the sustaining supplies. The truck — even though it could not negotiate in all areas — was a necessity.

The truck had to be rugged. The old stick-shift two-and-a-half was such a truck. U.S. servicepeople swore by it (and cussed and wept later in the early 1950s, when the new automatic-transmission models came in).

Do you remember those pictures of the U.S. supply bases for Russia in Iran? What did the pictures show? Trucks, trucks — and more trucks.

Trucks were the way we moved the supplies into Russia.

And trucks were part of the supplies!

Enormous numbers of trucks — way beyond the numbers of any other items shipped the Reds — went to help their cause and ours.

The War brought Russia into — or at least toward — the 20th Century.

But consider this: Long after the War, the Russians contracted with the Ford Motor Company to build for it the largest heavy truck plant in the world at that time, at the Kama River — capable of producing 100,000 heavy trucks per year.

At the same time, it came out that Russia still had a badly developed road system (although of course much better than the primitive years of 1941-45).

It came out that Russia in the *1960s* still lagged the world in automobile production — partly due to lack of roads outside the few main cities, and partly due to not wanting the workers to have anything!

In the 1960s, Russia was planning to develop its Siberian oil deposits. This would lead to products for surfacing roads — and to gasoline to power automobiles, and so on. The world could see that Russia was beginning to look in the direction of measuring up to a Western standard (and thus, hopefully, to a more enlightened system!) To develop its oil, it looked to American technology, hired U.S. firms, swiped U.S. drilling-bit technology, and got busy — twenty, forty, even sixty years behind everyone else.

Now it's the 1980s. Russia *still* has a lousy automobile industry!

All this confirms the case that Russia — although it has never wanted to admit it — did not have much truck-producing capability during the War. It received vast quantities of trucks from the U.S. during that time — and this materially helped it win its war.

500,000 trucks — outnumbering by dozens of times major armament items shipped the Reds — went to help them defeat Germany.

U.S. armaments didn't help Russia much. Yet, the U.S. *materially helped.* It may be unromantic, but the help was in truck transport.

Myth Fourteen

That The Bombing Of Germany Wasn't Effective

> For twenty-five years after the War, a school steadily developed which claimed the big strategic bombings of German military, industrial, and civilian targets (not battlefield close support, or medium-range tactical strikes such as bridges, etc.), had no real effect, and were instead *counterproductive* — actually helping the enemy against us. In reality the situation was the reverse — and much more devastating than even advocates believed.

After the War, a deep revulsion to the bombing of cities hit Great Britain (and, soon after, the U.S. in reaction to its bombing of Japan). Germany had been utterly devastated, but many chose to avert their eyes and minds. At some point, accurate statistics appeared which showed conclusively that German war production had *risen* during the last two years of the War. This made many people feel that the bombings had indeed been useless and unnecessary, as well as savage. As the school grew which claimed the bombings were ineffective, new voices added the concept that rubbleized cities had made Germany easier to defend, and had cost the lives of many invading Allied ground troops. (Some even claimed the rubbleized cities were easier for Germans to live in). A second great wave of revulsion hit (especially in the U.S.) in the late 1960s and early 1970s, when the general public there accepted the Dresden and Hamburg obliteration raids for the first time. When the War was rewritten in the 1970s, all factors concerning the bombings had surfaced — and it could be seen that the raids were not less, but far more effective than even many advocates had believed. ↓

Let's go back to the revulsion that set in after World War II.

From the "revulsion factor" — as much as from any other thing — stemmed elements of the myth of the ineffectiveness of the bombing.

The British were a lot closer to the War than the Americans. Their revulsion was deep. They had experienced the awful attacks on their cities in late 1940 and early 1941. Later — around D-Day and after — they underwent the horrible V-1 and V-2 rocketing of London and some other cities. So civilians there knew what it was like on the ground.

The British civilians also knew what the Allies were doing to German cities. Returning airmen told plenty of stories indicating that most bomb loads were not going on "military and industrial" targets (the main euphemism) at all, but on civilians. There was a growing sick feeling about the type of bombing.

Immediately after the end of the War, one of Britain's greatest heroes, General "Bomber" Harris, commander of the British effort, fell into disfavor and was not awarded the medals and positions that were expected.

In the U.S., the mythologizing press easily maintained the "shiny" concept of strategic bombing. Basically, fliers were glamorous and made "good copy." We were depicted as only hitting industrial targets with our precision Norden bombsight. The U.S. remained innocent, basically, of the horrors of its bombings in Europe until *long* after the War.

(However, the U.S. had more than a wave of revulsion following its use of the A-bombs on Hiroshima and Nagasaki — so it was no stranger to the factor of revulsion).

Let's take a brief look at the development of strategic bombing — its various theories and practices, and some of the coverups used to protect the home front publics from news of such violence carried out in their names.

It's probably correct to begin with pure theory. The sheer

essence was that air power could strike the enemy heartland with such a blow as to *win a war*.

The purest theory would use this as the *only* aggressive action. In other words, in the purest theory, nothing else was needed.

But immediately, the theory must divide as follows: Are we talking about eliminating the civilian heartland or the enemy's military might? Or a mixture?

In ancient sieges, the aggressors would surround the city and starve the population! So that was victory through eliminating the population or its will to fight. (Usually, there was also some military action, but the defeat was wrought upon the civilian population).

As wars grew bigger, the conquest of individual cities was less important in the overall scheme. World War I was fought out on the landscape. When planes were used, they were usually in "close-support" roles bombing and strafing the enemy military.

After Billy Mitchell sank the battleship, even the "Colonel Blimps" of this world changed over to the concept that air power could destroy military targets.

As aircraft ranges grew longer, and bombers were developed (the U.S. had the B-17 in the late 1930s, as an example), the concept of destruction of "military targets" rose quickly.

Three main classifications developed: battlefield close-support; medium-range tactical strikes such as against bridges, trains, troop support areas and ammo dumps; and, lastly "strategic" bombing of "military targets." This last would mean bombing of, for example, an aircraft factory making enemy warplanes. Hence the expansion of this term to "military and industrial targets."

This term, "military and industrial targets" was later to be used as the euphemism for bombing the hell out of civilians! It was the "cover term" for press releases for both Europe and Japan.

When World War II broke out in Poland, the Germans first used the "monster" — ruthless bombing of civilians in a city — in the destruction of a large part of Warsaw. The world agreed it was unnecessary. It was, though, an experimental testing of a new war method. The world then, as we know, turned its head. England and France declared war — but then did nothing, and the ensuing period of about seven months before the invasion of France was known as the "phony war."

On English cities late in 1940 and early in 1941, the Germans made an all-out use of the "monster." They had failed to destroy the RAF, and had internally decided to give up the invasion attempt. Then they launched a devastating attack upon civilian centers in the stated attempt to break civilian morale and bring about surrender.

(As a side note, there are important opinions regarding the beginning of the attacks on civilians. However, I think these (though worthy of study and mention) are incidental. Here they are: The British started bombing as early as May, 1940, after the invasion of France. Some say the first attack (by a mere handful of planes) was near Dusseldorf May 11-12. This was on industrial targets. However, as brought out earlier in this book, something like half the days of the year were overcast. Also, the British did not like day raids due to the exposure to fighter planes, and resultant big losses — so they bombed generally at night. Hitting a specific industrial plant was done only by luck — and if anything at all was hit, it was usually civilians. Thus, even from the start, Germany could — and did — claim that the British were raiding civilians! But of course, the Germans would say this anyhow, because it made "good copy" with which to stir up their "home front" and justify the war of plain aggression they were waging.

(On June 6, French bombers attacked *Berlin*. The plot was thickening.

(The Germans had been bombing British airfields and some industrial areas and London docks. On August 23-24, ten German bombers erred and laid their eggs in the heart of London's civilian areas. The British specifically and statedly retaliated by bombing Berlin. There were only eighty-one planes in the raid. To give an idea of the clumsiness of bombing at that time, only twenty-nine hit the city, while twenty-seven couldn't even find it. Eighteen bombed alternate targets (probably anything with lights burning, or a mere unloading of bombs and a report of "on an alternate target"), seven aborted, and five failed to return. *(Almanac).*

(Reports said this and subsequent raids infuriated Hitler, causing him to order the Luftwaffe to start bombing London civilians. He accused England of bombing "civilian residential quarters and farms and villages," thus earning a harsh "answer" from the Luftwaffe.

(According to the analysis in this book, however, Hitler had already used the "monster" in Poland, and had decided immediately after the failure to knock out the RAF (which date was August 18), to switch methods and attempt to win the war with England by destroying civilian morale through systematic civilian annihilation. The surface talk about "retaliation" for British bombings was just a convenient coverup for both a diabolic action and an action which went far beyond any retaliation and into the attempt to conquer a nation by destroying its civilian population by aerial strategic bombing).

By September, 1940, the fat was in the fire. The Germans bombed civilians deliberately, by day. The British took such a toll (of the not-large German fleet and its elite crews), that the Luftwaffe switched to night raids early in September — a practice that continued except for September 15th. The British had switched earlier.

The Germans couldn't miss London. It was just across the Channel and up the Thames. It was huge — way bigger than Berlin or any complex in Germany. It was impossible to miss.

On the other hand, the British had many problems finding and bombing targets. Cloud cover — shifting after planes left the ground for their long, slow, hazard-filled missions — was number one. Second was enemy action — flak and fighter planes. Third was navigation at night with no radio beacons on the ground, and no light from the ground. (Later, the British were to develop a two-beam system from the north and south of England, crossing at exact points and thus giving the nearly-blind bombers a navigational fix in a grid system). The Germans became adept at placing lights on the ground in such a way as to mislead the bombers and cause the bombs to fall harmlessly.

One pilot likened finding a *city* to finding a needle in a hay-stack. Imagine how much more difficult it would be to find and then accurately bomb a particular aircraft plant!

In those early days of 1940, 1941 and much of 1942, raids were not huge as they were later — and not as frequent.

One source says the British "Pathfinder" concept was not developed until 1942. However, earlier, they had some method of dropping flares to illuminate — hopefully — the city, and not just the top of some cloud cover. (The Pathfinder system would have special planes go in first, dropping flares).

In the meantime, the bombers hit whatever they could hit.

Naturally, the main concept was "industrial areas." Well, entire large sections of cities in the Ruhr, for example, were "industrial areas." If a specific plant was the main target, the idea was to get the bombs into the vicinity. Thus, even when bombing "industrial areas," masses of civilian residential areas were at risk. (The even crueler type of attack was to come later).

Strategic bombing took a giant leap forward with the first huge raid — 1,000 planes on Cologne in May 1942. You can bet a lot of bomb sticks went, essentially, into the "area around industry" — and a wide area at that!

The next great leap forward (or backward, depending on the reader's views), came with the first raid of the American Eighth Army Air Force in August 1942.

The British were determined that the U.S. bomb at night. The U.S. gradually asserted its determination to bomb by day.

The U.S. had the supersecret "Norden bomb sight," which enabled bombers to hit "pinpoint" targets. The U.S. heard about it every day — "pinpoint bombing by U.S. planes hit . . ." thus and such target.

The concept was clean and shiny. The U.S. would, with surgical accuracy, remove the cancer of evil from the world — and leave the worthwhile and helpless still standing, unharmed.

Not mentioned was the cloud cover obscuring targets more than half the time. Or flak or damage or other problems causing bombs to be jettisoned over anything below. Or unexpected crosswinds causing missing — or missing for any of several dozen other reasons.

Many Americans at home believed in their clean, shining, concept. They accepted heavy daytime losses from being over-exposed visibly to enemy flak and air attack, because they believed (mythologically) that they were not hitting anything below but evil war plants, rail yards, etc.

The British officially stated they were doing the same — but were cynical underneath. It was important to keep up appear-ances. The press was full of how bad Germany was to have bombed London, Coventry, etc. The air crews simply could not be told that they were preparing to do worse to the Germans! But the British air crews knew what they were about, despite official statements.

According to one source, experienced air crews (British and U.S.) loved to haze newcomers, initiating them into squadron fellowship by telling them harrowing tales of murdering civilians and meeting horrific conditions in aerial combat — with immense daily losses. Apparently, it was fun to tell the terrorized new-comers, preparing immediately for their first combat flight the very next morning, that they were the eighth new person that month for that job, that the possibility of escaping death, injury or capture was only 50-50 each day, etc.

Thus, even though being informed that they were not clean, impervious knights, engaged only in killing dragons, the new-comers didn't believe all they heard!

But the exaggerations were not so great! Conditions were not vastly different from the exaggerations! With a turnover rate due to failure to return from missions of more than four percent (milk runs averaged in), mere survival for the mandatory twenty-five missions was a mathematical long shot! Crews sat in their quarters at night and figured the odds, based on the latest casualty figures.

By the time most newcomers learned that they were hitting civilians most of the time — accidentally or by design — half had landed on enemy soil dead, prisoners, or fugitives.

After the big raids began, U.S. bombers were directed into mass-destruction efforts. Except for a few glaring — and the worst — examples (which will be discussed further toward the end of this chapter), these were centered on industrial "areas." But the entire Ruhr could be called an "industrial area." Civilians "became" harder and harder to differentiate from "military personnel." I mean, after all, if a skilled civilian is making guns or planes which will kill our military and civilian personnel, isn't that worker *an enemy militant?* Thus went the reasoning — and with many real justifications.

However, the mythologizing Government press departments didn't want all the facts known. Therefore, the coverups of "military and industrial targets" and "pinpoint bombing" were used throughout the War. The populace was not given an opportunity to adjust slowly to the horrible slaughters we were inflicting on Germany. Old illusions were maintained as much as possible.

Thus — immediately after the War — the early wave of revulsion hit.

This early wave of revulsion — followed between 1965 and 1970 by another tremendous wave of revulsion regarding WWII (the revelations in detail of Dresden and Hamburg) — provided much of the basis and atmosphere for the school that the bombing was ineffective and counterproductive.

When the European War ended, Germany lay in ruins — a ruination obvious to the eye. Miles of newsreel and military film shot from the air at low altitudes are on file and can be examined. It is irrefutable. One source gives the following figures for Germany's destruction: Hamburg 75%, Bremerhaven 79%, Frankfurt 52%, Dresden 59%, Kassel 69%, Dortmund 54%; and on and on. Berlin was rated at only 33%. *(Almanac).* However, a qualifier is that the figures are from aerial destruction — not from fighting Russians in the streets, which added more! ✔

(I was an eye-witness to Berlin's destruction. A few years after the War, and before the Wall, I drove for miles in East Berlin. Every single block for as far as the eye could see had been levelled totally. Bulldozers had mounded up the brick rubble into flat piles about fifteen feet high, with sloping edges, filling every block sidewalk to sidewalk. There had not been one building worth saving. Two or three miles inside, we came upon "Stalinallee" — the Potempkin village sort of thing running for a mile on each side of one street. This had been widely photographed as proof that Russia had "reconstructed" East Berlin!)

How, then, could a school arise that said Germany had not been destroyed?

And yet, it would be the 1970s before the obvious utter wartime destruction of Germany again "had the floor," so to speak, to testify on behalf of the truth of the effect of the bombing.

How, in light of such visual proof, could the school of "ineffectiveness" and "counterproductivity" of the bombing, arise? Some reasons appear below.

German war production rose dramatically during the last two and one half years of the War.

Not long after the War, some remarkable — and accurate — figures appeared which showed clearly that German war production rose dramatically during the last two and one half years of the war!

In other words, that could be taken as evidence that the strategic bombing of "industrial and military targets" was a big flop.

Let's look at the figures: Allied bomb tonnage on Euope was less than 100,000 tons in 1942, more than 200,000 tons in 1943, nearly 1,000,000 tons in 1944 (and at about that rate in the shortened year of 1945). *(Almanac)*.

German military aircraft production for those years went from roughly 15,000 in 1942, to 25,000 in 1943, to 40,000 in 1944 (and at a lesser rate in the shortened year of 1945). *(Atlas)*.

German tank production figures are more difficult to obtain by years, and made complex by inclusion of other armored tracked or rubber-tired vehicles. One source shows roughly 5,000 in 1942, 10,000 in 1943, and 13,000 in 1944 (no figures shown at all for 1945). *(Atlas)*. Another source says German tank production rose "sixfold" in 1943, 1944 and the shortened portion of

1945. ("U.S. Strategic Bombing Survey" shown in *Almanac*). This is inexact, but at least states the strong trend of *increase despite bombing*. (And again, are they talking pure tanks?)

(As a side note, all these figures tend to confirm a thesis of this book, that the Germans were not nearly as mechanized as the world had believed. The Germans put on a massive production drive late in the War — but it was too late. The Allies had taken them at face value and produced giant volumes of equipment to offset them. In all the War, Germany produced only 20,000 pure tanks, while Russia produced 55,000, the U.S. 60,000, and Great Britain 22,000 — for a total Allied production of 137,000 to 20,000. Toss in 5,000 Italian, and 2,500 Japanese — and the Axis was still outnumbered more than five to one in tanks! So I think Germany's "ass had had it" anyhow, before they put on their great production drive).

Albert Speer, German Armaments Minister in the last years, in his book and interviews confirmed that German armaments production rose in the last two years despite bombings.

But are increased figures alone conclusive of anything? Unfortunately not.

British historian R.J. Overy asks the question many have asked: How much greater would production have been without the bombings? The answer is, much greater — *and of more advanced models.*

There were many factors limiting the value of the increased German production.

For example, Germany desperately needed to produce advanced new weapons. The Allies had introduced superior tanks and planes. Germany had experimental models, and even early production models of advanced weapons — some of which were better than the Allies' latest equipment. One example was the jet plane, available in 1939, when Hitler turned it down because he had just equipped the Luftwaffe. In May 1941, the Me-163 jet was flown at 621 mph. They also had another jet — the Me-262. *(Almanac).* These were never put into full production. If the Germans had possessed them in quantity, no Allied bombers of that decade could have penetrated German airspace. Did bombing affect decisions about jet production late in the War, when Germany desperately tried to rearm with this plane? Certainly.

Bombing forced production to leave the shattered, big, obvious plants and disperse into small, more hidden, numerous factories, which could be quickly set up. It was nearly impossible to bring out revolutionary new equipment this way. Thus, the Nazis stayed with production of old products already inferior to the latest Allied equipment.

Numbers alone were not the key factor in the last two years of the War.

Bombings chopped into V-1 and V-2 production — and eliminated the possibility of a German "wonder weapon" in the rocket classification. A huge Allied raid putting 2,000 tons of bombs on Peenemunde in August, 1943, nearly wiped out the secret labs and testing facilities — and the experimental production areas. The raid also killed many of the scientists.

Everywhere, the Allied bombings cut into the skilled work force. Not only scientists, inventors, and designers of the futuristic products on which Germany had pinned its hopes, but everyday skilled workers, who could not easily be replaced, were killed or put out of action.

Most publicized — and most controversial — was the Allied attempt to destroy German ball bearing production. The theory was simple — Germany could not "roll" without ball bearings, and most of the production was at Schweinfurt. Two big raids (August and October, 1943) cost the U.S. daylight attackers about one-forth of their raiding force (about sixty planes) each time — and aroused such debate that big runs this deep (way beyond fighter cover) were terminated for a long time. (See a later section of this chapter about increases in fighter plane ranges).

Even more controversial than the losses was the question: Did the raids do any real damage to German ball bearing production? This was not to be settled for more than two decades.

At the time of the strikes, the Germans pretended they were not hurt. They said the roofs of the buildings were badly damaged but the equipment was all safe — and that some production remained there, while some was dispersed, and went on.

There was much controversy among the Allies, with one faction claiming that the raids were only costly failures.

Speer testified much later in his book and interviews that the Germans were badly hurt at Schweinfurt. Production was cut. But the Germans had an ace up their sleeves — Sweden. They bought a lot of ball bearings from that neutral country! The Germans also had production facilities near Berlin.

The Swedes cooperated with the Germans in many limited ways. Offsetting some of this were many advantageous uses to which the Allies put the special status of Sweden during the War.

Some diplomatic pressure on the Swedes might have had the effect of another raid on German ball bearing production!

Speer settled the matter for all history when he said that further pursuit of the destruction of ball bearing production — even one more smasheroo raid on Schweinfurt — could have put Germany out of business!

Petroleum was another item Allied bombers blasted into a bottleneck for the Nazis. Again, the Allied theorists felt they could topple Germany by concentrating on just one item — but lost their vision before the final killing blow! The concept, though, as events later proved, was sound. It began with Ploesti raids in August 1943. It continued with the systematic wrecking of rail yards, petroleum storage areas, tank cars — anything related to petrol.

Goebbels was to write, "What good is all this aircraft production when we have neither the petrol nor the air crews?" Petrol had been a direct victim of the bombings. (The loss of air crews had been an indirect effect, discussed later in this chapter).

Again, we see that mere numbers of planes or tanks (even if they had been new models, which they weren't), were limited in their effectiveness.

Transportation — which embraces both production and distribution — was *shattered* by the bombings. (Some of this was medium tactical bombing). The same source which seems to indicate that bombing was not effective (because tank production increased "sixfold"), says, "the attack on transportation was the decisive blow that completely disorganized the Germany economy," and, "Transport proved to be the weakest link in the [German] logistic chain. Its failure was the immediate cause of the breakdown of the supply system and consequently was a decisive factor in the collapse of the German Army." ("U.S. Strategic Bombing Survey" quoted in *Almanac*).

Thus, in retrospect, after the dust had settled, it can be clearly seen that German war production — despite the increase in some numbers in some categories — was badly harmed by Allied bombing. It was limited, crippled, immobilized, and could not supply the front.

Germany needed new models, but couldn't produce them due to the bombings — so made large numbers of old models.

Periodic follow-up raids after Schweinfurt would have put Germany out of business. (Speer).

"What good is all this aircraft production when we have neither the petrol [a direct victim of the bombings] nor the air crews [an indirect victim of the bombings]?" (Goebbels).

"The attack on transportation . . . the weakest link . . . was a decisive factor in the collapse of the [German economy] and the German Army." (U.S. Strategic Bombing Survey).

(There are three more interesting stories connected with long-range bombing. Way back in the late 1930s, Boeing's new early-model "Flying Fortress" had been designed, with so many gun turrets, to defend itself in the air on long missions. As masses of these began bombing Europe after August 1942, aerial battles developed which are mentioned in many accounts — but are never mentioned as a *distinct type of warfare*. Prophecy buffs may remember Nostradamus' quatrains about a very distinct new war manifestation — aerial battles taking place over great distances. When we think about "aerial battles" we focus upon the battle of getting the bombers to the target and back, and considering the ground attack from flak. That was indeed a struggle. But distinct from that was the separate battle form of large magnitude — the aerial battle unrolling over hundreds of miles.

(The range of fighter planes for cover was remarkably short. Spitfires could barely get over the coast of the Lowlands — not being designed for such offensive convoying duty, but as one of the world's all-time great defensive fighter planes. In June of 1943, U.S. Thunderbolts could escort bombers to the German border — but not to the Ruhr, not to Bremerhaven. This meant that for about a year after the U.S. Eighth Army Air Force started its daylight runs, there was virtually no fighter cover into Germany. The result was hundreds of miles of air-to-air combat against enemy fighters which would lie in the sky until the fighter escorts turned back — then pounce.

(Pouncing, however, guaranteed nothing! The massed firepower of the Forts took a big toll in downed and damaged enemy fighters. Something was happening which has not been fully credited as a separate and effective war activity — and a product of the aerial bombing. This product was the systematic (though painful to the bombers) *destruction of the Luftwaffe in the West.*

· (For that first year, the bombers "went it alone." The British thought the Americans were crazy — and sometimes, the Americans also thought so — raiding in daylight. The gun battles were awesome. Beirne Lay and others have more than adequately described them — however, not as the distinct and telling form of warfare that I believe should be given to the activity.

(By the end of the first year of Eighth Air Force raiding (by August 1943), Thunderbolts with belly tanks could go out beyond the Ruhr, but not to Schweinfurt. Both the August and October Schweinfurt raids were without fighter cover for much of the distance in and back. Peenemunde in August — farther out than Berlin — had no fighter cover.

(However, things were looking up. By November of 1943, Lightnings could range out 530 miles — or as far as Berlin! The huge volume of bombers, though, and the large number of raids, made accompaniment by adequate fighters seldom possible. Also, once engaged, a fighter could use up a lot of fuel and have to return. But any fighter cover at all made things hot for the Luftwaffe — and contributed to its destruction.

(Enter the saga of the Mustang! It was rejected by the U.S. in1941 (hard to believe). Maybe it was underpowered at the time. But later, when it was equipped with a Rolls Royce engine, it became the pride of both Allies for speed (500 mph plus), fighting ability, and range. By December 1943, the Mustangs were able to fly out beyond Berlin. (All range data from *Atlas*).

(Now the aerial war was in its titanic phase — with thousands of bombers and fighters roaming the skies over occupied and enemy territories, engaging the Luftwaffe both defensively and offensively!

(A recent Eighth Air Force history says a byproduct of the bombing raids was the destruction of the Luftwaffe. I believe the aerial battles should be treated as a distinct war form (not just an adjunct to another activity), and their unexpected but undeniable part in the destruction of the Luftwaffe in the West be credited).

One of the props of the "counterproductive" theory was that "rubbleized cities" were easier to defend — and even more livable than regular ones. The theory sprang from two military (not civilian) circumstances — Monte Cassino and Stalingrad. In Stalingrad, the Russians did better when the buildings were standing, but could, and did, fight in the rubble. The advantages of non-rubble are that a defender can easily get about, and can choose some elevated positions for observation and fire. But the attacker can identify this or that window, doorway, roof or building as the problem area and blow it up. So these factors cancel out. In rubble, the situation also cancels out: the defender more easily hides, but the hiding is usually ground level or below. The attacker can't easily locate or describe a trouble area — and an encounter is likely to be face-to-face. There is no special advantage to a defender in rubble. The advantage is to the infantry which likes face-to-face encounters! The Russians used the rubble of Stalingrad to force the Germans — who were reluctant to go gut-to-gut and preferred to stand off and fire automatic weapons — to die face-to-face.

Aha, but what about Monte Cassino? It has been established that the hilltop monastery was more defensible after being reduced to rubble than before!

But that is not the entire story. At Monte Cassino, the Allies made a very crucial error. Their ground attack should have immediately followed their air attack. Instead, there was a substantial delay — and the Germans reoccupied the rubble. This particular rubble was at a high elevation, so the rubble afforded views which ordinary "flattened" buildings don't afford. Monte Cassino is thus not an example which can be extended to flattened cities. Also, in the long run, the monastery itself was not attacked (until bombed), and there was no history of its defensible qualities prior to the bombing. In sum, it was a good observation post for the Nazis before the bombing, and both a good observation post and ready-made defensive position after. And it fell, for the first time, after the bombing.

Therefore, I don't believe all the connections and extrapolations some people make about rubble and good defenses.

Let's move this discussion to *German cities,* where advocates say the bombing was counterproductive because it rubbleized the cities.

I fail again to see any advantage to the Germans (and disadvantage to the Allies) in German rubble.

Ask anyone who lived in one of those cities. Transportation was paralyzed, food was short, most families had lost one or more members, hospital facilities were nil, water was cut off, sanitation was primitive, and on and on.

I firmly believe that the myth that I have actually read, that the Allied bombings made German cities *more livable* is absurd on its face.

As to defending these cities, who is going to do this — the civilian population? No (except the Volksturm in Berlin's rubble, where they didn't find things "easy").

Will the military find these cities "easier" to defend?

Only where the infantry is holed up in cellars and knows that the next face-to-face encounter is the last one — and likes this — is a city of cellars and pieces of walls "easier" to defend.

To the equipment-rich Western Allies, it made little difference. Their tanks crawled over the rubble and put cannon shells into the cellars. Ten grenades or a blast from a gooey flamethrower would precede infantrymen. Every crevice had automatic weapons fire poured into it before anyone entered.

As further proof that these rubbleized cities were not defensible, we have but to examine if Germany furnished any particular defense of these "easy to defend" places. It didn't. It fought hard for some cities — rubble or not — and left others. Rubble was never a factor.

I think the entire rubble theory is fallacious.

I don't believe it was counterproductive.

Furthermore, I believe that the reduction of German cities to rubble was a definite contributing factor in the defeat of that aggressor nation.

Anyone who saw Germany after the War, or examined films, could not believe otherwise.

In this regard, let us examine the opinions of two top Nazis: Goebbels wrote, of the week of Hamburg raids in July and August 1943, "A catastrophe, the extent of which simply staggers the imagination" *(Almanac);* and Speer, who later said that after the Dresden raid (February 1945), had the policy of obliteration raids, started at Hamburg, been pursued with one or two more cities, it would have ended the War.

The bombing of Germany was not only effective, it was much more devastating than we believe.

☆   ☆   ☆

Unknown to the U.S. general public, and at least partly hidden in Great Britain, was the fact that the Western Allies adopted the "monster" in the late summer of 1943.

That late summer brought a huge surge in strategic bombing. The U.S. Eighth Air Force had been operating in England for a year. Another U.S. Air Force was operating from the Mediterranean. A giant flood of new planes and crews was coming in everywhere. A number of risky ventures were now tried — Ploesti, Schweinfurt, Peenemunde, others. (Those three were hit in August, 1943. Schweinfurt II followed in October). The Western Allies had the planes to risk — and the long pent-up theories to test. They received some bloody noses, but dished out more than they took.

It was theory-testing time.

The most horrible theory kicking around was the "monster" — winning through *civilian annihilation.*

Up until August, 1943, the U.S. (and probably Great Britain) had not deliberately hit what would be called primarily residential areas, except by accident.

Bombings of civilians had become routine to the night-bombing British, who could always say they were trying to hit the Messerschmidt works, but couldn't see a damn thing, and "sorry, old chap."

Killing of civilians had become routine for Americans too — who would go by daylight with the pinpoint capability, but get thrown off course by flak, enemy aircraft, dead navigators, etc., and confused by cloud cover, enemy camouflage, etc., and wind up blowing hell out of something called "the industrial area." This became all the greater as the numbers of aircraft increased. It was a long way from the early days of ten planes hitting the submarine yard at Bremerhaven, to 250 aircraft hitting the whole industrial area along the river at Bremerhaven. In the latter, bombs are going to get scattered all over the place. (It is interesting to look closely at film clips in some of the documentary materials released. I've seen several where the bombs landed in open fields! Why would they show this? If that's the best accuracy they can depict, then what can be said for attempts to hit a certain plant or yard in the middle of a big city? The answer lies in what all know by now — bombs aimed at industrial areas blew up civilian residential areas *connected to* the industrial areas.

Something big and awful happened in the late summer of 1943.

A deliberate decision was made somewhere to bomb the residential areas in Hamburg that were primarily civilian residential areas not incidentally connected to industrial areas.

The concept was to bomb the cities' civilians day and night to create the now well-famed "firestorm" effect — to overwhelm the city's fire-fighting defenses (this was a specific part of the mission — as if fire-fighting defenses for civilians were like military defenses which should be overcome), and burn out the whole damn place.

This was done. Some sources say it was three days and three nights. One says off and on from July 24 through August 2, 1943. *(Almanac).*

It was passed to the press as another raid — a big one.

But it was really the exercise of the "monster" theory. That was not told the public.

I was in Hamburg a few years after the War. My cab-driver guide, who drove me around all day and answered a lot of questions about the perspective of the War from inside Germany, realized I didn't want to just see the standard things. He drove me off the main sightseeing paths to show me something — the area which he said had been ruined in the War. He told me, "They bombed here three days and three nights, to create a fire storm that would overwhelm the fire-fighting capability of the city, and burn it out — women and children." He said 30,000 died.

When I returned to the U.S. and spoke of this, no one would listen.

Fifteen more years passed.

Then, with the publication of Kurt Vonnegut's book, *Slaughterhouse-five,* the U.S. general public began to be able to receive the shocking truth about a later raid of the identical type, Dresden.

That year, 1969, the U.S. public was undergoing the "second revulsion wave" about the "monster" in any of its forms.

The earlier, first wave — revulsion about the A-bombs on Japan — was still in force, but the nation had still not accepted the truth about Germany. Acceptance of the truth about Germany became part of the "second wave" of revulsion.

Another part of the second wave of revulsion included the Vietnam bombings of all types: close-support, medium tactical (the main gripe), and the sparing use of what could be called long-range strategic. Throughout all three types, though, ran a thread — murder of civilians as a specific tool of winning the war. However, confusing that picture was the fact that the people we had decided were the enemy more often wore civilian clothes than uniforms! So that one is still hot in the debate fires. For this book, we'll stay away from it, because it is another vast subject area.

However, it was part of the "second revulsion wave."

Vietnam (and Watergate later), taught us to question intensely what our Government was telling the press! And this — plus Dresden — led to reopening WWII for some more examination!

Many myths fell — and many very ugly things came up — regarding the "monster" in WWII.

Some things, I believe, are focused and presented to the general public for the first time, in this book.

Surely our use of the A-bomb on Japan was our first use of *civilian annihilation* as a tool of winning the war.

And surely this was not anything we premeditated, but instead found as an irresistable opportunity to end the war.

Nope on both counts.

I charge in this book — and I challenge anyone to try to refute — that we were engaged in a deliberate use of the "monster" of civilian annihilation (mixed in with our other programs but *there*), from the late summer of 1943 forward.

Atlas puts Hamburg's "casualties" at 80,000. *Almanac* shows 42,000 dead, plus many more of the 37,000 injured who died later. *German General Staff* puts the dead alone at 56,000.

(It adds this information: On July 23 (1943), 800 air mines, 12,000 high explosive, 80,000 phosporous and 150,000 incendiary bombs were dropped).

Atlas puts Dresden's "casualties" (February, 1945), at 135,000. *Dictionary* puts dead alone at up to 100,000, "leaving too few able-bodied people to bury the victims." *Almanac* pegs dead at 35,000. (Differences in numbers can occur between sources using estimates made of dead the day (or days) of the raiding, compared with estimates made later after the rubble had been cleared and the mortally injured demised). *War Maps* calls Dresden the "war's most destructive."

Some have mentioned as justification for this raid that the Russians had specifically asked us to hit Dresden, where troops and supplies to be used against the Russians were being marshalled. One source, while commenting on the heavy casualties, mentions the Russian factor. It says the city was "swollen to 830,000 by the influx of 200,000 refugees. Such an attack was justified as being against the important industrial complex as well as the hub of communications for the southern sector of the Eastern Front, and was made at the request of Russia." *(Almanac)*.

The Russians may indeed have asked for a raid on military assembly points, but the raid itself was an obliteration type, or civilian annihilation type, plain and simple. Furthermore, the excuse that this was in some way an unusual raid for us doesn't hold water. We were actively engaged in a deliberate program of civilian annihilation aimed at winning the War.

Of Dresden, Churchill was to say that it raised "a serious query against the conduct of Allied bombing."

The raids are in the history books as raids by "conventional" means. Actually, the "firestorm" is a diabolical invention of ours in the war — as unique as the Blitzkrieg, or showerbaths with poison gas — and used primarily against civilians.

We were mass murderers.

But we couldn't accept this until about 1970.

To continue with "firestorm" (our invention for killing primarily civilians), B-29s (our shiny, pure planes) began using it against Japan from the Marianas in February, 1945 — the same month as Dresden.

We used horrible incendiaries against European cities. We also used high explosives, "block-busters" and the like. However, it was the incendiaries which caused the terrible fires. (Germans used them too). If water was put on them, the burning magnesium simply exploded some more — spreading more fire. They were too large for the myth that a "bucket or shovel of sand" was the best way to combat them.

Shifting "firestorm" to Japan, incendiaries were ideal, because the buildings weren't masonry, but wood and rice paper — real flammable stuff.

As our "cover" for what was, in the Pacific, overt civilian annihilation, we literally classified *every Japanese home* as a "military plant" in which Japanese people made munitions, guns, steel, etc., to bayonet our boys on the Bataan Death March. I'm not kidding — we were reminded continually that these civilians were the people who did it. *All* Japs were depicted as having buck teeth and slant eyes and being devious and cruel.

There were plenty of real military targets which we bombed. We just set fire to the entire city while hitting the shipbuilding, etc. The "industrial area" was expanded from the plants and incidental civilian areas (as it started out in Germany), to the entire cities. Hell, the entire nation.

In Japan, we deliberately and overtly went after the entire population as a means of ending the war — but we carefully first called every person a "war worker" and every home a mini war plant. *Then* we blew hell out of them.

Sometime in February or March, we began using *napalm* dropped from the high-flying B-29s. You can imagine what a fiery mess that made!

(Of course, we said all along that the enemy could quit anytime it wanted to — and that was true. Our terms, though, were unconditional surrender).

We were "doing" the "monster." We were up to our ears doing it. It was there — but we pretended it wasn't.

On March 9-10, we hit the hated Tokyo with a fire raid that caused 83,793 deaths. *(Almanac)*.

Now we must jump a few months ahead.

Hiroshima's deaths were 70,000.

Nagasaki's deaths were 20,000.

Now consider this: *The most murderous civilian annihilation air raid in history was* not Hiroshima in August 1945, but *Tokyo* in March of that year. And the second most murderous one was probably Dresden, in Europe, in February of that same year. Hiroshima would rank *third* in the War.

Furthermore, unless some other Japanese raids (and we're not through with Japan yet — we're just discussing individual or "continuum" two or three or several days' duration raids) had greater tolls, then Hamburg ranks fourth.

Where's that other "terrible atom bomb" (for which bombs the U.S. suffered much of its first wave of revulsion, before the truth in Germany and the second wave of revulsion set in?) Nagasaki is at least fifth — and possibly as much as several steps lower.

I still find it hard to believe.

However, there is no getting around it.

Along with other myths that can hit the bucket is the one that "we wouldn't have pulled the A-bomb on Europeans (our "own people") but only on "Asiatics." We've suffered a lot for that one. But the fact was this: *Dresden* may have resulted (by a month or so after the raid, when the badly wounded who couldn't be saved were added) in the highest death toll of any raid of the War! And those people were "our own people."

Now we must talk about something even more disagreeable. We have concentrated on individual or "continuum" raids up to one week.

But we have also tried to look at the losses in this city or that city.

The city with the worst loss of life in the entire War was *Tokyo*. It was hit and hit and hit. The program was primarily civilian annihilation by our new invention for killing — the firestorm, with, mainly (if my sources are correct) napalm — with the intention of ending the War. As evidence that we were engaged in civilian annihilation plain and simple at Tokyo from 1944 forward, were the results: *"More than a million* people lost their lives in the 1944-1945 Allied [U.S.] air attacks as 15.8 square miles of central Tokyo were completely destroyed." *(Almanac).*

The dark horror is that we used civilian annihilation as a deliberate policy for at least two years before the end of the War.

(Little known facts: We popularly believe the A-bomb on Nagasaki ended the War. It didn't. After Nagasaki (August 10), the Japs agreed to surrender — but not unconditionally! The emperor was to retain his authority. On the 11th, the U.S. said, No. Now for the surprise: on the 13th, 1,600 U.S. planes were back over Tokyo with firestorm. Did that produce final results? No. On the 14th, it was business as usual — B-29s over several Japanese cities — Kumagaya, Isesake, and Akita — with more firestorm. That did it. V-J Day was declared August 15th. *(Almanac).*

(Another little-known fact: The U.S. had only the two A-bombs — and didn't know when it would have more!)

☆   ☆   ☆

The strategic bombing of German military, industrial and *civilian population* targets was not less effective, but more effective then we popularly believe.

APPENDIXES
and
OPEN FORUM

BRITAIN'S CONTRIBUTION REEVALUATED

Britain's war contribution was second only to Russia's. Compared with the U.S., the British did more fighting; took more military deaths (about 3 to 1, or about 750,000 to about 250,000); landed more troops on D-Day (about 75,000 to about 57,000); convoyed most ships (by far — controlling all the Halifax-to-England convoys); lost the most merchant ships (about 5,000 to 500-600); lost the most merchant sailors (about 35,000 to about 5,000); invented more war-winning detection devices (radar, centimetric radar — several), HF/DF (High Frequency Direction Finder), MAD (Magnetic Anomaly Detector); destroyed more subs (500 of the 793 destroyed or captured); established the most amazing intelligence-gathering machinery and people the world has ever known — including the Enigma-decoding Turing Engine (the Bletchley Park "Bomb"), and a secrecy which was maintained until 1974-75; had almost all the intelligence data for the Western Allies (the U.S. had to go to British sources for nearly everything, if it was smart — because the British information was always well ahead of anyone else's); constructed and carried out numerous "war of deception" plots elaborate and simple — including "Fortitude South" which U.S. General Bradley said held "twenty" Nazi divisions immobilized for "months" after the Normandy landings; and set up and carried out the support of (and often organization of) resistance groups on the Continent (at high peril to extremely intrepid workers who went in and out of occupied countries).

FOUR TRENDS TO WATCH

The First World War was really the "European World." It was fought between military people, of which some 15,000,000 were killed. A few civilians were killed, but the war was fought on battlefields, with military people as the targets.

The Second World War was more a "world" conflict. It was fought between military people — of which some 20,000,000 fell. But, for the first time, civilian populations were involved in a big way. Some 40,000,000 civilians were killed. Some fell relative to the War — as hordes moved back and forth over nations. The remainder were killed deliberately, as animosities shifted so that only about half the targets were military, while the other half were civilian.

What of the Third World War? It will surely be more truly "global." Military people will punch the buttons and pull the triggers, but civilian targets will be the *main* thing attacked. Civilian annihilation will be the *main* purpose — the main way of winning the war. (Most missiles are pre-targeted today upon civilian populations). Military people may not engage each other with significance to the war's outcome — but the conflict will be between one side's military and the other side's civilians! Think about it.

OPEN FORUM

Readers are invited to comment. Please send written corroborations, rebuttals, additional commentaries, eyewitness
accounts, or discussions of anything pertinent to a better understanding of World War II to:

> Paragon Press/Dynapress
> GREAT MYTHS DEBATE
> P.O. Box 866
> Fern Park, FL 32730-0866

All letters, or other communications, or enclosed materials
become the property of Paragon Press/Dynapress, Karl
Roebling, Publisher. Please retain a copy for yourself, and do not
mail the originals of any documentation.